ΙΟΙΟΙΟΙΟΙΟΙΟΙΟΙΟΙΟΙΟΙ

Managing Technological Innovation

Organizational Strategies for Implementing Advanced Manufacturing Technologies

Donald D. Davis

and Associates

ЮЮЮЮЮЮЮЮЮЮ

Managing
Technological
Innovation

 Jossey-Bass Publishers

San Francisco • London • 1986

MANAGING TECHNOLOGICAL INNOVATION
Organizational Strategies for Implementing Advanced Manufacturing Technologies
by Donald D. Davis and Associates

Copyright © 1986 by: Jossey-Bass Inc., Publishers
433 California Street
San Francisco, California 94104
&
Jossey-Bass Limited
28 Banner Street
London EC1Y 8QE

Library of Congress Cataloging-in-Publication Data

Davis, Donald D., 1950–
    Managing technological innovation.

    (The Jossey-Bass management series)
    Bibliography: p.
    Includes index.
    1. Technological innovations—Management.
2. Manufacturing processes—Technological innovations—
Management. 3. New products. I. Title. II. Series.
HD45.D34   1986   658.5'14   86-15378
ISBN 1-55542-008-7

Manufactured in the United States of America

The paper in this book meets the guidelines for
permanence and durability of the Committee on
Production Guidelines for Book Longevity of the
Council on Library Resources.

JACKET DESIGN BY WILLI BAUM

FIRST EDITION

Code 8633

ıoıoıoıoıoıoıoıoıoıoı

The Jossey-Bass Management Series

Contents

ŧOŧOŧOŧOŧOŧOŧOŧOŧOŧOŧOŧOŧ

Preface

A revolution is occurring today in manufacturing. The changes being made are fundamental, and although their full impact may not be seen for decades, several implications are already apparent. Advanced computerized manufacturing technologies undoubtedly present new strategic opportunities for firms capable of using them. In order to take advantage of these new opportunities, however, firms must first change the way they organize to conduct their business; managers must replace some comfortable old beliefs with new concepts—and new practices. Realizing the potential the new technologies offer will require bringing computerized functions to the fore in the management arena.

This book is about the adoption and implementation of advanced technologies in manufacturing. Advanced manufacturing technologies such as computer-aided design and manufacturing (CAD/CAM), computer-aided engineering (CAE), robotics, flexible manufacturing systems (FMS), and computer-integrated manufacturing (CIM) promise to revolutionize manufacturing. These computer-based technologies herald the coming of the "factory of the future," an almost workerless, paperless, fully automated production facility. These changes will alter manufacturing at least as dramatically as large-scale industrialization changed earlier guild forms of industrial organization. Yet despite the promise they hold for productivity and quality, American firms have been slow to purchase and use these technologies. This reluctance stands in stark contrast to actions taken by foreign competitors, especially in Japan, who have rapidly adopted advanced manufacturing technologies. The discrepancy becomes even less understandable—and begins to be alarming—when we realize that most of the new technologies were invented and developed by American firms.

Widespread use of advanced technologies is essential if American manufacturers are ever to compete again internationally in terms of product quality and cost. Although strategies such as outsourcing (producing parts and subassemblies in countries where labor and manufacturing costs are low) seem today to provide a competitive edge in labor cost and product quality, the gains they offer will stand only for the short term. What is needed instead is a transformation of the production function so that American manufacturers can produce goods of high quality and low cost at home. This will require a long-term commitment to the use of advanced manufacturing technologies and to organizational modification that will allow changes to be made successfully.

Contrary to the belief of many managers and engineers, the purchase of new technologies does not ensure their successful use. In many cases, promises of productivity gains are only partly realized, often because the social organization of the firm cannot adapt to their use. Despite assurances of "turn-key" operation, successfully implementing these technologies frequently requires changing management methods, human resource allocation, and existing organizational structure and design. Too many managers see the "factory of the future" as a quick fix—a false and financially dangerous belief.

Two questions associated with the use of advanced manufacturing technologies are apparent: (1) How can the dissemination and adoption of advanced manufacturing technologies be facilitated in order to improve the productivity and international competitiveness of American firms? and (2) Once adopted, how can advanced manufacturing technologies be implemented and managed so as to achieve the maximum possible productivity gains? Answers to these questions require one to focus on the managerial and organizational contexts in which the new technologies are embedded. This book has such a focus and is designed to address these two crucial questions.

Managing Technological Innovation is intended for three audiences: (1) scholars who conduct research and teach classes examining the role of technology in organizations, manufacturing, and management; (2) managers who manage production with advanced manufacturing technologies, or manage human resources or marketing; and (3) policy makers who may influence the spread of advanced manufacturing technologies.

This book will not only help scholars understand more about introducing new technologies into organizations, it will also be useful in advanced undergraduate or graduate courses on technology management, engineering management, management of change, and in advanced courses in business, industrial engineering and human factors engineering, industrial/organizational psychology, and sociology. Most chapters contain suggestions concerning research needs and methods. All who have contributed to this book hope that it will stimulate creativity and new research.

This book will be valuable to managers. It will clarify for managers at all levels the unique factors that contribute to or impede the successful adoption and implementation of advanced manufacturing technologies. Contributors describe strategies that can smooth the implementation process as well as reduce the likelihood that the surrounding organization and managerial systems will retard the new technologies' productive potential. Some of the chapters detail specific steps to follow for successful implementation. This book will also prove useful to anyone who designs and presents professional workshops and continuing education classes for manufacturing engineers, industrial engineers, human factors engineers, and all managers who are considering adoption of, or must manage implementation of, advanced manufacturing technologies.

Policy makers in a variety of governmental areas will find this book a practical resource. The failure of American manufacturing has important implications for national defense, the balance of foreign trade, and other large-scale concerns. Continued inattention at the national level may speed the decline of America as an industrial power. This book demonstrates that the failure to use advanced manufacturing technologies is widespread among American firms, but it is not inevitable. What is needed is more attention focused on (1) organizational and managerial impediments to the new technologies, (2) impacts of

these technologies on existing workers and work practices, and
(3) policies for fostering dissemination and adoption. Chapters
in this volume discuss recommendations for changes in federal
and state government policies.

This book is unique in that it is the first to apply what is
known about innovation adoption and implementation in organizations to the special problems associated with advanced
manufacturing technologies. Furthermore, it is the first work to
emphasize the influence of the surrounding social system of the
organization on manufacturing capabilities and the employment
of advanced technologies. I believe that such a sociotechnical
analysis is essential to reveal how firms can achieve the productive potential that is possible using the new technologies.

Perhaps the most important feature of this book is the
quality of its contributions. Each contributor has been selected
because he or she is involved in research or application of concepts that are on the cutting edge of advances in technology.
As a result, recommendations in this volume concerning how to
manage advanced manufacturing technologies are derived from
contributors' scientific research studies as well as from their
practical consulting and management experience in hundreds of
firms throughout the United States. Among the useful information included in this book are contributors' descriptions of their
implementation experiences along with suggestions about how
readers can avoid making serious mistakes.

The contributors' diverse backgrounds include industrial
and electrical engineering and manufacturing, management,
public administration, marketing, and sociology and psychology. Their multidisciplinary points of view are important because successful use of the new technologies requires an appreciation of complexity that transcends any single professional
discipline. The spectrum of expertise the contributors offer will
enhance the volume's usefulness for a wide and diverse audience.

Overview of the Contents

Part One addresses the challenges the new technologies
present and exposes the need to examine organizational systems

and managers as impediments to the use of advanced manufacturing processes. Chapter One describes the importance of an organizational perspective to understanding the adoption and implementation of advanced manufacturing technologies. Chapters Two and Three, by John Kimberly and Jerald Hage respectively, enlarge this context. They show that a firm's speed and success in adopting and implementing new technologies relate directly to characteristics of the adopting organization, its managers, and the surrounding environment. Both authors provide models for understanding the adoption and implementation processes in organizations and industries.

Part Two describes empirical studies that examine characteristics of employees, managers, organizations, and organization environments that are related to the adoption and implementation of advanced manufacturing technologies. In Chapter Four, John Ettlie describes a national survey of vendors and users of advanced manufacturing technologies. He focuses particularly on aspects of the vendor-user relationship that contribute to successful implementation.

Ann Majchrzak, Veronica Nieva, and Paul Newman, in Chapter Five, describe a national survey assessing the extent to which new technologies are used and integrated into computer-controlled systems. Characteristics distinguishing different levels of successful use are described. Chapter Six, by Linda Argote and Paul Goodman, describes the authors' research on the implementation of robots. Argote and Goodman describe the results of several studies and provide suggestions for improving the successful implementation of robotic systems. Chapter Seven, the final one in this section, is written by James Taylor, Paul Gustavson, and William Carter. These authors describe the application of sociotechnical systems design principles to the implementation and adaption of a CAD system at Zilog, a manufacturer of microprocessors. They argue that these principles contribute significantly to the success of organizations that redesign themselves in order to employ new technologies.

Part Three of the book addresses the importance of the new technologies for business policy and strategic planning. Chapter Eight, by Dorothy Leonard-Barton and Janis Gogan, describes why the new technologies must be marketed differently than other types of industrial products and processes. The authors provide recommendations for a preferred market strategy. Mariann Jelinek and Joel Goldhar, in Chapter Nine, discuss the role advanced manufacturing technologies should play in contributing to the development of competitive strategy. They suggest that the new technologies provide competitive advantages not available with more traditional forms of automation and that managers need to view the new technologies differently if their strategic potential is to be fully realized. Chapter Ten, written by William Hetzner, J. D. Eveland, and Louis Tornatzky, concerns the role played by federal and state government in fostering the use of advanced manufacturing technologies. These authors provide a penetrating and unique perspective because their group at the National Science Foundation was responsible for coordinating and funding much of the research in this area during the last several years. They offer suggestions for new policy along with the caveat that businesses will need to help themselves. They are not optimistic about the ability of government to contribute solutions to these problems.

The book closes with a chapter that synthesizes earlier contributions. It states that advanced manufacturing technologies may be adopted and implemented more successfully when attention is paid to four strategic functions within the organization: technology, manufacturing, marketing, and human resource strategies.

All of us who have helped to shape this book hope that it will be provocative. It denies that high cost is the only major reason for the widespread failure to adopt the new technologies. It denies that advanced manufacturing technologies are ever "turn-key" systems that only need be purchased and plugged in to generate profits. We hope this book will make readers ask themselves questions like these: Is there really something new going on in manufacturing? Can I manage new technologies with old management practices? Are these new technologies simple extensions of past forms of automation—or are they something entirely new? How can all of us in American industry and manufacturing take advantage of this?

Acknowledgments

While I am thankful for the interest and support offered by many colleagues during this book's development, the contributions of Louis Tornatzky and William Hetzner have been both seminal and substantive. Many of the ideas developed in this book grew out of discussions with these two men over the last few years. Those discussions ultimately helped to shape this book. Tornatzky and Hetzner were also influential in helping to organize and fund a conference held at Old Dominion University in 1983, which focused on the dissemination and implementation of advanced manufacturing processes. Revised and expanded versions of some of the papers presented at that conference appear here as chapters. Other chapters have been specially prepared for this volume.

The National Science Foundation (grant no. ISI-8314184) and the Old Dominion University Research Foundation (grant no. 83-968) provided financial support for my work over the last few years, for which I am very grateful. Thanks are also due to Ben Morgan and Raymond Kirby who, as director of the Center for Applied Psychological Studies and chairman of the psychology department at Old Dominion University, respectively, provided resources to encourage this program of research. Finally, I thank my partner, Deborah Mack, for her patience and support over the lengthy and demanding duration of this project.

Norfolk, Virginia   Donald D. Davis
July 1986

ЮЮЮЮЮЮЮЮЮЮЮ

The Authors

Donald D. Davis is assistant professor in the Department of Psychology and research scientist in the Center for Applied Psychological Studies at Old Dominion University. He received his B.S. degree (1973) in psychology, sociology, and philosophy and his M.A. degree (1977) in experimental psychology from Central Michigan University, and his Ph.D. degree (1982) in industrial and organizational and ecological psychology from Michigan State University, where he also served as assistant director of the Center for Evaluation and Assessment. Davis was previously an economic and community development consultant for a private firm in the Midwest. He has consulted for ten years with more than seventy-five public- and private-sector organizations throughout the United States.

Davis's major research interests are organizational behavior, theory, and change, especially innovation processes. He has published many articles, chapters, and papers on these topics. He is currently preparing another book tentatively titled "The Psychology of Technological Innovation."

Recipient of the 1983 Dissertation Award of the American Psychological Association for his dissertation "Innovation Adoption and Organizational Change," Davis has received research fellowship awards from the National Institute of Mental Health and the Gerontological Society of America. His research has been supported by grants from the National Science Foundation and Department of Health and Human Services, among other private- and public-sector organizations. He is a member of the American Psychological Association, Academy of Management, American Sociological Association, American Association for the Advancement of Science, International Association for Applied Psychology, Southern Management Association, Southeastern Psychological Association, and Society for Industrial and Organizational Psychology.

Linda Argote is assistant professor, Graduate School of Industrial Administration and the Robotics Institute, Carnegie-Mellon University, Pittsburgh, Pennsylvania.

William S. Carter is engineering manager at Xilinx, Incorporated, Los Gatos, California.

John E. Ettlie is senior researcher, Industrial Technology Institute, Ann Arbor, Michigan.

J. D. Eveland is director of technology applications research at Cognos Associates, a research and consulting firm specializing in technology implementation and knowledge utilization, Los Altos, California.

Janis Gogan is a Ph.D. candidate at the Graduate School of Business, Harvard University, Cambridge, Massachusetts.

Joel D. Goldhar is dean of the School of Business, Illinois Institute of Technology, Chicago.

Paul S. Goodman is professor of industrial administration and psychology, Graduate School of Industrial Administration and the Robotics Institute, Carnegie-Mellon University, Pittsburgh, Pennsylvania.

Paul W. Gustavson is a principal of Organizational Planning and Design, Incorporated, San Jose, California.

Jerald Hage is director of the Center for Innovation, and professor of sociology, University of Maryland, College Park.

William A. Hetzner is manager of training and technical assistance for the Industrial Technology Institute, Ann Arbor, Michigan.

Mariann Jelinek is Lewis-Progressive Associate Professor of Management Policy, Weatherhead School of Management, Case Western Reserve University, Cleveland, Ohio.

John R. Kimberly is professor of management and health care systems, Wharton School, University of Pennsylvania, Philadelphia.

Dorothy Leonard-Barton is assistant professor in the Graduate School of Business, Harvard University, Cambridge, Massachusetts.

Ann Majchrzak is assistant professor of organizational behavior, Krannert Graduate School of Management, Purdue University, West Lafayette, Indiana.

Paul D. Newman is organizational research analyst, Westat, Incorporated, Washington, D.C.

Veronica F. Nieva is director of organizational research, Westat, Incorporated, Washington, D.C.

James C. Taylor is the principal with Socio-technical Design Consultants, Incorporated, New York City, New York.

Louis G. Tornatzky is director of the Center for Social and Economic Issues, Industrial Technology Institute, Ann Arbor, Michigan.

To Vito and Jennie Saurini

ΙΟΙΟΙΟΙΟΙΟΙΟΙΟΙΟΙΟΙ

Managing Technological Innovation

Organizational Strategies for Implementing Advanced Manufacturing Technologies

ꙮ ONE ꙮ

Technological Innovation and Organizational Change

Donald D. Davis

> Who the hell wants to hear actors talk?
> —*Harry M. Warner,*
> *Warner Brothers Pictures,*
> *circa 1927*

The future is never what it is expected to be. Technological innovation abruptly destroys the present while creating the future. New technologies force organizations to reconsider their purpose and methods of operation. Organizational strategies receptive to new technologies contribute to successful adaptation. Organizations that do not modify themselves to absorb newly adopted technologies never achieve their technological promise. Many American firms have disregarded these basic facts.

International competition in manufacturing has awakened American managers from a decades-long slumber induced by unprecedented international success and almost smug self-confidence. American products are no longer assured of market dominance. "Made in America" no longer signifies unparalleled quality. Foreign products such as automobiles, shoes, consumer electronics, steel, and textiles, to name only a few, take bigger and bigger bites out of American and international markets. Many factors have contributed to this trend, but higher quality and lower cost derived from the use of advanced manufacturing technologies must appear on any list. Although aided by cheap labor and capital and government protection, foreign manufacturers have been quicker than their American counterparts to

1

adopt and use advanced manufacturing processes, despite their invention and early development in the United States.

Two problems are apparent. First, with some exceptions, American manufacturers have been slow to adopt advanced manufacturing technologies. Second, in cases where advanced manufacturing technologies have been purchased, they have frequently been perceived as turnkey systems, requiring little or no modification of other practices in the adopting organizations. Because of this naiveté, the performance of these technological systems has often been retarded by their surrounding social system.

Need for an Organizational Perspective

The characteristics of the adopting organization must be considered when implementing advanced manufacturing technologies. This organizational perspective requires attention to the firm's managers, human resources, structure, strategy, and context. Calls for fresh thinking about the role and practice of manufacturing are not new. Skinner (1969) has been sounding this clarion call for almost two decades. Skinner (1985) describes how the managerial infrastructure of most factories reduces the potential benefits of new forms of automation. He argues that the concept of the factory has become anachronistic and must be reconsidered. Factory improvement can no longer be conducted piecemeal but, instead, must be conducted systemically, focusing on practices such as production and inventory control systems, cost and quality control systems, work-force management policies, and organizational structure (Skinner, 1985, p. 94).

An organizational perspective is necessary to understand the factors related to successful use of advanced manufacturing technologies and to achieve the level of performance they are capable of providing. Unlike numerically controlled equipment and other simpler forms of automation, computer controlled technologies such as robotics, computer-aided design/computer-aided manufacturing (CAD/CAM), computer-aided engineering (CAE), flexible manufacturing systems (FMS), and computer-integrated manufacturing (CIM) are so complex that they stretch the ability of managerial and organizational systems to absorb them. This problem becomes particularly apparent when "islands of automation" are integrated into information-structured production systems. These new technologies are too often embedded in organizations designed and managed in a fashion more suitable for older, simpler production methods. The Taylorist approach to shop-floor management and the Weberian approach to organizational design, while sensible for earlier forms of production, are less appropriate for today's advanced manufacturing technologies. Necessary, then, is a rethinking of the purpose of manufacturing organizations and how best to organize them.

The chapters in this book provide different views regarding the redesign of manufacturing organizations and change in their practices to make them receptive to innovative ideas and processes such as advanced manufacturing technologies. These views stress managerial, organizational, and contextual factors related to the adoption and implementation of technological innovations such as new forms of computerized automation. They stress as well changes in human-resource practices that are important for the successful use of these new technologies; marketing practices necessary to sell these new technologies, as well as the proliferation of products made possible with these computerized production methods; and the implications of these new technologies for business policy and strategy.

Management, Organization, and Context

Advanced manufacturing technologies are for most organizations a radical process innovation. They represent a production process that is often a considerable departure from previous production experience in the firm. Their purchase and use are an example of the adoption and implementation of innovations.

Organizational scholars have studied such adoption and implementation for several decades. Hundreds of studies have revealed several characteristics of managers, organizational structure and processes, and organizational context that are related to the adoption of innovations (Hage, 1980; Kimberly, 1981; Tornatzky and others, 1983). Examples include the values and attitudes of top managers, the form of decision making, the extent of rules and regulations, the proportion of technical personnel who are specialists and professionally active, and the form of strategic planning. Organizations are likely to adopt innovations when they have strategies that stress technological advancement, structures that allow decentralized decision making, limited formal rules and regulations, high proportions of managerial specialists who are professionally active, and managers who value new ideas and are receptive to change. Characteristics of the innovation itself, such as cost, are also important.

Traditional organizational forms that stress functional differentiation often reduce the likelihood of adoption of advanced manufacturing processes. Restricting decisions regarding the purchase and implementation of advanced technologies to technical professionals such as engineers limits potential success. Only infrequently are those responsible for the development and use of technologies knowledgeable about the social and organizational factors that limit their effectiveness. Seldom, for example, are human-resource professionals involved in the planning and implementation of new technologies, yet implementation will almost surely cause severe disruptions among employees. Whether to retrain old workers to use the new technology or to hire and train new workers is one of the obvious questions. The question of how the new technology fits existing social relationships is also important. Yet, frequently, only after the new equipment has been purchased and installed are these questions addressed.

Equally unlikely is the involvement of marketing professionals in the decision to purchase new manufacturing technologies. If the firm does not consider new market segments that are capable of exploitation with computerized automation, cost justification for the purchase of the new automated processes becomes difficult (see Blumberg and Gerwin, 1984; Kaplan, 1983). Indeed, marketing techniques useful for selling products produced by typical mass production methods may not be as effective for selling small batches of highly specialized products made by using new forms of computer-integrated automation (Hayes and Wheelwright, 1984, pp. 197-228). As a consequence, previous marketing practices of the firm must be changed to take full advantage of new forms of automation. Increased integration of engineering and design, production, human resources, marketing, and other professional functions is therefore necessary.

Adoption and implementation of advanced manufacturing technologies are thus facilitated by certain configurations of management attitudes and values, organizational structure and practices, and organizational context and environment. But precise delineation of the most appropriate configuration is difficult because of gaps in our knowledge about organizations and technology. New forms of computerized automation only partly fit existing knowledge about organizational behavior and theory. Empirical data describing the operation and organizational consequences of new forms of computerized automation such as robotics and CIM have only recently been collected.

In addition, ideas concerning technology and its management generally held by organizational theorists may be only partly appropriate for new forms of computerized automation. Classic contingency views of technology may be incomplete for understanding the relationships among strategy, structure, and organizational adaptation involving new forms of automation. For example, the contingency view states that successful firms have structures that match their production processes at the unit or organizational level, depending on the size of the organization (Hickson, Pugh, and Pheysey, 1969; Woodward, 1965). Woodward (1965, pp. 50-80) reports several ideal relationships between organizational structure and unit-batch, mass, and continuous-process forms of production. She states that mass production organizations typically have mechanistic structures, where tasks are fragmented, roles are specific, spans of control are wide, communication is formal, standard control procedures are used, and production administration is separated from actual supervision of production operations. Batch and continuous-process firms, by contrast, possess more organic structures, where role ambiguity concerning duties and responsibilities is greater, verbal communication is preferred to written communication, direct labor is greater than indirect labor, narrower spans of control exist, and there is a greater ratio of manual workers to clerical and administrative staff. Successful firms tend to be those that have complementary structures and technologies. (See also Burns and Stalker, 1961.)

Traditional methods for measuring technology may also be limited. For example, work-flow integration, a frequently used measure of technology, assumes that automation, work-flow rigidity, and specificity of assessing organizational activities are positively related (Hickson, Pugh, and Pheysey, 1969). New forms of automation, however, permit an inverse relationship between automation and work-flow rigidity—flexibility can increase with increased automation and integration.

Thus, the relationships between technology and its management become blurred with new forms of automation. The distinctions do not neatly fit manufacturing firms with fully integrated automation. These firms share characteristics of both batch and mass production. They have the flexibility of batch processing but are also capable of long production runs of standardized products. They have a high degree of automation and specificity of evaluation, but knowledge and equipment may display little rigidity because of the ease of changing software-encoded instructions. Tasks may be enlarged and roles may be increasingly ambiguous as in batch firms, yet software-contained communications and control procedures can be more standardized than currently used written forms. Ratios of direct labor to indirect labor and manual work to clerical and administrative functions can change. With CIM, highly controlled batch production becomes possible with few direct and manual workers (and managers). Order quantities previously possible only with mass production may be completed alongside small-volume, custom orders, all using the same production system. Is this now a mass production, batch, or continuous-process form of production? Should the organization be mechanistically or organically structured to achieve top performance? Answers to questions such as these will require fresh thinking about the ideal relationship between organizational structure and technology in firms using new forms of computerized automation.

These considerations have important consequences for strategy formulation and competition. Traditional views regarding the role of manufacturing in business policy and strategy need reassessment. Advanced manufacturing technologies require that new production possibilities be considered when trying to establish a competitive advantage. Approaches to strategic planning that view new forms of automation simply as extensions of past technological capability will underestimate their potential.

The chapters in this book address some of these concerns and discuss some of the changes required in the infrastructure of the factory to make it less anachronistic than it now is. Managerial, organizational, and contextual factors related to successful adoption and implementation of advanced manufacturing technologies are discussed. Suggestions are provided for change in management practice.

Plan of the Book

The parts of this book represent four areas of study believed important for an understanding of the adoption and implementation of advanced manufacturing technologies. The first part describes two ways of understanding innovation processes in organizations. The second part reports on national surveys of usage rates and organizational features related to usage. The third part describes factors related to successful implementation of advanced manufacturing technologies. Finally, the implications of advanced manufacturing technologies for strategic planning are discussed.

In the first part, John R. Kimberly presents a general model for understanding innovation processes. He examines five different classes of technological innovation: the organization as user of innovation, as inventor of innovation, as both user and inventor, as vehicle for innovation, and as the innovation itself. This classification is useful because it helps us understand that barriers to change are different for different types of innovation. Organizations such as Cincinnati Milacron, which invent and sell advanced manufacturing technologies, will confront problems different from those encountered by firms such as

Zilog, Inc., which must adopt and implement advanced technologies for the production of microprocessors. Some firms may cut across several of these classifications. In the case of the joint venture between General Motors and Fujitsu-Fanuc, for example, new technologies are simultaneously invented (robots and other computerized forms of automation) and implemented (General Motors is one of the largest users of advanced manufacturing technologies). The joint venture also is a vehicle for innovation and is an innovation in itself. These two firms will need to address barriers to creating new technologies, implementing and managing these new production processes throughout their own plants, marketing these systems to other firms, and managing the integration of two firms with different traditions and cultures.

Jerald Hage extends this analysis by examining the adoption of new manufacturing technologies throughout entire industries. Hage's industry-level analysis complements Kimberly's analysis at the level of the firm. Hage examines why entire industries have been slow to adopt advanced manufacturing technologies. He applies a new paradigm in organizational theory called population ecology. This approach studies factors contributing to the emergence and decline of populations of organizations, much as a biologist or botanist might study the birth and death of species of animals or plants. To illustrate his discussion he describes a case study of the American shoe industry. The study reveals how characteristics of an industry's managers, structure, and environment can reduce the likelihood of adopting new manufacturing technologies. His analysis demonstrates that the industry's ontogeny, much like human development, shapes later growth and adaptive capability. This perspective is an important addition to the organizational theory of innovation and adds to other life-span contributions (see Kimberly and Miles, 1980).

Taken together, the chapters by Kimberly and Hage provide a context for subsequent chapters. They demonstrate that the failure of American firms to adopt advanced manufacturing technologies can be understood by examining characteristics of each firm's managers, structure, strategy, and environment—factors that have been associated with the adoption of other types of innovations.

The second part of the book focuses on the usage rates of advanced manufacturing technologies and characteristics related to this usage. National surveys of usage rates for computerized design and manufacturing technologies portray an American manufacturing Methuselah. Bylinsky (1983) cites some illustrative data. Over 34 percent of U.S. machine tools are twenty or more years old, more than in any other industrialized nation in the world. Fewer than one third of the machine tools used by American firms are less than ten years old. Numerically controlled machine tools, a technology available for several decades, constitute only about 4.7 percent of all machine tools in the United States (*American Machinist,* 1983), demonstrating little growth from previous levels of about 4 percent (*American Machinist,* 1978). In Japan, by contrast, only about one fifth of the machine tools are more than twenty years old. Moreover, and more significantly, almost two thirds of Japanese machine tools are less than ten years old. Japan is not the only modernized manufacturing competitor of the United States. The United States has the lowest percentage of machine tools less than ten years old among seven other major, industrialized nations (*American Machinist,* 1978).

American use of robots is no less discouraging. Although robots were originally developed in the United States by firms such as Unimation, American companies, especially small firms, have lagged in their adoption. Survey data reported by Ayres and Miller (1983, p. 7) reveal that although the U.S. robot population is larger than that in other Western industrialized nations, its placements are outpaced in Japan by more than three to one. Although the number of robots has increased in the United States in recent years, it has also grown in other nations. The percentage of world robotic placements accounted for by U.S. firms has declined slightly from about 17 percent of the world total to about 13 percent (Robot Institute of America, 1982, 1983). On considering the prevalence of modern machine tools and advanced manufacturing technologies among Japanese firms, David Nitzan, director of industrial robotics at

SRI International, states, "We are facing another Sputnik—a Japanese Sputnik" (cited in Bylinsky, 1983).

Although public opinion in the United States, currently fueled by the imbalance of foreign trade, strength of the dollar, loss of jobs, and a small amount of xenophobia, is pressing for trade tariffs and other protectionist measures, these provide no long-term solution to the problem. It is also necessary to modernize American manufacturing capabilities.

National studies conducted by John E. Ettlie and by Ann Majchrzak, Veronica F. Nieva, and Paul D. Newman reveal in detail the extent to which the new technologies are being used. Examined is whether adoption and use of computerized forms of automation are similar to the patterns for other radical process innovations such as computers and stand-alone automation. These two studies are important because they empirically delineate the factors associated with the increased and successful adoption and implementation of advanced manufacturing technologies. Their results are at two levels of detail. The study by Ettlie is a national survey of vendor and user firms. His discussion focuses on the interpersonal relationship between vendors and users. The study by Majchrzak and her associates is also a national survey, but it examines users exclusively. The two studies complement each other. The qualitative methods used by Ettlie provide rich details illuminating the special nature of the vendor-user relationship and how this relationship may be one of the critical ingredients of successful implementation. The quantitative survey methods used by Majchrzak and her associates provide a precise study of a sample of the population of users in three industries throughout the United States. Their results yield substantial evidence to demonstrate that integrated automation is rare in American firms and that firms that employ these technologies are different from those that do not.

It seems clear after viewing these data that increased attention must be paid to dissemination and implementation strategies. The third part of the book examines efforts intended to foster the use of advanced manufacturing technologies. This problem has two parts. First, methods for increasing the purchase of these new technologies must be tested. Second, successful implementation procedures must be used once they are purchased. The first portion of the problem is answered, in part, by marketing.

A major problem in the marketing of advanced technologies is that products and processes are designed first; marketing is usually an afterthought (New and Schlacter, 1979). That is, technology drives marketing—a technology-push orientation. An alternative is to let markets inform the design of technology—a technology-pull orientation. The logic of technology pull is that users can contribute productively to the new technology design because they are most familiar with the uses to which the technology will be put (von Hippel, 1976, 1977a, 1977b). Users can effectively shape technology design, even through the creation and initial testing of prototypes. Disregarding this role of the market in creating new technologies can be expensive. Many failures are not eliminated until after full production has begun (Myers and Sweezy, 1978).

Dorothy Leonard-Barton and Janis Gogan suggest in their chapter that advanced manufacturing technologies require special marketing sensibilities and applications. Leonard-Barton and Gogan provide an analysis of how the marketing of advanced manufacturing technologies is different from marketing consumer products. Some practices, such as segmentation, are similar in meaning but take a different form when applied to industrial marketing. The authors describe a nested approach as a powerful method for market segmentation. Other ideas, such as the need to educate users about the capabilities of these new technologies, are contrary to standard marketing practice. For example, in many cases the marketer of advanced manufacturing technologies must reduce and make realistic expectations about the new technology held by the prospective buyer in order to diminish the risk of disillusionment. Reducing expectations has seldom been a problem for consumer-marketing giants like Procter & Gamble. Another important aspect of marketing is difficulty in justifying the purchase of these large and expensive systems. Accounting perspectives that stress quarterly returns and neglect the profit potential of added flexibility or expanded production have limited utility, although they often still guide the purchase decision (Gold, 1982a, 1982b; Kaplan, 1983).

Potential problems do not cease, however, once advanced

manufacturing technologies have been disseminated and purchased. Equally important is attention to factors that contribute to successful implementation. The complexity of these new
systems requires change in other organizational practices and
processes. Workers and managers have to adapt to the new systems. In most cases, there is no organizational memory recording changes of similar technological and cognitive magnitude to
guide the implementation effort. New ideas and tactics are required. This effort is complicated by the fact that the characteristics that make organizations most receptive to innovations
such as advanced manufacturing technologies may be different
from the characteristics related to their successful implementation (Zaltman, Duncan, and Holbek, 1973).

Organizational features such as centralized decision making, reliance on formal rules and procedures, and fewer occupational specialties may reduce the probability that the organization will adopt new technologies. This phenomenon has been
documented in the shoe industry (Cohn and Turyn, 1980), hospitals (Kimberly and Evanisko, 1981), and health and welfare
organizations (Hage and Aiken, 1967), among others. The relationship between these factors and subsequent implementation,
however, is not clear. Once the decision to adopt has been
made, strict adherence to written rules and decisions made at
the top may ensure that the new technology is implemented
easily (Zaltman, Duncan, and Holbek, 1973). However, participative decision making and the possibility for local adaptation
of the new technology may engender shop-floor support, leading to effective and complete use. These propositions are mostly conjecture at this point and require further testing. What
seems clear, however, is that characteristics of the organization's managers, structure, and practices will determine the
success of the implementation effort. Adoption of advanced
manufacturing technologies does not ensure their successful
implementation. Advanced manufacturing technologies are not
turnkey systems.

Successful implementation also requires attention to the
needs of employees using the new systems. Individual workers
are strongly affected by the characteristics of their job (Griffin,

1982; Hackman and Oldham, 1980). Task characteristics such as autonomy, feedback, and skill variety can increase job satisfaction, commitment to the organization, and productivity, and they can decrease absenteeism and turnover. Advanced manufacturing technologies significantly change these task characteristics, altering the balance between the worker and the immediate work environment. The technology constrains the manner in which individual jobs can be designed (Oldham and Hackman, 1980). For example, the software built into computerized forms of automation can significantly reduce the amount of autonomy that can be exercised. Workers now spend a greater amount of time tending and monitoring production and less time picking, placing, cutting, assembling than they do in less automated systems. This usurpation of skills and responsibilities can significantly reduce job satisfaction and commitment to the organization. In its most dramatic form, workers' worst fears are realized: They may be laid off or replaced.

Fears of job displacement are not groundless. Hunt and Hunt (1983, p. 69) estimate that each robot displaces about two jobs. This displacement is especially likely in functions such as painting, welding, and loading/unloading. As many as 45 percent of all jobs in the United States could be affected by office or factory automation, with major consequences for individual workers (Office of Technology Assessment, 1983, p. 14). Successful implementation of advanced manufacturing technologies requires attention to human-resource issues associated with their use. Whether new forms of automation have traumatic effects on workers will depend on the human-resource practices undergirding their implementation.

Chapters by Linda Argote and Paul S. Goodman and by James C. Taylor, Paul W. Gustavson, and William S. Carter describe two implementation cases that shed light on the factors important to successful implementation—in the first case, implementation of robots, and, in the second case, implementation of a CAD system. It is clear in both cases that successful implementation requires attention to the needs of employees using the new systems.

Argote and Goodman provide a general framework for

understanding the relationship between robots and the organization using them, especially the conditions under which the use of robots will enhance outcomes such as productivity. They point out that use of robots does not lead inevitably to any particular set of outcomes; these outcomes depend instead on the interaction between characteristics of the technology itself (robots), the manner in which it is implemented, the larger organizational context and structure, and the people who actually work with the robots. Using this fourfold framework, the authors discuss the results of several studies that have tracked the implementation of robotic systems. Their discussion demonstrates clearly that advanced manufacturing technologies cannot be installed in a turnkey fashion to increase productivity automatically. Instead, certain configurations among the new technology, organizational structure, and human-resource practices are needed to produce desired outcomes.

A major feature associated with the successful implementation of new technologies is the fit between them and their surrounding organizational context. This thinking has given birth to a stream of ideas and action originating in England known as sociotechnical systems design (SSD) (Herbst, 1974; Pasmore and Sherwood, 1978). This view of organizations is at the same time a set of concepts for understanding how they work, a set of beliefs and values suggesting how they ought to work, and a set of practices for guiding the redesign of organizations so that they might work more effectively than they now do. SSD interprets organizations as open systems operating within a complex web of environmental relationships that influence outcomes (see Emery and Trist, 1965). The firm uses the technical system (technology and procedures) and the social system (people and their interrelationships) to process inputs (raw materials, labor, and so forth) to produce outputs (products or services). Implicit in SSD thinking is the concept of equifinality—the belief that organizations can reach the same end state although starting from different initial conditions and following different paths of action (see von Bertalanffy, 1956). The key is to identify the initial conditions, examine paths of action, and discover variances in performance that contribute to undesired outcomes. The organization is then redesigned to eliminate these variances and jointly to optimize the social and technical systems. Several reported cases describe the effectiveness of SSD in improving organizational performance (Cummings and Molloy, 1977; Davis and Cherns, 1975).

The chapter by Taylor, Gustavson, and Carter describes one of the first applications of SSD principles to the implementation of advanced technologies—in this case, a CAD system implemented at Zilog, Inc., a microprocessor manufacturer. They describe the application of SSD principles and techniques to the redesign of an engineering unit responsible for circuit design. The social and technical systems were analyzed and the roles and relationships of unit members (the social system) were changed to fit the demands of the new CAD system (the technical system). Engineers no longer worked individually, separated by function. Instead, individuals were organized into teams, with the common goal of designing and supporting a new integrated-circuit product. Previously existing functional boundaries were blurred to increase the level of support from other units, such as marketing, that typically are not involved in product design. Rearrangement of the social system to fit the technical system is the most common type of intervention in SSD approaches (Roitman and Gottschalk, 1984). The authors report encouraging increases in productivity and decreases in turnover, an especially severe problem among Silicon Valley firms.

A final area of concern important to the success of advanced manufacturing technologies is an understanding of their role in the larger firm. The contribution of these new forms of automation to the firm's success will be limited if they are seen only as extensions of past technology rather than as qualitatively new approaches to production that affect the firm's very foundation and purpose. Part Three of this book discusses strategic and policy questions related to advanced manufacturing technologies.

The competitive advantage to be derived from the use of new computerized forms of automation must be considered during the earliest stages of strategic management, in the formulation of goals and objectives. Such strategic planning plays a crucial role in aiding the firm's adaptation to change. The importance of strategic management may be appreciated by examining those firms with assets of more than $20 million that existed in 1917 and firms that exist today (Chandler, 1977, App. A). This comparison will reveal many firms that were successful earlier but that have failed to survive to the present. Firms continuing to exist today are usually those that have succeeded in matching organizational structure, technology, and strategy—firms such as General Electric, Eastman Kodak, John Deere, and Burroughs Adding Machine (later Burroughs Corporation). Firms that plan strategically generally perform better than those that do not (Davis, in press).

Neglect of the role of technology and manufacturing in strategic management has been the subject of much recent writing (for example, starting with Skinner, 1969; and, more recently, Buffa, 1984; Skinner, 1985; Hayes and Wheelwright, 1984), although, as revealed by Ettlie (1985), few managers adopting advanced manufacturing technologies read this literature. The theme running through these critiques is that American managers have been slow to consider production methods as a tool for achieving competitive advantage. The contribution of advanced manufacturing technologies to competitive advantage is discussed in this book in chapters by Mariann Jelinek and Joel D. Goldhar and by William A. Hetzner, J. D. Eveland, and Louis G. Tornatzky.

Jelinek and Goldhar argue that the mission and purpose of the firm must be reinterpreted in light of the new opportunities for control, flexibility, accuracy, and market responsiveness made possible by these new technologies. These new technologies carry with them the possibilities of new economies—economies of scope (Goldhar and Jelinek, 1983)—resulting in a degree of integration previously only dreamed of. This level of integration has major consequences for other functions of the firm such as design and marketing. Reduction in design time through CAD and the possibility of inexpensive production changes through linkage with CAM provide new opportunities for marketing. The flexibility of these new systems allows proliferation of product designs and product lines, resulting in increased responsiveness to customer needs. Responsiveness and custom production become strategic strengths rather than the costly liabilities they are in traditional production systems emphasizing long runs of standardized products.

Another perspective on this problem is provided by examining the role of federal, state, and local governments in fostering the use of advanced manufacturing technologies (see Tornatzky and others, 1982). The government can provide great leverage in the dissemination of technologies through taxes and regulations. A direct role may be played as well. For example, the U.S. Air Force was influential in fostering the development of numerically controlled machinery. The Air Force continues to underwrite the development of computerized automation through its Integrated Computer-Aided Manufacturing (ICAM) program. The National Bureau of Standards, through its Center for Advanced Manufacturing Processes, also exerts influence by developing and testing hardware and software. The U.S. Agricultural Extension Service has long acted to disseminate new agricultural technologies. The question that emerges is: Should government at various levels use its power to enhance the international competitiveness of American firms by fostering the dissemination of advanced manufacturing technologies? This debate resembles the national debate on industrial policy, where it is advocated that the federal government provide broad, long-term support for entire industries (see Reich, 1983). Most federal efforts thus far to foster advanced manufacturing processes have been concentrated in a few agencies and have emphasized short-term, defense-related applications (Hetzner, Tornatzky, and Klein, 1983). The government has made little effort to study manufacturing as a system or the managerial, organizational, and contextual variables likely to act as barriers to widespread use of advanced technologies.

The chapter contributed by Hetzner, Eveland, and Tornatzky examines this trend and discusses some of its consequences. They argue that the failure of the federal government to address the question of advanced technologies comprehensively reinforces the lack of strategic vision among manufacturing managers. They contend that the federal government can

and should play a wide role in fostering the development and
dissemination of new knowledge about these computerized
technologies, especially among small and medium-sized firms
that have lagged in their adoption but could benefit from their
use. They also advocate a type of technology extension service
to disseminate more widely than now new technological practices.

The chapters in this book provide a perspective on the
use of advanced manufacturing technologies by expanding the
focus of study to include managerial, human-resource, organizational, and contextual factors related to their adoption and
implementation. This wide focus is required to achieve the production potential made possible by these new technologies.
Attention only to hardware and software will reduce performance of these systems. Scholars wishing to understand the
relationship between organizational strategy, structure, and
technology must reshape their theories in light of these new
technologies. Managers wishing to gain and sustain competitive
advantage must adopt and implement advanced manufacturing
technologies. They must also go beyond considerations of hardware and software; they must consider the social context of
advanced manufacturing technologies.

References

American Machinist. "The 12th American Machinist Inventory
    of Metal-Working Equipment." *American Machinist,* Dec.
    1978, pp. 133-148.
American Machinist. "The 13th American Machinist Inventory
    of Metal-Working Equipment." *American Machinist,* Nov.
    1983, pp. 113-114.
Ayres, R. U., and Miller, S. M. *Robotics: Applications and So-
    cial Implications.* Cambridge, Mass.: Ballinger, 1983.
Blumberg, M., and Gerwin, D. "Coping with Advanced Manu-
    facturing Technology." *Journal of Occupational Behavior,*
    1984, 5, 113-130.
Buffa, E. S. *Meeting the Competitive Challenge: Manufacturing
    Strategy for U.S. Companies.* Homewood, Ill.: Dow Jones-
    Irwin, 1984.

Burns, T., and Stalker, G. M. *The Management of Innovation.* London: Tavistock, 1961.

Bylinsky, G. "The Race to the Automated Factory." *Fortune,* Feb. 21, 1983, pp. 52-64.

Chandler, A. D., Jr. *The Visible Hand: The Managerial Revolution in American Business.* Cambridge, Mass.: Belknap Press of Harvard University Press, 1977.

Cohn, S. F., and Turyn, R. M. "The Structure of the Firm and the Adoption of Process Innovations." *IEEE Transactions on Engineering Management,* 1980, *EM-27* (4), 98-102.

Cummings, T. G., and Molloy, E. S. *Improving Productivity and the Quality of Worklife.* New York: Praeger, 1977.

Davis, D. D. "Designing Organizations for Productivity, Technological Innovation, and Quality of Worklife: A Human Resource Perspective." In D. Gray, T. Soloman, and W. A. Hetzner (Eds.), *Strategies and Practices for Technological Innovation.* Amsterdam: North-Holland, in press.

Davis, L. E., and Cherns, A. B. (Eds.). *The Quality of Working Life.* Vols. 1 and 2. New York: Free Press, 1975.

Emery, F. E., and Trist, E. L. "The Causal Texture of Organizational Environments." *Human Relations,* 1965, *18,* 21-32.

Ettlie, J. E. "The Implementation of Programmable Manufacturing Innovations." In D. D. Davis (Ed.), *Dissemination and Implementation of Advanced Manufacturing Processes.* Washington, D.C.: National Science Foundation, 1985.

Gold, B. "CAM Sets New Rules for Production." *Harvard Business Review,* 1982a, *60* (6), 88-94.

Gold, B. "Robotics, Programmable Automation, and International Competitiveness." *IEEE Transactions on Engineering Management,* 1982b, *EM-29* (4), 135-146.

Goldhar, J. D., and Jelinek, M. "Plan for Economies of Scope." *Harvard Business Review,* 1983, *62* (6), 141-148.

Griffin, R. *Task Design: An Integrative Approach.* Glenview, Ill.: Scott, Foresman, 1982.

Hackman, J. R., and Oldham, G. R. *Work Redesign.* Reading, Mass.: Addison-Wesley, 1980.

Hage, J. *Theories of Organization: Form, Process, and Transformation.* New York: Wiley, 1980.

Hage, J., and Aiken, M. "Program Change and Organizational

Properties: A Comparative Analysis." *American Journal of Sociology,* 1967, 72, 503-519.

Hayes, R. H., and Wheelwright, S. C. *Restoring Our Competitive Edge: Competing Through Manufacturing.* New York: Wiley, 1984.

Herbst, P. G. *Sociotechnical Design.* London: Tavistock, 1974.

Hetzner, W. A., Tornatzky, L. G., and Klein, K. J. "Manufacturing Technology in the 1980's: A Survey of Federal Programs and Practices." *Management Science,* 1983, 29, 951-961.

Hickson, D. J., Pugh, D. S., and Pheysey, D. C. "Operations Technology and Organization Structure." *Administrative Science Quarterly,* 1969, 14, 378-397.

Hunt, H. A., and Hunt, T. L. *Human Resource Implications of Robotics.* Kalamazoo, Mich.: Upjohn Institute, 1983.

Kaplan, R. S. "Measuring Manufacturing Performance: A New Challenge for Managerial Accounting." *Accounting Review,* 1983, 58 (4), 686-705.

Kimberly, J. R. "Managerial Innovation." In P. C. Nystrom and W. H. Starbuck (Eds.), *Handbook of Organizational Design.* Vol. 1. New York: Oxford University Press, 1981.

Kimberly, J. R., and Evanisko, M. J. "Organizational Innovation: The Influence of Individual, Organizational, and Contextual Factors on Hospital Adoption of Technological and Administrative Innovations." *Academy of Management Journal,* 1981, 24, 689-713.

Kimberly, J. R., and Miles, R. H. (Eds.). *The Organizational Life Cycle: Issues in the Creation, Transformation, and Decline of Organizations.* San Francisco: Jossey-Bass, 1980.

Myers, S., and Sweezy, E. E. "Why Innovations Fail." *Technology Review,* 1978, 80, 40-46.

New, D. E., and Schlacter, J. L. "Abandon Bad R&D Projects with Earlier Marketing Appraisals." *Industrial Marketing Management,* 1979, 8, 274-280.

Office of Technology Assessment. *Automation and the Workplace: Selected Labor, Education and Training Issues.* Washington, D.C.: Office of Technology Assessment, 1983.

Oldham, G. R., and Hackman, J. R. "Work Design in the Organizational Context." In B. M. Staw and L. L. Cummings

(Eds.), *Research in Organizational Behavior.* Vol. 1. Greenwich, Conn.: JAI Press, 1980.

Pasmore, W. A., and Sherwood, J. J. (Eds.). *Sociotechnical Systems: A Sourcebook.* San Diego, Calif.: University Associates, 1978.

Reich, R. B. *The Next American Frontier: A Provocative Program for Economic Renewal.* New York: Times Books, 1983.

Robot Institute of America. *Worldwide Robotics Survey and Directory.* Dearborn, Mich.: Society of Manufacturing Engineers, 1982.

Robot Institute of America. *Worldwide Robotics Survey and Directory.* Dearborn, Mich.: Society of Manufacturing Engineers, 1983.

Roitman, D., and Gottschalk, R. *Job Enrichment, Sociotechnical Design, and Quality Circles: Effects on Productivity and Quality of Worklife.* Washington, D.C.: National Science Foundation, 1984.

Skinner, W. "Manufacturing—Missing Link in Corporate Strategy." *Harvard Business Review,* 1969, *37,* 136-145.

Skinner, W. *Manufacturing: The Formidable Competitive Weapon.* New York: Wiley, 1985.

Tornatzky, L. G., and others. "Fostering the Use of Advanced Manufacturing Technology." Unpublished paper, Innovation Processes Research Section, National Science Foundation, 1982.

Tornatzky, L. G., and others. *The Process of Technological Innovation: Reviewing the Literature.* Washington, D.C.: National Science Foundation, 1983.

von Bertalanffy, L. "General Systems Theory." *General Systems: Yearbook of the Society for General Systems Theory,* 1956, *1,* 1-10.

von Hippel, E. "The Dominant Role of the User in the Scientific Instrument Innovation Process." *Research Policy,* 1976, *5,* 212-239.

von Hippel, E. "The Dominant Role of the User in Semiconductor and Electronic Subassembly Process Innovation." *IEEE Transactions on Engineering Management,* 1977a, *EM-24,* 60-71.

von Hippel, E. "Transferring Process Equipment Innovations

from User-Inventors to Equipment Manufacturing Firms." *R & D Management,* 1977b, *8* (1), 13-22.

Woodward, J. *Industrial Organization.* Oxford, England: Oxford University Press, 1965.

Zaltman, G., Duncan, R., and Holbek, J. *Innovations and Organizations.* New York: Wiley, 1973.

ΙΟΙ TWO ΙΟΙ

The Organizational Context
of Technological Innovation

John R. Kimberly

It is often alleged that the United States has lost its competitive edge in the global economy, that it has let other nations assume the preeminent position that it historically enjoyed (Hayes and Abernathy, 1980). Although many explanations are offered for the decline, diminished productivity is generally seen to be a major part of the problem.

What lies behind the relative decline in productivity? The explanations are varied and complex. Congress is struggling both to define the problem and to develop remedies. Discussions of industrial policy are but one example of the search for viable answers (Reich, 1983). At this point, it appears safe to say that there are many hypotheses but few, if any, generally accepted explanations.

Prominent among the hypotheses is the relatively low rate of use of the latest advances in production technology by U.S. manufacturing firms. Advanced manufacturing technologies are available, the argument goes, but are underutilized, at least relatively speaking. (See Chapter Five.)

This chapter does not confront this allegation directly. Rather, my assumption is that there will always be a significant gap between technological innovations and the ability of individuals or of organizational or social systems to use them effec-

Note: Preparation of this chapter was supported, in part, by a grant from the National Institute of Education, School Organization and Management Program, John R. Kimberly and Janet A. Weiss, coprincipal investigators.

tively and fully. Our technical capacity will always lead our organizational capacity. Our ability to develop technological innovations will always outstrip our ability to develop the social and
organizational arrangements to ensure their rapid and widespread use. The managerial challenge is to keep the gap as small
as possible.

This chapter focuses on the relationship between technological innovation and organizational systems, and, particularly,
on what existing research has to say about this relationship. A
framework for classifying this research is elaborated, based on
the type of relationship that obtains, and a number of questions
are then raised about each type of relationship and the answers
are compared across types. Implications for the full and effective use of existing advanced manufacturing technologies are
then explored.

Types of Relationships

The subject of innovation has fascinated researchers and
managers alike, albeit for quite different reasons. Researchers
are attracted by the insights into the process of change that the
analysis of innovation promises. Managers are drawn by the potential improvement in performance that innovation implies.
Both goals have been to a certain extent illusory, of course, but
this drawback has not dimmed the enthusiasm of researchers for
the subject or the aspiration of managers for improved performance.

One result of virtually incessant attention has been volu-
minous writing on the subject. Everett Rogers has performed
heroically in cataloguing and synthesizing the research on innovation, and his 1983 book was a much-welcome update of his
previous synthetic efforts. Those interested in developing an
appreciation for the broad sweep of research on the general
topic would do well to familiarize themselves with this book.

All of this attention, of course, is a mixed blessing. One
particularly troublesome consequence has been a proliferation
of perspectives on and definitions of innovation itself. Most
people who work in the area are aware of the problem (see, for

example, Kimberly, 1981; Daft, 1982), yet definitional variety persists. To confuse the issue further, much of the research on innovation—however defined—has an organizational cast to it. Organizations are frequently the context of or for innovation, yet no generally accepted convention has been developed to sort out this research in a conceptually meaningful and empirically useful way.

This chapter proposes a framework for doing just that, the basic argument being that the type of relationship between innovation and organization varies and that five substantively significant types can be distinguished: the organization as user of innovation, the organization as inventor of innovation, the organization as both user and inventor of innovation, the organization as vehicle for innovation, and the organization as innovation. Barriers to ensuring a maximally productive relationship between organization and innovation exist in all five types; however, the barriers differ by type, as will be shown in the discussion of each that follows.

Type I: The Organization as User of Innovation. The organization as user of innovation is the type of relationship that researchers have most often examined, typically by using an adoption or diffusion perspective or both. Why is it that some organizations more quickly adopt a given innovation or set of innovations than other organizations? How can we account for patterns in the way in which a given innovation spreads in a population of potential user organizations? In either case, the implicit assumption seems to be that innovation is good and more innovation is better; the practical concern, then, is how to increase the receptivity of given organizations to a particular innovation or set of innovations (that is, how to increase the organization's adoption potential) or how to speed up the process by which an innovation spreads within a population of potential adopters/users. The federal government often encounters this diffusion problem as it tries to encourage, for example, the widespread use of innovations in medical technology developed with federal funding or the use of innovations in educational technology similarly supported. And as the authors of Chapter Eight point out, both perspectives are central to the concerns of marketing, where the issue is to increase the rate of use of certain products throughout a population of organizations or individuals.

Type II: The Organization as Inventor of Innovation. In the Type I relationship, organizations are the consumers of innovation. By contrast, in the Type II relationship, organizations are the producers of innovation. In this case, the principal research question is how to account for differences in the rates, types, and quality of innovations produced by a sample of organizations or departments. In the research literature, this problem has generally been referred to as one of research creativity. In the practitioner-oriented literature, it is generally referred to as the problem of the management of research and development (R&D) or of new-product development. Chapter Seven, with its focus on how principles of sociotechnical design were used to restructure an R&D unit to improve performance, provides one example of the Type II relationship. Here again, the implicit assumption appears to be that innovation is good and more innovation is better, and the search is for ways to increase the volume of innovations produced by a particular department or organizational system.

Type III: The Organization as Inventor and User of Innovation. Organizations often invent solutions to specific problems that they have. Not every organization has the capacity or the resources to do this well or frequently, but the normative position seems to be that they should. When they do, they are both inventing and using innovation.

Researchers have referred to this particular relationship between organization and innovation as innovation *in situ* (for example, Kanter, 1983). Although not widely researched, the frequency of this type of relationship is undoubtedly high. One example is the development of software in-house to meet what are believed to be idiosyncratic needs. The motivation is real-time problem solution rather than new-product development for an external market. It is not unusual, however, for a company to become aware of the market potential of an innovation initially developed for its own use and to move it into the marketplace. General Motors and IBM have done this with robots, for example, as has General Electric with flexible manufacturing systems.

The prevalence of "user-dominated innovation" (von Hippel, 1976)—that is, the development of new products in response to specific demands from users—would lead one to suppose that organizations are often able to solve particular problems with home-grown remedies. One might predict that the incidence of innovation *in situ* varies inversely with the capital cost of the solution. One might also believe, therefore, that this type of relationship is relatively rare when hard technology is involved. A firm would not, for example, be likely to invest heavily in the development of its own advanced manufacturing system (unless it was extremely large, as is the case with General Motors and robotics or General Electric and flexible manufacturing systems).

The Type III relationship is certainly interesting and worthy of considerably more attention from researchers than it has received.

Type IV: The Organization as Vehicle for Innovation. In the first three types of relationships, the organization is directly involved with the innovation in question, either as a producer or a consumer or both. In the fourth type of relationship, the organization's relationship to the innovation is that of carrier, or vehicle, rather than producer or consumer and is therefore less direct (although no less central).

Certain kinds of innovations require new organizational forms to ensure their application. Without these new forms, the innovations would not be available to potential users. Consider, for example, the innovation of prepayment in medical care, a significant departure from the more usual fee-for-service mode of payment to physicians. Prepayment cannot be simply willed into use. It requires that a rather complex set of relationships be developed among physicians, hospitals, and employer groups—relationships that are themselves somewhat novel. The health maintenance organization (HMO) is one specific organizational form that was created in order to make it possible for this innovation in mode of payment to become available. The HMO in this example, then, is the vehicle for innovation—prepaid medical care.

What is particularly interesting about this type of relationship between organization and innovation is the fact that
frequently the organizations that act as carriers of or vehicles
for innovation are themselves new forms. Joint ventures are
good examples. Both the research opportunities and the managerial challenges are magnified considerably when novelty is so
abundant. To the usual concerns on the part of potential users
about the innovation (Will it work? Is it really better than what
I've been doing all along? What do I have to do differently in
order to use it?) are added concerns arising from the unfamiliar-
ity (and hence the questionable legitimacy) of the new organizational form.

Type V: The Organization as Innovation. In some cases,
the organization itself is the innovation, that is, a new organizational form is invented to solve a particular problem or set of
problems. This type of relationship between organization and
innovation differs from the previous one in that the organization that is the vehicle for innovation need not necessarily be
innovative itself (although it frequently is).

A particularly interesting example of the organization as
innovation is the educational service center in the field of education. Historically, a great deal of tension has existed between
state education agencies, such as a department of education,
and local school districts. The local school districts tend to be
fiercely autonomous and to regard the state educational bu-
reaucracy with suspicion and mistrust. They generally consider
initiatives from the state level inimical to local interests, almost
by definition; the amount of cooperation between the state and
local authorities thus tends to be highly variable. Historically,
too, there has been relatively little cooperation between and
among local districts. They tend to staunchly defend boundaries
and to maintain their independence by whatever means necessary.

This situation was tolerable in an era of abundant resources for elementary and secondary education. As resources
became scarce, both state and local education officials had to
find new ways to fund existing programs and to develop new
programs and services. One solution was the creation of a new

organization, the educational service center, located between the state and local levels and requiring the cooperation of several school districts. The idea was that these organizations could provide services to local districts that might be too expensive for any single district (Kimberly, Norling, and Weiss, 1983). In this case, an innovative organizational form was the response to the problems of the agencies involved.

Examples of the organization as innovation in the context of advanced technology are the public or quasi-public organizations created to foster links between industry and universities in order to generate research funds and develop new technical breakthroughs. One such organization is the Industrial Technology Institute in Michigan, whose mission is to promote the adoption of advanced manufacturing technologies through a combination of technical assistance and basic and applied research.

Analytical Issues

Identifying these five types of relationships between innovation and organization is useful only to the extent that these distinctions add analytical power to frameworks for understanding innovation. The contention here is that these five distinct organizational contexts for innovation vary with respect to five key questions: What phenomenon is being examined? What perspective or set of lenses has been brought to bear on the phenomenon? What definition of innovation is typically used? What outcomes are of primary interest? What are the key managerial problems?

The distinctions among the five types of relationships are useful precisely because the answers to these five questions vary depending on which type of relationship is of concern. Because the term *innovation* is so widely used, it is essential to clarify its use in any particular instance. The typology proposed here does that and helps the researcher or manager to locate specific cases more precisely within the wide range of alternatives than is otherwise possible. To amplify and illustrate this point, each of the five questions will be considered in turn.

The Phenomenon of Interest. What particular phenomenon are researchers or managers interested in? It turns out that
the phenomenon is different depending on the type of relationship being examined. When the concern is with the organization as user of innovation, adoption or diffusion of innovation
or both are the phenomena of interest. One might be interested
in why one organization adopts more innovations than another
or different innovations than another, or why one innovation
spreads more rapidly within a population of potential user organizations than another. When the concern is with the organization as inventor of innovation, however, the phenomenon of
interest is new-product development. In the case of the organization as both inventor and user of innovation, researchers and
managers are interested in understanding creative internal problem solving. Where the organization is a vehicle for innovation,
the concern is with effective organizational design; and in those
instances where the organization itself is the innovation, the interest is in how and why new organizational forms are created.

Each of these phenomena—adoption (or diffusion) of
new technologies, development of new products, creative internal problem solving, effective organizational design, and generation of new organizational forms—is quite different, and it is unrealistic to expect, therefore, that a single theoretical perspective would be capable of illuminating each one with equivalent
power and precision.

Perspective Used. In fact, quite different perspectives have
been brought to bear on understanding the different organizational contexts for innovation. In the case of the organization
as user, for example, the marketing perspective has dominated.
The problem attacked by the preponderance of research here
has been either how to enhance the ability of a given organization to adopt innovations or how to speed up the spread of a
given innovation to a population of potential users. With the
adoption perspective, researchers have tended to concentrate on
the appropriate mix of employee and organizational attributes,
the assumption being that the right people with the right values
and motivations in the right kind of organizational setting will
result in an organizational system with a good potential for

adopting innovations. With the diffusion perspective, the focus has, by contrast, been on the attributes of innovations, the assumption being that certain attributes enhance the attractiveness of an innovation to a set of potential users and that if you know what these attributes are you can speed up the process of diffusion.

Whether the problem is defined as one of adoption or of diffusion, a marketing orientation seems to lie behind most of what has been written. Three points should be made briefly here. First, when the organization is the user of innovation, both adoptor attributes and innovation attributes influence the outcome. It is unrealistic to consider them in isolation from one another. Second, it is not obvious that research should uncritically accept the marketing orientation that is implicit in much of this work. As I have argued elsewhere (Kimberly, 1981), not everything that passes for innovation is necessarily desirable, either from the perspective of a single organization or from that of society as a whole. What organizations (and societies) need is the capacity to evaluate innovations—be they innovations in manufacturing technologies, medical technologies, or entertainment technologies—and to embrace those that offer particular promise and reject those that do not. As a practical matter, making these decisions is enormously complex. Conceptually, however, the distinction needs to be made. Finally, researchers need to concentrate as much on the actual use of innovations as they do on adoption. As we all know, the mere fact of adoption does not by any means guarantee use. How many small business computers, for example, lie unused after purchase? Research tends to stop with adoption. In many respects, however, adoption is just the beginning of the most interesting part of the story.

In the case of new-product development, where the organization is the inventor of innovation, a combination of consumer behavior and industrial economics tends to drive research. The questions asked have to do with the kinds of new products that are developed and with the rate at which they are developed. For the individual firm, the issue tends to boil down to the extent to which it should be directly involved in R&D or should be positioning itself to capitalize quickly on new prod-

ucts developed by others. At a macro level, researchers have
been interested in the relationship between expenditures on
R&D and rates of new-product development or profitability or
both; on a micro level, they have concentrated on the kinds of
organizational arrangements that appear to be associated with
highly productive R&D efforts.

Until quite recently, relatively little attention has been
paid to the organization as inventor and user of innovation.
Hence, not much research has been done on this particular
relationship between organization and innovation. However,
Kanter (1983), Ouchi (1984), and Peters and Waterman (1982)
all focus in one way or another on the issue of how organizations can unlock the creative potential of their employees,
potential that is often inhibited or frustrated by bureaucratic
systems that take on a life of their own. We can reasonably anticipate, therefore, that a significant perspective on this relationship will be that of human-resource management—what kinds
of human-resource management procedures and policies are
likely to stimulate creative internal problem solving, and how
can they be most effectively implemented?

If there has been little research on the organization as inventor and user of innovation, there has been virtually none on
the organization as vehicle for innovation. Yet it is conceivable,
even likely, that recent experiments linking universities and
firms through various state and private initiatives may lead to
alteration not only of methods for financing innovation in advanced manufacturing technology but also of the traditional
and time-honored roles of faculty. These experiments need to
be carefully watched and evaluated; they provide a rich setting
for researchers interested in the general problem of change and
innovation.

Researchers concerned with the invention of new organizational forms have been interested in the organization as innovation. Perhaps the classic statement of the problem is contained in Stinchcombe's (1965) analysis of the relationship between social structure and organizations, where he hypothesized
that new organizational forms are invented to meet particular
configurations of social and economic needs at particular points

in time and, once founded, tend to perpetuate their basic forms relatively unchanged over long periods of time. A different point of view is found in the work of the population ecologists, who seek to apply bioecological theory to the study of human organizations (Hannan and Freeman, 1978). And a third perspective—itself eclectic—can be inferred from the work of those interested in the phenomenon of entrepreneurship, where the invention of a new organizational form is defined as the consequence of the efforts of a particular highly motivated individual with the prescience to see a particular niche in the marketplace and to fill it in a unique way. Viewed as a whole, research on the organization as innovation is by far the most diverse of the types of research discussed here and comprises at best a loosely related set of perspectives on the problem.

The aim here is not to go into great detail about any single perspective but rather to make the point that many perspectives have been brought to bear on the five types of relationships between organization and innovation and that this diversity underscores the need to take a differentiated view of these relationships.

Definition of Innovation. Given the diversity of phenomena and of perspectives found in research on the organizational context of technological innovation, it should come as no surprise that researchers and managers alike use the word *innovation* to refer to many different things. This point has been made elsewhere (for example, Kimberly, 1981; Daft, 1982) and need not be rehashed in detail here. Some general discussion, however, is useful.

The term has been used principally in three ways: to refer to a process ("the process of innovation is notoriously difficult to predict"), to refer to a specific item ("CAD/CAM is an innovation whose potential is enormous"), and as an adjective to describe individual people or organizations ("Hewlett-Packard has the reputation of being a highly innovative organization"). In analyzing the relationship between organizations and innovation, the second of these definitions is the most appropriate. And, for the purposes of this chapter, we are interested in particular innovations in manufacturing technology such as numerical control systems, just-in-time systems, or robotics; the second definition is clearly the most relevant.

Even when referring to a specific item as an innovation, we need to be aware of a conceptual issue. What is the frame of reference by which the specific item is judged to be an innovation? There are at least two possibilities. One is field based—that is, the item is judged to be a significant departure from the state of the art in a given field at the time it appears. Thus, for example, computer-aided design/computer-aided manufacturing (CAD/CAM) might be judged to have been a significant departure from the state of the art in design and manufacturing at the time it was developed and therefore could rightfully be called an innovation as opposed to an incremental improvement.

A second possibility is that the frame of reference be organization based—that is, the item is judged to be a significant departure for a particular organization. A particular word-processing system, therefore, might be judged to be an innovation for one organization but not for another.

For four of the five types of relationships between organization and innovation described, the definition of innovation is field based. The only exception is the case of the organization as inventor and user of innovation, where it is clear that, by definition, the item has to be significantly new to the organization. The item may also qualify as an innovation according to field-based criteria as well, but it need not.

Outcomes. As the discussion thus far implies, the outcomes that researchers are interested in understanding and that managers are paid to achieve vary depending on the type of relationship that is the focus of attention. In the case of the organization as user of innovation, the outcome is typically rate of adoption. When the organization is the inventor of innovation, the outcome is the rate at which new products are developed and, sometimes, their eventual rate of success in the marketplace. In the case of the organization as inventor and user, the outcome is the rate of innovation *in situ,* however measured (and such measurement, of course, is no small problem). Where the organization is the vehicle for innovation, the outcome of interest is effectiveness: How well does the organization do what it is supposed to do? And, when the organization itself is the innovation, the outcome is its survival: Will it pass the fitness test, and is it well adapted for the purpose(s) for which it was created?

This diversity in outcomes of interest to researchers and managers again bespeaks the utility of a framework that usefully differentiates among the various types of relationships among organizations and innovation rather than implicitly treating them as all the same.

Managerial Issues. The phenomena, the perspectives, and the outcomes are different across the five types. So, too, are the kinds of issues that confront managers working in these different contexts. Where the organization is user of innovation, the managerial challenges are to identify innovations of particular promise, no small task, and then to build support for those identified, get them adopted, and ensure that they are used productively. Also, in the long run, the manager must attempt to avoid having the organization become overinvested in any particular innovation so that it may be receptive to the next generation of innovations.

In the case of the organization as inventor of innovation, the managerial challenge is nurturing creativity and productivity among R&D personnel. The manager must understand how to influence the climate and how to structure rewards in ways that positively influence the process of scientific development. This challenge is quite obviously of a different sort from that of the manager in an organization that is a user of innovation.

The problem in the case of innovation *in situ* from a managerial perspective is how to get people to develop and forward ideas for internal improvement in the first place and then how to choose among these ideas in a way that continues to motivate employees to search for new solutions. Some have called the issue here building the capacity for self-renewal into an organization. Managers are caught in a dilemma. They have to balance needs for control with needs for innovation. The knee-jerk response when the two conflict is to tilt in the direction of control at the expense of innovation. The challenge is to develop an internal climate and supporting structures that reward innovation and that do not reward excessive control. With all its flaws, the research on excellent companies (Peters and Waterman, 1982) does strongly suggest that the capacity for creative internal problem solving distinguishes high-performing firms from others, and the implication is that managers need to think about how to encourage this capacity in their own organizations or subunits.

The managerial issues when the organization is the vehicle for innovation and when the organization is itself the innovation are similar, particularly when a new form of organization is developed to be the vehicle for the innovation. The principal problem confronted by managers in these cases is to develop some stability internally while creating public understanding of the organization externally. A new organizational form necessarily creates uncertainty in the outside world. People do not know what to expect from the new organization or how to behave toward it. The managerial challenge here, then, is creating legitimacy for the enterprise—that is, doing what is necessary to reduce the level of ambiguity in the outside world regarding what the enterprise is and what it does. At the same time, the manager needs to nurture the internal sense of adventure and uniqueness that goes with creating a new organizational form and that motivates many people to join the organization in the first place. The dilemma here, of course, is balancing internal pressures toward emphasizing the unique with external pressures to describe the organization according to existing and widely accepted models. The tendency is to tilt in the direction of responding to external pressures and, in this quest for legitimacy, to lose distinctiveness.

Spread and Use of Advanced Manufacturing Technologies

How does the preceding discussion relate to present concerns about the spread and effective use of advanced manufacturing technologies? Perhaps most significantly, although the organization as user is the type of relationship between organization and innovation of greatest interest to those concerned with this question, exclusive focus on this type inevitably omits important influences on outcomes. In other words, one reason that research results on the adoption and use of innovation are inconclusive may be the way researchers have chosen to frame the questions they investigate. There is research on the process of invention and research on the process of adoption, but these two are generally treated as unrelated, at least implicitly. Research on invention tends to end with the development of a new product or products; research on adoption tends to begin with awareness of and end with a decision to purchase the innovation in question. Considerably less attention is paid to how invention influences adoption or, conversely, to how adoption influences invention.

How an innovation fares in the marketplace is a function of numerous factors—its performance, how effectively it is marketed, and its comparative advantage, to name just a few—but many of the factors that connect invention with adoption are notably absent in research on innovation. In the case of advanced manufacturing technologies, and probably in the case of most other kinds of innovations as well, the fate of any one organizational effort to use it hinges on considerably more than the attributes of the organization and its employees. A complex web of relationships between and among both individuals and organizations, taken together, ultimately determines the outcome. Chapter Four suggests one, the relationship between the vendor and the user, and this one may well be the most important. The key, however, is that researchers recognize the connectedness of invention and adoption—each is truly context for the other—and develop their strategies accordingly.

The basic point, then, is that much research on technological innovation has had a strong organizational cast. Upon close examination, five distinct types of organizational contexts for innovation can be identified in the extensive amount of work that has addressed the general topic. These five types are characterized by differences in phenomena, perspectives, the way innovation is defined, outcomes, and managerial issues of greatest import. The problem, however, is that while it is unlikely that any single theoretical perspective will be able to encompass all five, each of the five is limited in its ability to capture important aspects of, for example, the spread and effective use of advanced manufacturing technologies. The theoretical conundrum revolves around breadth. The argument here is that increased breadth would be preferable.

The case of advanced manufacturing technologies illustrates the point well. To understand why existing technologies have not achieved widespread acceptance and use, one needs to look not only at potential users but also at the contexts in which they are enmeshed. Because patterns of spread and use derive from aggregating decisions made at the level of individual firms, it makes good sense to view the problem from the firm level. The intention here is to suggest three sets of variables that together influence the effective use of advanced manufacturing technologies and ultimately to argue that although we are interested primarily in understanding the organization as user, to gain such an understanding requires going beyond what researchers working in this domain have typically done.

The three sets of variables are the place of manufacturing technology in the firm's competitive strategy, the nature of the relationship between the firm and the vendor of new technology, and the firm's strategy for integrating the new technology with its existing organization. The following discussion, although oversimplified, illustrates the general direction of the theoretical argument.

Place of Manufacturing Technology in the Firm's Competitive Strategy. Being at the technological forefront in manufacturing processes may or may not be central in the overall competitive strategy of any given firm. To the extent that it is, one can anticipate that the probabilities that the firm will adopt innovations in manufacturing technologies and will see them through are higher than if it is not. In some respects, this variable is similar to what other researchers have called top management support. (For a detailed discussion of this variable, see Chapter Four.) However, the difference is that the focus on strategy connects the firm with its environment. Top management support does not exist in a vacuum. It is motivated, presumably, by the role of technological sophistication in manufacturing in management's overall plan for the firm. Thus, support inevitably is based on management's assessment of the competition and on how important management believes advanced manufacturing processes are for meeting that competition. An assessment of the competition invariably requires some familiarity with what competitors are doing as well as some understanding of the range of technological alternatives available. Therefore, what may appear at a relatively superficial level to be top management support is, in reality, a complex set of variables that reflects the place of manufacturing technology in the firm's overall competitive strategy.

Nature of the Relationship Between the Firm and the Vendor. As noted earlier in this chapter, it is the rare firm indeed that is both the inventor and the user of innovations in manufacturing technology. Innovation *in situ* in most instances is unlikely given the substantial research and development costs associated with developing a new manufacturing technology from the beginning. Thus, most firms contemplating new technology in this area are likely to use products that are available in the marketplace and hence work with vendors. The nature of the relationship between the firm and the vendor has a major impact on how effectively the firm is able to use the new technology. Chapter Four captures a number of the significant attributes of this relationship, and they will not be repeated here. The theoretical point I would make is that the probability of effective use in any particular instance is enhanced substantially by a mutually supportive and satisfactory relationship between the firm and the vendor. Again, even though we are interested in the organization as user of innovation, the nature of the relationship between the firm and the vendor forces us to look beyond the firm's boundaries and toward variables not typically included among those found in research on the organization as user.

Firm's Strategy for Integrating the New Technology. Most typical of the variables used by researchers interested in the organization as user of innovation is the third set we propose, the firm's strategy for integrating the innovation with its existing organization. Successful introduction and effective use of advanced manufacturing technology are heavily dependent on the fit between the new technology and the system in which it is being used. Although this point may seem obvious, as a practical matter it tends often to be overlooked. *Fit* here refers to a broad spectrum of both organizational and technological variables. Although most managers are reasonably adept at ensuring technical fit, at solving the engineering problems, they seem often to be bedeviled by organizational fit, by problems of social or human behavior. This observation has been made by many others (Kimberly and Quinn, 1984), and the intention is not to dwell at length on it here. Rather, the theoretical point is that the probabilities of effective use of advanced manufacturing technologies are enhanced by firm-level strategies for integrating the technology fully with the existing organization; such strategies are described in Chapters Seven and Eleven.

Evidence that these strategies exist would include (but most certainly is not limited to) adequate time for shaping employee expectations, provision for adequate technical training, flexible reward systems built on how introduction of the new technology will affect traditional measures of output, careful consideration of how introduction and use of the new technology will be communicated both to the rest of the organization and to the outside world, and provision of adequate slack for dealing with the inevitable adjustment problems—both technical and human—that will occur as the new technology is introduced and used. Chapter Six presents some support for the importance of these kinds of variables.

Conceptually, each of these three sets of variables can be dichotomized: the role of manufacturing technology in competitive strategy can be central or not; the nature of the relations between the firm and the vendor can be mutually supportive and thus positively evaluated by both parties or not mutually supportive; and the firm can have a well-articulated strategy for integrating the new technology or not. Cross-classification of these three dichotomized variables yields the eight situations depicted in Table 1.

The theoretical argument sketched out here leads to some relatively straightforward predictions about the relationships among the three sets of variables defined as central and the

Table 1. A Framework for Analyzing the Spread and Effective Use
of Advanced Manufacturing Technology.

| | Role of Manufacturing Technology | | | |
| | Central | | Peripheral | |
	Integrating Strategy	No Integrating Strategy	Integrating Strategy	No Integrating Strategy
Firm-Vendor Relations				
Good	1	2	3	4
Poor	5	6	7	8

probability in any given instance of the effective use of advances in manufacturing technology. The probability of effective use is unquestionably greatest when manufacturing technology occupies a central place in the firm's overall competitive strategy *and* the relations between the firm and the vendor are positive from both points of view *and* there is a clearly articulated strategy by the firm for integrating the new technology with the existing organization—that is, in cell 1 of Table 1. The probability is clearly lowest in cell 8—that is, when manufacturing technology plays a peripheral role in the firm's competitive strategy *and* relations with the vendor are poor *and* there is no integrating strategy. The remaining cells are in some respects the most interesting because the predictions are not as straightforward. The theory being proposed here would attribute the greatest predictive power to the variables reflecting the firm's competitive strategy, the next greatest to firm-vendor relations, and the next greatest to the firm's integrating strategy. Thus, cell 2 would rank right behind cell 1 and would be followed by cell 5. Conversely, cell 7, where the place of manufacturing technology is peripheral in the firm's strategy and the relations between the firm and the vendor are poor, would be a case in which the probability of effective use of advanced manufacturing technology would be low despite the development of a strategy for integrating it into the organization. And cell 3 would rank next to cell 7 because of the peripheral place of manufacturing technology in the firm's strategy despite positive firm-vendor relations and a strategy for integration.

There is room for much discussion of the situations represented in cells 2 through 7. The purpose here has been to provide a theoretical foundation on which debate about the relative importance of variables can be built. In so doing I hope both to have broadened the theoretical context in which analysis of the spread and use of advanced manufacturing technologies is carried out and to have contributed to a sharpening of the theoretical focus.

References

Daft, R. "Bureaucratic Versus Nonbureaucratic Structure and the Process of Innovation and Change." In S. B. Bacharach (Ed.), *Research in the Sociology of Organizations*. Vol. 1. Greenwich, Conn.: JAI Press, 1982.

Hannan, M. T., and Freeman, J. H. "The Population Ecology of Organizations." In M. W. Meyer (Ed.), *Environments and Organizations: Theoretical and Empirical Perspectives*. San Francisco: Jossey-Bass, 1978.

Hayes, R. H., and Abernathy, W. J. "Managing Our Way to Economic Decline." *Harvard Business Review*, 1980, *58*, 67–77.

Kanter, R. M. *The Change Masters*. New York: Simon & Schuster, 1983.

Kimberly, J. R. "Managerial Innovation." In P. C. Nystrom and W. H. Starbuck (Eds.), *Handbook of Organizational Design*. Vol. 1. New York: Oxford University Press, 1981.

Kimberly, J. R., Norling, F., and Weiss, J. A. "Pondering the Performance Puzzle: Effectiveness in Interorganizational Settings." In R. H. Hall and R. E. Quinn (Eds.), *Organizational Theory and Public Policy*. Beverly Hills, Calif.: Sage, 1983.

Kimberly, J. R., and Quinn, R. E. (Eds.). *New Futures: The Challenge of Managing Corporate Transitions*. Homewood, Ill.: Dow Jones-Irwin, 1984.

Ouchi, W. G. *The M-Form Society*. Reading, Mass.: Addison-Wesley, 1984.

Peters, T., and Waterman, R. *In Search of Excellence: Lessons from America's Best Run Companies*. New York: Harper & Row, 1982.

Reich, R. B. *The Next American Frontier: A Provocative Program for Economic Renewal.* New York: Times Books, 1983.

Rogers, E. M. *Diffusion of Innovations.* (3rd ed.) New York: Free Press, 1983.

Stinchcombe, A. L. "Social Structure and Organizations." In J. G. March (Ed.), *Handbook of Organizations.* Chicago: Rand McNally, 1965.

von Hippel, E. "The Dominant Role of the User in the Scientific Instrument Innovation Process." *Research Policy,* 1976, *5,* 212-239.

THREE

Responding to Technological and Competitive Changes: Organization and Industry Factors

Jerald Hage

A rapid transformation of American industry is occurring (Reich, 1983). Many industrial sectors are doing quite well—computers, chemicals, missiles, aircraft, and other high-tech areas. Many other industrial sectors—shoes, consumer electronics, steel, tires, cement, and other low-tech areas—are being invaded by foreign products and disappearing. Although many assume that this is a problem of labor costs and the high price of the dollar, in each of these industrial sectors process technologies are available that would make the United States much more competitive than it now is. The objective of this chapter is to explain why whole industries are doing poorly, especially when alternatives are available. To handle such a complex issue requires that we attempt to integrate three different levels of analysis—organizational, managerial, and market or environmental. Once an analysis is made, survival advice for managers logically follows and can be provided.

How serious is the decline of American economic power? The slip in economic performance is measurable in three ways: our present trade imbalance, our present investment in new process technologies, and the foreign ownership of American firms, land, and stocks. The first point, trade balances in certain industrial sectors, is a familiar problem. Less well known is how

44

much we lag behind the Japanese in investment in process technologies. Finally, the United States is now a debtor nation, which means a lower standard of living for future generations.

Although in some industrial sectors the United States still reigns superbly, such as computers, synthetic fibers, and drugs, in many sectors foreign imports or foreign-owned companies in the United States account for a substantial share of the national market—shoes, steel, rubber tires, television sets, china. In most but not all of the areas where foreign penetration is large, new process technology is available but remains unpurchased and unutilized. In the areas of tires, steel, cement, automobiles, electronics, and the like, foreign firms have bought American-produced process technologies such as robots, computers, and automated assembly lines, and have used them to produce superior products at low cost. And the United States has not faltered only in the area of hardware technologies. Managerial technologies such as quality work circles and worker-participation schemes have also been invented here but are more successfully implemented elsewhere. We have a paradox! The new process technologies—both machines and managerial—are developed in the United States and yet ignored by the companies that need them for survival. How can we explain how whole industrial sectors disregarded these new process technologies and failed to adapt to changing economic conditions and new competition?

Presently the Center for Innovation at the University of Maryland is analyzing data from a matched comparison of what happened to 50 plants in Japan and 110 plants in the United States in comparable regions and across a wide spectrum of industrial sectors during the decade 1972–1982. About one third of the American plants closed, whereas only 5 percent of the Japanese plants did. More ominous is that the Japanese firms invested much more heavily in automation and new process technologies than did the comparable American firms. Equally revealing is the role of human capital. Many more Japanese workers than American workers are involved in quality work circles; there are ten times as many suggestions per worker in the Japanese plants as there are in the American. Not only are we losing the hardware race, but we are way behind in the use of human potential, which will probably be the decisive factor in the current competitive struggle.

More worrisome than the nonadoption of new process technologies is the response of American companies and industries to the problem of foreign penetration of markets. The chairman of U.S. Steel asked the American government to invent a new process technology that would allow the steel industry to leap-frog over the Japanese competition, something the company should have been doing for itself before 1983. In addition, many of the large companies are abandoning their traditional businesses and purchasing companies in the high-tech area. But if they could not manage their own businesses, it does not seem reasonable to expect them to do better in businesses in which top management has little technological expertise (Chandler, 1962).

Foreign purchase of American companies, land, farms, and the like has accelerated considerably; in 1981 it was almost on a par with American investment overseas. To be specific, foreign investment of all kinds in the United States hit $500 billion in 1980 and went up another 18 percent in 1981 (*U.S. Statistical Abstract,* 1983). We are now a debtor country—that is, foreign investment is greater than American investment overseas. Although this situation is caused partly by the large deficits and paradoxically by the strength of the dollar, it does not bode well for the long term in the United States.

The foreign presence beyond mere imports is much greater than appreciated. The English operate Safeway, while the Germans run A&P. The French have purchased a major American cement factory and have installed computer processing technology in it. They build French-designed cars in Kenosha, Wisconsin. Michelin Tires has captured a significant share of the American market mainly because American manufacturers said the American consumer would never pay more for quality. The French also purchased the nuclear-energy division of Westinghouse, primarily because of Westinghouse engineers' refusal to improve the design of nuclear-energy plants. Sanyo, a Japanese firm, bought out a division of Whirlpool that makes television sets for Sears and turned it around, in this case with managerial technologies such as quality work circles. More dramatic than these examples are the partnerships between American car manufacturers and the Japanese. One could list many other examples, but these provide a sense of how common foreign presence is now.

One objective of this chapter is to classify industrial sectors to help explain why some are doing well and others poorly. One basic dimension is investment in research and development (R&D). Another is size. Where does the American economy remain strong? Most of the large companies that are successful invest heavily in basic research or product development or both. They accommodate technological change, and product innovation occurs in them every three to five years (*Science Indicators*, 1984). The performance of IBM, for example, has been impressive, although it too has in some cases faltered. IBM has defeated not only General Electric and RCA but also the major efforts of both the French and German computing companies (including the giant Seimens), to say nothing about its considerable penetration of the Japanese market. It has done so by heavy investments in both R&D and human capital. It is not well known, but IBM spends more on education than R&D as a percentage of its sales dollar. Although General Electric faltered in the production of mainframe computers, it too has demonstrated remarkable adaptability to many changes in its business environment. For example, after the energy crisis of 1973, General Electric redesigned all its electrical products and was able to reduce its energy consumption by 50 percent in the space of seven years. Although these are examples of specific companies, much could be said for whole industrial sectors where the investment in R&D is large. They are successful, and we are exporting products in these areas.

Why do whole industries fail to adapt to changing market and technological conditions while others are flexible? Once one poses the problem at an industrial level, or in economic terms at the market level, the problem becomes more interesting than when considering individual companies. It is not a single company that fails to change with the times but instead entire industries. (For simplicity, I will use a seven-digit Stan-

dard Industrial Classification code as a definition of an industrial sector; for government agencies the term *bureau* or *institute* is roughly equivalent.) What makes analysis at this level
more attractive than analyzing individual companies is that it
casts some doubt on several microeconomic assumptions about
competitive forces. These failing industrial sectors are by and
large markets that are not heavily regulated, pollution laws
being the major exception. Although some are oligopolistic,
such as steel, not all are. Even in those markets that are dominated by several large firms, when new forces of competition
enter the market, the large firms do not compete. Worse, the
means for survival exist—namely, new process technologies—
and yet they are not acquired. Why are these firms or their
managements so nonrational?

My interest in this problem is in adding to a new paradigm in organizational theory called the population-ecology
perspective (Aldrich, 1979; Hannan and Freeman, 1978). Simply put, it examines the factors contributing to the emergence
and disappearance of populations of organizations. Can we explain why some are endangered and perhaps even speculate on
how to save them?

I will use a fourfold typology of organizations that has
proved useful in handling a number of problems—from markets to hierarchies (Williamson, 1975) and from stagflation to
class-economy theory (Hage, 1980; Hage and Clignet, 1982;
Hage, 1985)—to analyze why some populations of organizations
fail to adopt the new process technologies. This typology explains the historical development of various industrial sectors
and indicates how the American economy is now rapidly altering as one form of organization disappears and another becomes
dominant.

Knowing the characteristics of forms that have survival
potential has a number of practical advantages. These advantages need to be indicated, and they are. But because this analysis is important for managers, I want to integrate these ideas
from organizational theory with those of both microeconomics
and industrial psychology. How could managers in these failing
industries, some of the best and brightest, trained at Harvard,

Carnegie-Mellon, and other leading business schools, remain opaque and not change with the times? Their failure says something about cognitive structure. I want to speculate about the causes of this mental rigidity because it helps to understand their economic nonrationality. We can, therefore, further advance our microeconomic, organizational, and cognitive paradigms by analyzing this critical test of American industry and its failure to adapt.

This chapter has three parts. The first describes an in-depth study of the American shoe industry and why it failed to adopt new process technologies. The study involved case reports of the managerial decision-making processes, which provided a number of insights. The second part locates the shoe industry in a larger framework of a fourfold typology of organizations. This part explains why different industries have evolved in different ways. The third part then draws a number of conclusions from the previous two parts and lists a number of recommendations for manufacturers and especially managers in large firms. In this part, several popular books such as those by Ouchi (1981) and Peters and Waterman (1982) are evaluated for what they say about how to survive. The first and third parts of the chapter are intended for managers, while the first and second parts are of interest to organizational researchers.

The Shoe Industry: A Case Study

To get an intellectual grip on these issues, we will examine an in-depth study of an entire industry experiencing heavy penetration of foreign goods where sophisticated process technology was available (Cohn, 1980; Cohn and Turyn, n.d.). In the shoe industry, a number of quite sophisticated machines were available; if purchased, they would have made the products competitive with foreign imports. The task of the study was to explain why the machines were not purchased. Essentially three ideas were explored: Did the companies know about the machines? Did the companies have the money to purchase the machines? Did the companies have an organic structure that would make the purchase likely?

The researchers discovered that the companies did know about the machines and that they either had capital or had access to bank support, but they still would not buy them. The crucial factors determining whether a firm purchased advanced equipment were structural features of the firm, especially managerial specialization. The first important general finding was that the firms that were less likely to adopt new process technologies had few managerial specialists and were more likely to be centralized—that is, decision making was concentrated at the top. One might ask why having more managerial specialists results in more adoption of new process technologies. Specialists monitor the environment and seek information. They know about new machines and are likely to understand their advantages and limitations; they become advocates for the equipment. A large study of hospitals (Moch, 1976), for example, found that the presence of a department of specialists in a specific area meant much higher adoption rates for new process technologies in that area compared with areas without departments of specialists. Another large research tradition that one can cite and integrate is the diffusion literature (Rogers, 1983). Early adopters of new products display many of the characteristics of specialists—for example, higher levels of communication and education, which themselves correlate.

Another reason the number of specialists affects the adoption of new technologies is the probability that they will act as technological gatekeepers. Their presence increases the probability that new ideas will enter the organization (Allen, 1977). (To my knowledge, no one has done any research on how to select and train technological gatekeepers. We just know that they exist and have an impact on the organization's effectiveness.) Certainly, the number of specialists is related to involvement in professional meetings where ideas are being circulated.

Not only is the concentration (the proportion) of managers critical but so is the diversity or variety of specialties. Each contributes to explaining the rate of innovation. In the shoe industry, those firms with a variety of specialists purchased more different kinds of new sophisticated process machines, some revolutionary and others not, than firms without a variety of specialists. This finding indirectly demonstrates the role of specialists as advocates when they hear about new ideas. Managerial specialists thus are likely to know about new ideas and become advocates for them. With a larger number of specialists, the probability is greater that one of them will be a technological gatekeeper, especially for the purchase of new process equipment.

But to have their input count, the decision-making structure also has to allow for the specialists to participate. In detailed studies of the decision-making process in the shoe industry, the researchers found that those firms that did not purchase much equipment had centralized decision making. Production managers made the decisions to purchase new machines without consulting with marketing. In contrast, in those companies where new equipment was purchased, marketing was involved in the decision-making process. The implications of new process technologies for handling rapid shifts in market tastes can be appreciated better by marketing than by production. Production managers in the firms that purchased little equipment defined their job as simply taking orders from marketing and filling them. With this view, the purchase of automated equipment did not make sense or appear rational.

In some cases, centralization was associated with the purchase of new equipment but not automation or radical machines. The purchase of radically new equipment, however, is especially interesting because it represents a quantum leap in production flexibility and productiveness. This equipment was purchased only when the authority structure was decentralized. Then the managerial specialists had an opportunity to express themselves.

Why can centralization result in the lack of recognition of advantages of the equipment? It is helpful in understanding why bright people fail to see the obvious and make major errors. I would suggest that centralization produces what Janis (1965) has called group think—everyone defines a problem and its solution in the same way. Group think is especially likely to occur when one occupation dominates the decision making at the top of the organization. An example is John DeLorean's discussion of General Motors (Wright, 1980). The domination by accountants led to a short-term focus on profits rather than a broader, more long-term perspective. DeLorean comments on the lack of innovativeness in the firm during the 1960s and early 1970s as a consequence. The same problem occurred in the shoe manufacturers that were centralized, with decisions made exclusively by production managers; they too adopted a short-term view that made the purchase of new and especially radically new equipment appear to be nonrational. Group think is most likely when a single occupation dominates; which occupation this is does not make that much difference.

Even more important than the number of occupational specialists and decentralization is participation in extraorganizational professional activities. In my own research, I have found that frequent attendance at professional meetings is positively related to high rates of innovation (Hage and Aiken, 1967). Similarly, studies of school districts have found that simply requiring faculty to attend one professional conference a year increases the adoption rate of new ideas (Daft and Becker, 1978). This finding also holds for the shoe industry. Firms that had managers involved in industrial conferences were much more likely to purchase the new process technologies than those that did not. Conferences provide opportunities to hear pros and cons and reinforce the decision to go ahead.

There is a difference between knowing about the machines and knowing the machines, a difference in level of comprehension. Sales personnel explain the virtues of their equipment—this is knowing about. But as individual managers hear about the equipment from a variety of sources, including ones they trust, they know in a much more profound sense of the term. A trivial example among academics and also managers is how many times they have to hear about a personal computer before becoming persuaded to buy one. Managers are likely to be convinced when they hear that others have tried the machines and found them successful. If a firm does not have technological gatekeepers, attendance of managerial specialists at meetings exposes them to new ideas of many kinds and leads to an openness in general. Studies of differences in technology (Rogers, 1983; Hage and Aiken, 1970) have indicated how much reading and travel influence one's acceptance of new products.

Another factor that positively influences the decision to purchase new process technologies is informality. In the shoe industry, organizations that had a flexible structure and were nonbureaucratic were much more likely to adopt the equipment than those that were inflexible and bureaucratic. This is very much a theme of *In Search of Excellence* (Peters and Waterman, 1982), which stresses the need to constantly shake up the structure.

These four characteristics—managerial specialists, decentralization, attendance at meetings, and informality—result in a diversity of theses and antitheses that can be combined in a new synthesis. They also result in a complex perception of the organizational environment. Thus they influence both cognition and perception.

In sum, at least in the shoe industry, the concentration and variety of specialists, the extent of centralization, attendance at extraorganizational meetings, and informality help explain why some companies survived. It was not the market and its competitive forces—firms went out of business while the study was in process—but instead the characteristics of the firms that influenced their capacity to adapt to changing circumstances and to adopt new machines.

We can draw three important managerial conclusions from this study. First, the problem is not the creation of process technologies but the failure of companies to purchase them. The issue is not invention but implementation. Second, the problem is not a lack of money but a lack of managerial wit —a managerial problem not a financial one. Third, managers work in environments that have helped to mold their ways of thinking.

The argument thus far is at the organizational level. It helps explain differences between organizations but not necessarily between industrial sectors, unless all organizations within an industrial sector have the same characteristics. If so, then we must attempt to identify the causal variables that influence these characteristics. What aspects of the market, the technology, and other contextual or environmental factors might explain why a whole industry would have either many or few managerial specialists, be more or less centralized, have a high or low attendance at extraorganizational meetings, and be more or less informal?

When we take these empirical findings and apply them to other industrial sectors such as automobiles, steel, and rubber tires, we are left with the conclusion that the same pattern does not necessarily hold. The steel industry, which along with textiles is perceived to be the industry that sets the tone for the first industrial age, has been slow to implement new process technologies (Landes, 1969). We should note, however, that the population of steel organizations is different from that in the shoe industry, at least until recently. There are or have been only a few large companies, about twelve. Most of these have been highly resistant to adopting new process technologies. In addition, many new, small steel companies have emerged. These are located in the South and produce small-batch specialty steels with the new process technologies. Thus, in one sense, we see the steel industry as a more extreme case than the shoe industry, with even larger companies being even more nonadaptive to technological change, but with smaller companies using newer technologies.

But when we look at the computer or electrical-products industry (firms such as IBM, General Electric, and Westinghouse) or at the chemical industry (small, high-tech plastics companies or the giants like Dow, Monsanto, and DuPont), we find a great deal of interest in and adoption of new process technologies. The adaptiveness of IBM to the growth in the personal-computer market is well known. Although it took IBM some five years to decide that it should compete in the personal-computer market, its speed of adaptiveness was still much faster than that of U.S. Steel or General Motors or many of the shoe companies. I have also noted the adaptiveness of General Electric during the energy crisis. Admittedly, this is a different kind of adaptiveness, one involving market changes, but even if we were to focus on process technology, we would find the same result. General Electric offers to sell the design of entirely automated plants. I am using these two firms as examples; the conclusions are largely the same for the entire computer, chemical, and electrical industries.

To use another example, one that falls somewhere between shoes and steel, on the one hand, and computers and electrical products, on the other, we can examine the automobile industry. In the late 1960s, Japanese investment per worker, an indicator of investment in process technology, passed that of the American automobile industry. In particular, the Japanese invested in new stamping machines that worked much faster than the old ones. The Japanese development and use of robots on the assembly line have also been widely publicized. Although much has been made of the Japanese management style (Ouchi, 1981) to explain greater productivity, let us also not lose sight of the fact that new process technologies contributed mightily to these improvements.

Perhaps the difference between American and Japanese automotive firms in adaptiveness is best illustrated by their response to American legislation on pollution control passed in the fateful year 1973. The Japanese hired a number of engineers and tried to design cars that would meet the standards. The Americans, most notably General Motors, hired a number of lawyers and tried to repeal the legislation. The American companies claimed the standards could not be met by 1985. The Japanese just went ahead and did it. New process technologies helped to determine their success.

How does one account for the differences between General Motors and General Electric? Between the steel industry and the chemical industry? While we are awash in bulk steel imported from various countries, our drip-dry shirts are being shipped throughout the world. We are the world's leader in man-made fibers. In one case, size seems detrimental and in another it does not. I started by stating that I would like to add to the population-ecology model. Apparently describing populations by the number of companies and their relative size is not enough. Small is beautiful only some of the time. We must look for still other dimensions to differentiate populations of organizations.

Technological and Market Determinants of Adaptiveness

Except for a few studies, such as an early one by Stinchcombe (1965), the level of the industrial sector has been largely ignored in organizational theory. One advantage of the population-ecology perspective is that it poses a new set of macroquestions about the context or environment. Among others, the following characteristics seem critical about a population or species of organizations: the number of organizations in the population or task environment; the proportion of large and small organizations in the population; the number that account for 50 percent of sales or more. These three characteristics let us know how much competition will actually occur. If the industrial sector is dominated by a few large firms that are price leaders, then the companies are generally not so likely to be dynamic.

We want to understand how population characteristics influence the adaptability or survivability of the population. The connecting link is the internal or structural characteristics of the species, which I will call *form* (Hage, 1980). The most important issue is what organizational forms are likely to adopt new process technologies. Because adoption of new process technologies is affected by the kind of organizational form, we can label some forms as adaptive—because they adopt new technologies—and others as nonadaptive. (The term *adoption* means the purchase of new equipment or the provision of new products. The term *adaption* means a fundamental change in the level of automaticity as measured by the Amber scale. When there is a qualitative shift from assembly-line production to continuous-process production or automation, the alteration in process technology is large enough to be called an *adaptation*.)

One might argue that the large organizations will survive because they have more resources (Aldrich, 1979). Or one might argue that the small ones will adapt because they are more flexible, the small-is-beautiful thesis. In the case of the shoe industry, generally the smaller companies have survived.

My position is a different one—namely, that some small ones do and some large ones do. What makes the difference is the level of technological sophistication.

We can rely on organizational theory to help explain which forms are most likely to adopt new process technologies. Burns and Stalker (1961) studied electronics firms in Scotland and discovered that they had two different ways to organize in order to attain two different objectives. First, organizations can be organized along *mechanical lines* to achieve high productivity. This type of organization involves a hierarchy of authority, communication, and control—that is, features of classic bureaucracies. Second, organizations can be organized along *organic lines* to achieve high rates of product innovation. This type involves a network of authority, communication, and control. Subsequent research has demonstrated that even more critical is the variety of managerial specialists, especially relative to the size of the organization (Hage and Aiken, 1967, 1970; Hage and Dewar, 1973; Pelz and Andrews, 1966; also see the review of the literature in Hage, 1980, chap. 6; for an exception, see Kim, 1980). The shoe-industry study demonstrates how the organic form is more open to new process technologies than is the mechanical form. The link to the environment, however, is not completely clear in the Burns and Stalker (1961) formulation.

In Table 1 I make this link by delineating four environmental contexts and four organizational forms. The environmental contexts are technological sophistication—low and stable or high and changing—and market demand—small and changing or large and stable. The organizational forms (as described later) are mechanical, organic, traditional, and mixed mechanical-organic. The origins of these dimensions are in the work of Blau (1970, 1972, 1973), Duncan (1972), Hull and Hage (1982), Lammers and Hickson (1979), Mintzberg (1979), Perrow (1967), Thompson (1967), as well as others.

When the market is characterized by large and stable demand, we find that the mechanical form is most appropriate. This context is what economists call the monopoly market, where industrial concentration is quite large. What the econo-

Table 1. The Relationship of Environmental Characteristics
and Organizational Form.

| Technological | Market Demand | |
Sophistication	Small, Changing	Large, Stable
Low, Stable	Traditional form Independent, machine production system Competitive market Price and tastes impor- tant	Mechanical form Assembly-line or chain production system Oligopolistic market Price and quantity im- portant
High, Changing	Organic form Team production sys- tem Custom-made market Individualization im- portant	Mixed mechanical-organic form Reciprocal or continu- ous-process produc- tion system Semi-oligopolistic mar- ket Price and quality im- portant

mists have not emphasized is that technological sophistication is
low and the technology is relatively stable in monopoly markets. Under these circumstances, economies of scale are important. The dominant production mode is the assembly line.
Examples of this industrial sector are steel, tires, cement, cig-
arettes, railroads, department stores, grocery chains, and the
Post Office.

At the other extreme are small, high-tech companies,
which invest heavily in R&D. The technology is changing rapidly, as are consumer tastes. Indeed, the emphasis is on producing products to meet custom-made specifications (Perrow,
1967; Hull and Hage, 1982). The organic form is the most appropriate structure, and the production system is organized as
a team.

Beyond the continuum of mechanical-organic are two
special forms. The traditional form exists where the technology
is stable but consumer tastes are continually changing because
of fads and fashions. Craftspeople, artisans, and semiprofession-
als work in these organizations, largely independently.

The mixed mechanical-organic form engages in a large amount of research but also produces products in large quantities. This firm is usually the one described in Peters and Waterman (1982). The production system is highly automated. The firms in this quadrant are usually multidivisional ones and are described by Chandler (1962).

In my analysis, I want to concentrate attention on only the large firms. The general thesis is that the mechanical form has been nonadaptive to changing consumer demand and the appearance of new technologies. The mixed mechanical-organic form has been most adaptive. But the reasons for the differences lie in the historical origins of these forms and how they have evolved over time.

Two Patterns of Growth and Evolution. In attempting to explain why industries adapt or do not adapt to changing environments, we must ask ourselves what factors cause a company to have more managerial specialists and to be more decentralized and informal than others—that is, to have an organic or mixed mechanical-organic form. One factor is the level of technological sophistication required in the production process. General Electric, which was founded prior to General Motors, was built on science and started with research labs and managerial specialization (Freeman, 1982). The consequence was the steady proliferation of new products and process technologies. The road to profits was via innovation.

In contrast, the automobile industry began essentially with craft knowledge about how to build a car. Henry Ford's assembly line resulted in a great gain in productivity (Chandler, 1977). Afterward, there was a rapid growth in demand, and the automobile industry became dominated quickly by a few large companies and a few small ones producing specialty products. Despite all the model changes, the number of different cars is few. Given its starting point, there was not much need for the automobile industry to engage in research except of an applied kind. (See Landes, 1969, for a discussion of the electrical and chemical industries.) The consequence was the steady rationalization of the production process to produce ever larger economies of scale. The road to profits was via efficiency.

Thus, from the beginning, the electrical industry evolved differently from the automobile industry.

Some companies today are more adaptive than others to the new process technologies because their origins have affected the role of research and the interest in innovation. Large companies that started with craft technologies, moving from the traditional form to the mechanical form in Table 1, evolved a structure that is resistant to adopting new process technologies. When there is a demand for high productivity and little product differentiation, or when managers are concerned with this objective, centralization occurs, reducing specialization. This change makes the company less adaptive to radically new technologies such as robots or automated assembly lines. This process is seen clearly in the evolution of General Motors (Wright, 1980), where research and development was deemphasized and engineers gradually lost power. General Motors often developed new products, but they were not adopted because power had become so concentrated at the top of the pyramid. Centralization works best when markets are stable and there is little technological change. Then production is easy to program. In dynamic environments characterized by technological change, centralization reduces the flexibility of the firm and diminishes its adaptability.

Another factor is, of course, the relative demand for new products. As demand for innovation increases, which currently appears to be the case, it too stimulates higher innovation rates. In the shoe industry, consumer demand shifted from large demand for a few basic styles to demand for small batches of many different kinds of styles as the American consumer became increasingly fashion conscious. The radically new process technologies provide this flexibility. We also see this shift in demand occurring in the automobile industry. (See the appendix in the Abernathy, Clark, and Kantrow, 1983, study of the automobile industry.)

Much depends on the type of market demand as well. When customers want low price relative to the amount of product, then obviously those companies that are the most efficient will gain in the marketplace. Chandler (1977) documents this evolutionary process in a number of industries where Americans succeeded very well in the nineteenth century. Because of our large population of immigrants, mass-produced, low-cost products were pioneered largely in this country. Because of our decentralized political system and lavish attention to education, we invented products and process technologies and the large firms to go with them. It is an irony that our free, competitive economy produced monopoly capital and economic oligarchy.

Large companies have thus evolved in two ways. Organizations have grown via the development of new products. Procter & Gamble is an example. It does extensive research, develops a product, market-tests it, and, when convinced it can capture a large segment of the market, launches the product. Organizations have also grown via the development of low-cost manufacturing or efficient operations. For example, Singer Sewing Machine built a low-cost product, provided good customer service, and dominated the market for about a century, earning profits even during the Great Depression (Chandler, 1977).

One way of achieving lower costs is via the purchase of sophisticated process technology. Thus we are led to a certain paradox. The companies and industries that should be more open to new process technologies are the ones less likely to adopt them. Why is this so?

One answer is structural and the other is psychological and economic. As organizations get larger in size, they have fewer managers per number of employees, especially if their technology is not very sophisticated. The large number of managers at General Motors is insignificant when one realizes that the key is the ratio and the denominator is 400,000 employees. But as organizations grow and centralization occurs, an inner elite emerges (Thompson, 1967). The company becomes large and successful, success institutionalizes stability and, in the process, denies the need for new managerial specialties or decentralized decision making. It is difficult to fault the most successful automotive company in the world. Thus we are led to the conclusion that nothing fails like success! It prevents the kind of managerial questioning that is needed for a flexible and dynamic organization. Barnard (1946) wrote long ago about the pernicious problem of success and how it encourages hierarchical systems that resist change and veto new ideas. What he did not do is ask why some organizations, as they grow, evolve in this direction.

The analysis in this chapter suggests that industries that are nonadaptive now were successful over a long time period and slowly evolved toward increased centralization and few managerial specialties because of stable technologies and markets. When the technological base changes radically, however, such as with the invention of automated equipment, organizations with a mechanical structure tend not to adapt to this radically new technology. In contrast, organizations with an organic model adapt quite easily. We now have an explanation of why General Electric and IBM have not always been successful. They lie in between the organic and mechanical, having an admixture. Thus, they are sometimes slow to adopt, but when they make the decision to go ahead, they do so quickly and usually effectively.

This analysis leads to the important conclusion that, as these technologies and markets change, there are new opportunities for further concentration or deconcentration. We see this shift presently occurring in the railroad industry as well as elsewhere. Utterback (1983) reports that each new breakthrough in process technology produces a further shrinkage in the number of firms because only some adopt the new technology and because it usually allows for increased economies of scale. We are presently seeing this process occur in many of the sectors where the mechanical organization has been the dominant form.

Why is Japan doing better than the United States in world markets? In part, because it is investing more in the new equipment, especially automation. This investment allows for a flexible production system and the ability to produce products of high quality. The Center for Innovation is currently investigating whether Japanese organizations have a managerial structure that is more like the mixed mechanical-organic form or the organic form.

Psychological and Economic Underpinnings. Parallel to the tendency for some organizations to evolve in a centralized direction, the mechanical form, are psychological and economic factors that also increase resistance to process technology. If market demand remains stable, there is little need to have much participation. It is easy to plan for the future: more of the same. This lack of change, in turn, leads to the selection of personnel who like stability and to the promotion of "yes" men, a process described by DeLorean (Wright, 1980). Obviously, this process promotes a simplistic cognitive structure on the part of managers and a trained incapacity to change—the origin of group think. Therefore, when new machines are invented, they are rejected even by bright managers. When polluting laws are passed, the battle becomes a legal one rather than an engineering one. All of these are psychological dynamics that parallel and reinforce the structural dynamics described previously in this chapter.

Economic processes also reinforce an industry's tendency to resist technological change. The greater the fixed or sunk costs in the production system, the greater the tendency to want to maintain long production runs. This tendency is logical if in fact there is little change either in technology or in market demand, the mature stage in Utterback and Abernathy (1975). (Also see Utterback's 1978 model of the evolution of industrial sectors.) Their model argues that in the first stage there is a lot of product innovations as an industry moves from the craft to the mechanical form. In the second stage there are a large number of process innovations. As this innovation occurs, there is industrial concentration. Finally, in the mature stage, there are few new process innovations. Most of the American industrial sectors that did not adapt well to the technological and market changes of the 1960s and 1970s were industries in the mature stage. Now, with new process technologies in many of the sectors that are in the mature stage, a problem arises with the Utterback and Abernathy (1975) model. With radically new process innovations such as automation, robots, and CAD/CAM, and with a change in the nature of the market, do companies start over again in the second stage? It would appear that we are on the verge of a whole new wave of transformation. If so, these changes cast doubt on their model.

Organizations evolving toward increased productivity thus

become resistant to change for various reasons. Organizations that grow via the development of new products have a different history. Most chemical, electrical, and drug companies started out with a high proportion of specialists because of their research departments. In turn, there was continual production of new products. As the companies grew, they had to develop new divisions to handle the new technologies in a form of federal decentralization. These divisions are best treated as separate companies, which in turn means that smaller size and higher concentration of managerial specialists are maintained. General Electric has 125 divisions, which makes General Motor's design look simple in comparison—and it is. Thus, companies that started with an applied science not only remained in the first stage of the Utterback and Abernathy model (1975) much longer but proliferated new companies that are divisions in a decentralized structure. This is not just a peculiarity of General Motors and General Electric. Contrast Westinghouse and Ford. Or shift to the steel industry and the chemical industry. Again, steel is characterized by few divisions and relatively few products, chemicals by many divisions and technologies.

With many divisions, companies are less likely to recruit only a single type of personality. Companies that grow via new products select different types of personalities. General Electric calls them entrepreneurial managers and specifically tries to recruit people with this managerial style. It has also set up its own venture-capital center. Both policies are mechanisms for the maintenance of a dynamic company—or, I should say, division—and of the capacity to adjust to changes, whether in the marketplace or in the knowledge base. These companies also develop a special and distinctive culture, as we have seen in Peters and Waterman (1982).

In summary, big is not necessarily bad. Two different evolutionary patterns have occurred. With unsophisticated technologies, growth meant a movement toward oligopoly stopped only by the technical limits of managerial coordination, market differentiation, and the availability of process technology. Parallel to this movement were a number of psychological and economic processes that institutionalized the structure. For managers concerned with increasing openness to new process technologies, these processes constitute a series of "don't's."

By contrast, with highly sophisticated technologies, growth meant a concentration of managerial specialists, and in many cases a decentralized multiorganization. Again, parallel processes constitute a series of "do's" for managers, as summarized later in this chapter. One of the most interesting is the establishment of new companies to house new technologies. We can now move back to our leitmotif about the problem of large size, or is small beautiful? If divisions are kept small, companies can grow to a large size. The cognitive abilities of the managers are not overwhelmed, and the divisions can adapt to changes in the environment. General Electric is thus not big but small because it has continued to differentiate its structure. Now, it is experimenting with the development of separate companies with its venture-capital unit. Again, we are led to the conclusion that the problem is not one of technological invention as much as it is one of managerial vision. We need to change our managers—not just their attitudes, but the variety and concentration of specialists in the organization.

Recommendations for Managers

The major recommendation for managers in the large, low-tech area is to convert their organizational forms from mechanical to mixed mechanical-organic. This general, overarching recommendation can be broken down into a series of specific ones.

1. Increase the diversity of managerial specialists. Large firms, of course, frequently do have managerial specialists. Here we are referring to their diversity and relative proportion to the work force of the company. Among these specialists, it would be desirable to have engineers and others knowledgeable about advanced process technology. Another specialty that is important is research, both pure and applied.

2. Create an R&D department if one does not already exist. Researchers provide new products. They also keep a company abreast of new technologies. Increasingly in postindustrial

society, the only way a company will be able to survive is through the development of new products.

3. Create a department for process technology. Although such a department would be quite distinctive, it would speak to a major issue in American industry. We have research departments for products but not for processes. The advantage would be to have equipment champions as well as product champions. Companies increasingly need to upgrade their process technology. The old argument was to protect the technological core (Thompson, 1967). The new argument should be continual change.

4. Send managers frequently to national conferences and invest in their continued education. IBM's policy on human capital is a wise one and should be emulated. Research on innovation shows that people who read more and travel more are more open to new ideas than those who do not.

5. Hire technological gatekeepers. As yet we do not know how to select such people, but the concept from Allen's (1977) work is an important one. Some individuals are especially adept at finding new ideas that improve the success of R&D units.

6. Eliminate formal rules and keep the structure flexible. Again, this is the advice that flows from the shoe study, and it is also one of the themes in Peters and Waterman (1982). Informality increases communication and the circulation of ideas.

7. Decentralize the decision-making processes and especially include different specialties. A diversity of perspectives will not make much difference if the perspectives are not taken into account in the decision-making process, as we have seen in the shoe study.

8. Create performance measures in the area of process technologies. Again, the point is to sensitize managers to the need to continually improve their process technology. One might assume that improvements in technology are directly measurable by productivity, and this assumption is partly true. But new process technologies are also important for flexibility and quantity, and in the marketplace these factors are increasingly important.

9. Involve workers in quality work circles. Such involvement is one way of continually upgrading the performance of the process technologies, and it is one of Japan's strengths.

10. Use task forces to redesign the organizational structure, to facilitate the movement from mechanical to mechanical-organic, and to facilitate the implementation of automation. Peters and Waterman (1982) point to the importance of such task forces. General Motors is a concrete case of an organization that is transforming itself with the help of task forces.

11. Use techniques to help break down group think. A number of techniques can help management change its cognitive structure (Huse, 1975; Beer, 1980).

12. When resources permit, put new products and process technologies in new units or divisions. General Motors is using this tactic with its Saturn project. It is much easier to start afresh with radically new technologies than to attempt to convert existing structures.

13. Automate as rapidly as resources and the labor force allow. The obvious implication of this book is that automation is coming, but the speed of its approach does require concern about employment.

I could add other recommendations, but these cover both the managerial and organizational level and include an attention to design, process, and structure. We might also ask about their relationship to current proposals such as those by Ouchi (1981) and Peters and Waterman (1982). Both these books discuss the concept of culture. Ouchi's *Theory Z* stresses providing job security and other benefits that are likely to build trust between workers and managers. These are important aspects of culture and may be necessary before quality work circles can be effective. We need research to be sure about this suggestion. Several ideas of Peters and Waterman (1982) have been incorporated in these recommendations. Flexible structures and task forces are useful ideas. However, neither of these books looks at technology or the need to automate, the concern of this chapter.

Given the propositions of books such as Toffler's *The Third Wave* (1980) and Naisbitt's *Megatrends* (1982), now would appear to be an age when it is important for managers to rethink their organizational structure and culture. The draconian solutions are for companies to change their form and process technologies along the lines I have recommended here.

References

Abernathy, W. J., Clark, K. B., and Kantrow, A. M. *Industrial Renaissance: Producing a Competitive Future for America.* New York: Basic Books, 1983.

Abernathy, W. J., and Utterback, J. "Patterns of Industrial Innovation." *Technological Review,* 1978, *80* (7), 40-47.

Aldrich, H. E. *Organizations and Environments.* Englewood Cliffs, N.J.: Prentice-Hall, 1979.

Allen, T. J. *Managing the Flow of Technology: Technology Transfer and the Dissemination of Technological Information Within the R&D Organization.* Cambridge, Mass.: MIT Press, 1977.

Barnard, C. "Functions and Pathologies of Status Systems in Formal Organizations." In W. F. Whyte (Ed.), *Industry and Society.* New York: McGraw-Hill, 1946.

Beer, M. *Organizational Change and Development: A Systems View.* Glenview, Ill.: Scott, Foresman, 1980.

Bell, D. *Post Industrial Society.* New York: Free Press, 1973.

Blau, P. M. "A Formal Theory of Differentiation in Organizations." *American Sociological Review,* 1970, *35,* 210-218.

Blau, P. M. "Interdependence and Hierarchy in Organizations." *Social Science Research,* 1972, *1,* 1-24.

Blau, P. M. *The Organization of Academic Work.* New York: Wiley, 1973.

Burns, T., and Stalker, G. M. *The Management of Innovation.* London: Tavistock, 1961.

Chandler, A. D., Jr. *Strategy and Structure.* New York: Doubleday, 1962.

Chandler, A. D., Jr. *The Visible Hand: The Managerial Revolution in American Business.* Cambridge, Mass.: Belknap Press of Harvard University Press, 1977.

Cohn, S. F. "Industrial Product Adoption in a Technology Push Industry." *Industrial Marketing Management,* 1980, *9,* 89-95.

Cohn, S. F., and Turyn, R. M. "Organizational Structure, Decision Making Procedures and the Adoption of Innovation." Unpublished manuscript, Department of Sociology, University of Maine, Orono, n.d.

Daft, R., and Becker, S. *Innovation in Organizations: Innovation Adoption in School Organizations.* New York: Elsevier, 1978.

Duncan, R. B. "Characteristics of Organizational Environments and Perceived Environmental Uncertainty." *Administrative Science Quarterly,* 1972, *17* (3), 313-327.

Freeman, C. *The Economics of Industrial Innovation.* (2nd ed.) Cambridge, Mass.: MIT Press, 1982.

Hage, J. *Theories of Organization: Form, Process and Transformation.* New York: Wiley, 1980.

Hage, J. "Sociological Trends and General Equilibrium Cycles or a Sociological Explanation for the Shifts in the Phillips Curve." Paper read at the American Sociological Association meetings, Aug. 1981.

Hage, J. "Shifts in the Phillips Curve: Sociological Factors in the Causes of Stagflation." Unpublished working paper. Center for Innovation, University of Maryland, College Park, Md., 1985.

Hage, J., and Aiken, M. "Program Change and Organizational Properties: A Comparative Analysis." *American Journal of Sociology,* 1967, *72,* 503-519.

Hage, J., and Aiken, M. *Social Change in Complex Organizations.* New York: Random House, 1970.

Hage, J., and Clignet, R. "Coordination Style and Economic Growth." *Annals of the American Academy of Political and Social Science,* 1982, *459* (1), 77-92.

Hage, J., and Dewar, R. "Elite Values Versus Organizational Structure in Predicting Innovation." *Administrative Science Quarterly,* 1973, *18,* 279-290.

Hannan, M. T., and Freeman, J. H. "The Population Ecology of Organizations." In M. W. Meyer (Ed.), *Environments and Organizations: Theoretical and Empirical Perspectives.* San Francisco: Jossey-Bass, 1978.

Hull, F., and Hage, J. "Organizing for Innovation: Beyond Burns and Stalker." *Sociology,* 1982, *16* (4), 464-577.

Huse, E. *Organization Development and Change.* St. Paul: West, 1975.

Janis, I. *Group Think: Psychological Studies of Policy Decisions and Fiascos.* Boston: Houghton Mifflin, 1965.

Kim, N. "Organizational Innovation and Structure." *Journal of Business Research,* 1980, *8* (2), 225-245.

Lammers, C., and Hickson, D. J. (Eds.). *Organizations Alike and Unlike.* London: Routledge & Kegan Paul, 1979.

Landes, D. *The Unbound Prometheus: Technological Change and Industrial Development in Western Europe from 1750 to the Present.* Cambridge, England: Cambridge University Press, 1969.

Mintzberg, H. *The Structuring of Organizations.* Englewood Cliffs, N.J.: Prentice-Hall, 1979.

Moch, M. "Structure and Organizational Resource Allocation." *Administrative Science Quarterly,* 1976, *21,* 661-674.

Naisbitt, J. *Megatrends.* New York: Warner Books, 1982.

Ouchi, W. G. *Theory Z: How American Business Can Meet the Japanese Challenge.* Reading, Mass.: Addison-Wesley, 1981.

Pelz, D., and Andrews, R. M. *Scientists in Organizations: Productive Climates of Research and Development.* New York: Wiley, 1966.

Perrow, C. "A Framework for the Comparative Analysis of Organizations." *American Sociological Review,* 1967, *32,* 194-209.

Peters, T., and Waterman, R. *In Search of Excellence: Lessons from America's Best Run Companies.* New York: Harper & Row, 1982.

Reich, R. B. *The Next American Frontier: A Provocative Program for Economic Renewal.* New York: Times Books, 1983.

Rogers, E. M. *Diffusion of Innovation.* (3rd ed.) New York: Free Press, 1983.

Science Indicators. Washington, D.C.: National Science Foundation, 1984.

Stinchcombe, A. L. "Age and Structure of Organizations." In J. G. March (Ed.), *Handbook of Organizations.* Chicago: Rand McNally, 1965.

Thompson, J. *Organizations in Action.* New York: McGraw-Hill, 1967.

Toffler, A. *The Third Wave.* New York: Morrow, 1980.

U.S. Statistical Abstract. Washington, D.C.: Department of Commerce, 1983.

Utterback, J. M. Personal communication, 1983.

Utterback, J., and Abernathy, W. J. "A Dynamic Model of Process and Product Innovation." *Omega,* 1975, *3* (6), 639-656.

Williamson, O. *Markets and Hierarchies: Analysis and Antitrust Implications.* New York: Free Press, 1975.

Wright, J. P. *On a Clear Day You Can See General Motors.* New York: Avon Books, 1980.

♢ FOUR ♢

Implementing Manufacturing Technologies: Lessons from Experience

John E. Ettlie

In the midst of the publicity about and enthusiasm for the factory of the future, an important principle of the management of the innovation process has been all but overlooked or forgotten: Radical process innovations in organizations do not adopt and implement themselves. Successful innovation is not inevitable. Most manufacturing firms, not only in the United States but also in the other industrialized countries of the world, have not adopted programmable manufacturing innovations, such as robotic cells and flexible manufacturing systems (FMS) (Miller, 1983). These systems present a formidable challenge to manufacturing management and raise serious policy issues for general management about the role that manufacturing innovations ought to play in business strategy.

In the past, organizations had only two general production alternatives available: line, or continuous-process flow, organized around products; and job-shop flow, organized around equipment groupings like milling machines and lathes. The disadvantage of the job-shop alternative is high work-in-process

Note: This study was supported in part by the National Science Foundation, Grant No. ISI 8218494, and DePaul University, Chicago. The views in this chapter are mine and do not necessarily reflect the official position of the National Science Foundation. Elizabeth O'Hara and Jan Eder were graduate assistants at DePaul University on this project. I gratefully acknowledge comments and revision suggestions by three anonymous reviewers and, especially, by Donald D. Davis.

(WIP) inventories. The disadvantage of continuous process is the difficulty of changing over from one product to another. In the late 1960s, new flexible systems began to appear. Called by various names, these systems linked general-purpose equipment together with materials-handling systems and overall programmable control, and ushered in a new, mid-volume production-process alternative (Jablonowski, 1980).

As was the case with other radical process innovations in the past, like computers adopted for electronic data processing in the 1950s and 1960s (Mann and Williams, 1960), stand-alone automation in various industries like steel (Czepiel, 1974), and discrete-parts manufacturing, there has been considerable resistance to the adoption of these new programmable manufacturing innovations. What is more important, perhaps, and what forms the major assumption of this chapter is that firms that attempt to implement these systems experience considerable variance in success.

Another important principle that innovation research teaches is that there is rarely a single sociotechnological solution to a problem. Organizations typically try to select technologies for their future that conform with certain internal values and experiences, and that are consistent, within limits, with the technologies that will later become available. Some of these technologies constitute radical, or discontinuous, departures from the experience in the firm, the industry, or even the world. Other technologies are incremental departures.

My study takes these principles as assumptions. The purpose of my overall research effort is to determine the causes of the relative degree of implementation success of advanced programmable manufacturing systems in the United States; it ultimately aspires to contribute to a general theory of implementation. This chapter is a report on the first phase of the study. The general hypothesis of the study is that a successful implementation strategy is matched with the characteristics of the manufacturing innovation being introduced. One of the most important of these characteristics is the degree to which the new technology represents a radical, as opposed to an incremental, departure from existing practice.

Hage (1980) gives examples of this fit between implementation strategy and technology. Radical process innovation is hypothesized to require an off-line, special site and a team to install the new process, which is subsequently integrated into the firm's work flow. The major question being posed by the present research is: What are the key elements of a successful implementation strategy?

I expect both strategic and structural variables are important in a successful implementation strategy (Ettlie, 1984). However, in the first phase of this study, which employed a qualitative, grounded-theory approach (Das, 1983; Glaser and Strauss, 1967) to the use of implementation, I placed no limitations on the crucial variables. This approach was rewarded with some surprises in the resulting data. The two most commonly mentioned variables in the literature of implementation tend to be top management support and participation. Results of previous studies of the implementation of process innovation in manufacturing (Ettlie, 1973; Ettlie and Rubenstein, 1980) suggested also that strategic commitment to the new manufacturing approach, integration of the process innovation into the work flow, and the relationship between the supplier and the user of the new system, among others, would be mentioned frequently. The methodological approach and the results are presented below.

Method

The overall, organizing methodology of this study is probably best described by Miller and Friesen (1982). This methodology involves longitudinal replication of results with multiple-panel data collection using both respondents and informants. The specific study design employed here included an initial qualitative phase of data collection, followed by three annual panels of data collection during a longitudinal, quantitative phase of the study. This report is limited to the first, or grounded-theory, phase of the study. The purpose of this phase was to focus the theoretical approach of the study and to generate candidate variables.

Interview Schedule. An interview schedule was developed

with five main questions, including an introduction that was used, in part, to guarantee confidentiality to respondents and to test the primary assumption of the study—that there is variance in the degree of implementation success for advanced programmable manufacturing systems. The first question is the key question of the interview: What factors of the implementation strategies selected by firms distinguish the successful and unsuccessful attempts? The second question asks what is the most valid measure of implementation success. The third and fourth questions focus on major and minor problems during implementation and on how major problems were overcome in successful cases. The final question asks respondents what the best method would be to select firms for the second, longitudinal phase of the study and is not reported on here. (A copy of the interview questions is available from the author.) In addition to these questions, several others were asked, when time permitted, about opinions regarding the factory of the future, training, simulation, and greenfield versus existing-plant automation.

Sample. A total of forty-one organizations participated. All were either suppliers (twenty-four) or users (seventeen) of programmable manufacturing innovations. Of these, twelve were visited primarily because they were users of flexible systems. Twelve of the twenty-four suppliers were machine-tool suppliers, and the balance were nine robotics suppliers and three consultant or system-supply organizations.

A total of fifty-five respondents were systematically interviewed in these forty-one organizations: fifteen (27.3 percent) were top managers (general manager or above); thirty-three (60 percent) were middle managers; and seven (12.7 percent) were technical personnel (for example, engineers). Specific issues were taken up with an additional set of participants, and the total number of individuals generously donating their time exceeded one hundred. I conducted interviews in these organizations between July 1983 and January 1984.

Factors in a Successful Strategy

The first and most important question on the interview schedule asks respondents to report on the differences between successful and unsuccessful implementation attempts, with an emphasis on differences in the implementation strategies of these firms. The responses were grouped by content into categories, which are listed in Table 1. The interrater agreement

Table 1. Correlations of Organizational Type (Supplier Versus User) and Technology Grouping (Machine-Tool Suppliers Versus Robot Suppliers) with Content Categories (N = 41).

Content Category[a]	Machine-Tool Suppliers User (Scored 0) Versus Supplier (Scored 1)[b]	Robot Suppliers User (Scored 0) Versus Supplier (Scored 1)
1. Supplier-customer relationship (22)[c]	−.09	−.05
2. Product-process dependency (19)	−.01	−.15
3. Strategy (17)	.00	−.08
4. Training (15)	.22	−.01
5. Computer-integrated manufacturing (10)	.25	−.05
6. Incremental implementation strategy (10)	−.10	.19
7. Human-resource policy (10)	−.15	.12
8. General management support (10)	−.39[b]**	.12
9. Champion (user) (7)	.25	.08
10. Participation (7)	−.28[b]*	.08
11. Justification (6)	−.21	.01
12. Organizational culture (4)	.28*	−.06
13. Size, structure (3)	.05	.19

[a]If organization reported this factor, score = 1; if not, score = 0.

[b]A negative correlation indicates that users were more likely to report this content category than were suppliers.

[c]Numbers in parentheses are the number of respondents naming each category as important to successful implementation.

*p < .05.

**p < .01.

with a second judge for the first four categories averaged 77 percent for the first thirty-seven firms sampled. The average correlation for measuring interrater agreement (compare Jones and others, 1983) for the same data was $r = .47$ ($p < .001$). These statistics are impressive considering that there were no protocol and no predetermined categories for respondent quotations. Category labels did vary somewhat between myself and the second rater, but the results indicate a reasonable degree of convergence in the interpretation of the most important of these results.

Results. The most frequently mentioned factor that accounts for success or failure in implementation of these advanced, usually multiple-machine, systems was the nature of the *supplier-user relationship.* It was mentioned in twenty-two (54 percent) of the cases. Respondents used many words to describe this relationship in the successful cases or lack of it in the less successful cases. *Marriage* was often used—a long-term, mutual commitment. Respondents differed on whether there is a "chemistry" in this relationship or whether it can be developed in spite of personality differences. Regardless, there were always at least two (and maybe that's the optimal number) key people, one from the vendor firm and one from the user, who worked hardest at building a team to integrate the technology in the user's plant. They worked long hours; the experience was usually unique in their careers; and they were changed when it was over —much like a soldier returning from a war. These systems do not implement themselves. They are complex enough and tailored enough so that there are no turnkey installations. Having a customer who expects a turnkey installation is probably one of the best indicators that the storm clouds are on the horizon for the installing firm. Vendor service after the installation, no matter how quick and expert, cannot carry the day. The user has to assimilate the system. As one supplier said, "Two-way cooperation between OEM [original equipment manufacturer] and buyer is needed. Appoint two project managers—one from each side—then get married." Another supplier (an FMS supplier) and buyer remarked, "You have to be able to bare your soul to your customer." And from a robot-cell user: "A good marriage—60% + 60% = 100% . . . , in bed with vendor and long-term."

After examining the comments of respondents on this

issue, one reaches the tentative conclusion that team building across organizational boundaries is the key. The one word that comes to mind to describe this relationship in the successful cases is *friendship*. This interpretation is reminiscent of the findings reported by Czepiel (1974) that information on the adoption of process innovation in the steel industry was passed on friendship networks.

These data also reinforce Hage's (1980) hypothesis of separate-site, off-line implementation for a radical process implementation. However, based on the importance of this factor, it might well be that it would make some sense to talk about the implementation strategy of the vendor-user team rather than that of the user organization. One supplier said that successful installations are "user driven and vendor guided," which summarizes this interpretation.

Product-process dependency was mentioned as a factor in nineteen (46 percent) of the cases. This variable, first suggested by one of my respondents, refers to the relationship between products and manufacturing processes, especially its complexity. (An anonymous respondent in this study planted the seeds for the idea of the label of this category in an interview.) One of the great paradoxes today is that these complex systems can usually be justified only when a new product is launched. That is asking an organization to do a lot in a short time. It takes a special effort and a successful vendor-user team to do it. In one case, by the time the FMS was installed and running, only 65 percent of the parts originally scheduled to go on the system were still in sufficient demand to be produced in that plant. The product is a moving target, and flexibility has limits. The robotics people and cell installers are sensitive to this issue too. One often finds that the operator is visually inspecting during processing, which most robots cannot do yet or cannot do fast enough to meet cycle-time requirements. As a former FMS user said, "They [top management] changed the rules . . . part family you had to make went from a variety of low volume to making a large number of a few."

Many firms simply buy the wrong system. What they end up learning in the process is valuable, but the price is high. If the vendor and user truly have a good working relationship, the system design can be changed once it is ordered. This change saves some of the systems from failure or greatly reduces the cost of technical success.

Another category to emerge from the content analysis, with seventeen (41 percent) mentions, was user *strategy*. The key to this variable appears to be the planning horizon for which the firm is truly serious—the longer the better—and the degree to which manufacturing is a part of the long-range plan. (See Chapter Nine.) The academician quoted most, albeit infrequently, by respondents was Skinner (1978), and many of the comments illustrate Skinner's theme of elevating manufacturing in the corporate strategy.

Some of the earlier work conducted in the area of technology policy (Ettlie, 1983b) should be helpful in delineating this construct. In a review of three empirical studies, it was consistently found that firms with an aggressive technology policy tried out new processing equipment when it became available; actively recruited the best possible technical, production, and marketing people available; and were strongly committed to technological forecasting (Ettlie, 1983a). One buyer responded, "We think every company should have a vice-president in charge of change." And an FMS supplier and buyer said, "FMS is a good example of something you can't buy for financial reasons alone. It has to fit strategy."

Training is a reasonably straightforward factor and was mentioned in fifteen (37 percent) of the cases. It involves both education of the organization and training in specific technical skill areas—for example, operation, programming, and maintenance. Early commitment to training and education is important, and perhaps it is a factor in establishing a readiness for change and participation. It appears that the success of participation in decision making depends on a true understanding of the potential and appropriateness of programmable automation for the given product and user setting. An interesting combination of the training and vendor-user elements of implementation strategy was suggested by one respondent: Vendor and users conduct training schools together after the initial batch of user personnel has been trained. The user could then pace the training to the strengths and weaknesses of the personnel involved in the implementation.

Another category of implementation strategy to emerge from content analysis was *computer-integrated manufacturing (CIM)*. Integrative aspects of successful implementation were mentioned in ten (24 percent) of the cases; these aspects are related theoretically to Hage's (1980) reintegration of radical process change into the organization; Ettlie's (1973) work-flow integration of numerically controlled (NC) machines for highest utilization; and the ideas in Chapter Five. That is, when you have an island of automation, programmable or not, it is only as good as the materials-handling system and production-control system that integrate it with the rest of the process-control system in the organization. This integration includes general support of the system too, not just materials handling. Tooling support usually has to be improved; and quality of material input—for example, castings for unmanned systems—usually has to be upgraded. Often it is recommended that group-technology (GT) concepts are necessary before true flexibility of a system can be obtained because part families have to be specified to utilize the system effectively. There is often pressure to integrate design—for example, linking computer-aided design with programmable manufacturing. This puts pressure on the design function to include manufacturability as a design criterion. Shared, common, utility data bases for the manufacturing, design, finance, and marketing functions in the firm of the future seem desirable.

A category tied in importance with the previous category and the next one, based on frequency of mention, ten (24 percent), is *incremental implementation strategy*: Don't try too much too fast. It is wise to take a strategic approach to phased adoption and implementation for these major, multimachine, multicontrol systems. Allow sufficient time (equal in importance for people and financial resources) to implement. Many of the organizations visited during this phase of the study simply could not afford a major FMS or robotic cell, so it had to be assembled incrementally over time. One organization planned to spend about $1 million a year and would have the desired FMS in six to seven years. In other organizations anticipation of adding (or having the option of adding) more machines later was emphasized during the shop tour.

One of the issues that emerges with this category is the leap-frogging approach to innovation. The consensus of respondents on this issue is that it is not desirable or really possible to leap-frog over competition. The firm will not have learned enough to adopt and implement a new generation of the technology when it is ready if it has not had experience with the previous generation.

This strategic category is reminiscent of one of the measures I used to delineate the management-commitment variable in an earlier study of the implementation process (Ettlie, 1973). There was a significant correlation (Kendall tau = .72, $p < .01$) between the plans a firm had for the future adoption of other NC machines and utilization of the NC machine studied. There were various degrees of commitment. Some plans were vague; others included very specific purchase orders for various types of machines. But all these indicators pointed to a commitment of management to the NC concept of production—a new philosophy of producing parts in small batches—that differed drastically from the existing average practice in the firm.

It is quite possible that this variable could be incorporated into the strategy category described previously. Incrementalism can work only if there is a plan for phased adoption and implementation. This concept is important because it gives most domestic small-batch producers—small and medium-sized firms—the hope of participating in the factory of the future. The extent of incremental adoption among firms in three industries in the United States is described in Chapter Five.

Human-resource policy was mentioned in ten (24 percent) of the forty-one cases. One of the most consistent problems that was mentioned under this category is bumping of hourly employees by those with more seniority because of a lay-off or preferred access to overtime—for example, a weekend job assignment. The person bumped is often the one who knows the most, is the most trained and committed, and works best with other members of the production team. Bumping also occurs when there is turnover on the installation or production team. These systems rev up and then drop off substantially over long periods of time, often in phase with top management changes. Because turnover cannot be universally prevented, a prudent human-resource policy makes accommodations for this possibility. A contingency plan of this type may turn out to be crucial to implementation.

Some job protection for special categories was discussed by respondents, but in the case of this issue and every other major human-resource issue—for example, training, selection, compensation, work rules, union negotiations—the human-resource experts in the organization did not substantially influence implementation, were never consulted, or were only marginally involved as an afterthought. Many times, it appears, human-resource experts in an organization are expected merely to rationalize and justify human-resource decisions made by operating personnel. These personnel experts have little or no influence on what is perhaps one of the most important aspects of their profession—the long-term personal growth and stability of people in the organization.

A further category of comments related to implementation strategy was *general management support*. Respondents in ten (24 percent) of the forty-one cases said such support promoted implementation of programmable manufacturing. This factor is. one of the most prevalent in the literature on implementation (see Chapter Two), so it is not surprising that people mentioned it. What is surprising is that this factor and participation (discussed later in this chapter) were not mentioned more often.

There are two probable reasons for these results. First, most studies of implementation, even when the change was truly radical for the organization (Mann and Williams, 1960; Williams and Williams, 1964), focus exclusively on the implementing organization and ignore the supplier of the technology or the other change agents involved. In this study, which gave equal weight to supplier and user opinion, factors that represent the combined views of the implementation process are most important: vendor-user relationship and product-process (radical) dependency.

Second, top management support and participation are likely to be conceptually incorporated into one of the elements of implementation strategy already mentioned. For example, participation is very much a part of the supplier-user relationship in organizations (Woodman and Sherwood, 1980). And top management support is probably very much a behavioral manifestation of policy or strategy implementation, which suggests that general management support might be incorporated into the variable of user strategy. I discuss combining these categories later.

It should be noted, however, that top or general management support is the first of the categories on the list to exhibit any differentiated reporting tendencies. In this case, users in the sample were significantly more likely to report general management support as a factor. The correlations for all the categories are reported in Table 1 and are discussed later in the chapter.

I have labeled this category as *general* rather than *top* management support, because it became clear during about the middle of this phase of the study that the appropriate unit of analysis for a study of this type is the plant rather than the organization. More will be said about this point later in the chapter, but, given this conclusion, top management as perceived by the implementation team may be local highest management, which usually does not include corporate managers. In addition, support needs to be differentiated from involvement. (One of my colleagues, Barbara Gutek, made me keenly aware of this point in a conversation we had on this subject early in the design stage of this study.) Support is essential; involvement limits success. One example should suffice here. In a robotic cell application, the standing joke during start-up was that bleachers would have to be set up outside the cage in order to accommodate the visiting brass.

Innovation *champion* appears next in the list of factors with seven (17 percent) mentions. "A person has to love it— [has to be] a champion, an advocate; and they're not the same as a product champion" is the way one respondent described this element of implementation strategy. Some innovation champions were respondents in this first phase of the study, and they do have this characteristic of extreme commitment to the project—sometimes they are also the project managers. How extreme is this commitment? One champion said at the end of the interview that "I have my heart in this system." In another case, the champion's subordinate described the boss when he returned from seeing an FMS in another plant as looking as though "he had been at a revival meeting."

Champion commitment is deep and apparently is a key to success in many applications. A top manager of a supplier compared two plants of an automotive company; both plants made essentially the same drive-train parts. In one plant, after two years, they still called for service and were down for days or more at a time with their system. In the other plant, they wanted to place another major order. The difference between the two plants was that the second one had a well-placed champion of these programmable systems.

This and another case suggest the focused proposition that the more sophisticated the system, the more elevated in the hierarchy the champion must be in order to ensure success—an extension of the hypothesis of top (general) management support. Less clear than the placement of the champion in the hierarchy are the experience and training necessary for a successful champion. At a recent professional meeting, two colleagues from large manufacturing organizations agreed that process champions "come out of the woodwork" when they are needed. In most other cases it would seem, however, that prudent management might consider facilitating, through the reward structure, the emergence and maintenance of process championship.

Participation, mentioned previously in the discussion of general management support, was cited in seven (17 percent) of the cases and is significantly ($p < .05$) more likely to be mentioned by users. One clear emergent pattern concerning this much discussed managerial style and dimension of organizational structure is that a minimum amount of knowledge about a significant, radical shift in processing technology is necessary for people to be even adequate participators. Perhaps for this reason, the early literature on organizational change, from the 1940s and 1950s, said that forewarning was as significant a predictor of implementation success as participation.

It would seem an unwise implementation strategy to involve people in the decision to adopt a radical process technology if they know nothing about the technology and do not have an important stake in the success or failure of the new system. People who do not have a stake in participation will be angry when asked to participate (Alutto and Belasco, 1972), and people who do not know anything about the technology are being asked to expose their ignorance—at least at first. It is not surprising, and certainly it is not shocking, then, that this sample included only one case of the involvement of an hourly employee at the early stages. Without the preliminaries of education and training to establish readiness, participation is not a recommended course of action. It is highly likely that participation will be merged with team-building concepts of the vendor-user relationship.

Participation is often used as a method of overcoming resistance to organizational change. There is a tendency, although not marked, to report that the greatest resistance to these new programmable manufacturing systems in organizations is at the middle of the hierarchy. In successful cases, top management is usually committed—although this commitment may not be effectively incorporated into strategy. Hourly employees are often just not affected by the system—and those who will be are brought onto the team out of necessity. But when the system is finally loosed onto the shop floor, the production-control people, quality-control people, materials-supply people and a legion of other middle-management professionals are left scratching their heads wondering what happened or what is about to happen. This problem has been neither adequately dealt with in the literature nor adequately explored with the representatives of firms studied in this sample. It is a prime candidate for research.

Justification procedure appears next in the list of elements of implementation strategy, with six mentions (15 percent). Clearly, justification is one of the hottest and most controversial topics for the factory of the future. Little systematic work has been done on the topic of economic justification and accounting for advanced manufacturing systems. Exceptions are Gold (1981) and Kaplan (1983). Therefore, no widely accepted accounting model exists for these systems. Most respondents said that these systems cannot be justified on direct labor savings alone—especially when interest rates are high. I will remark later about measuring the success of the implementation of these systems. The upshot is that manufacturing people and financial people in organizations are at odds over these systems—before, during, and after installation and production release. Rate assignment is a sticky issue for people who do not understand these systems and their ultimate purpose—which may be vague at the outset of configuration and design. Purchasing people in potential user organizations are particularly vulnerable on this issue. Excited vendors are critical of these user representatives who approach the quotation process for procurement of an advanced, complex, programmable manufacturing system in the same way they would for replacement of a machine using fifty-year-old technology.

The more commitment of resources to planning and the more flexible the vendor-user relationship, the more likely that the evolving justification process will yield the correct design. This outcome is very much a function of the supplier-customer relationship and product-process dependency, characteristics described previously. (Also see Chapter Two.) If the design is fixed at the outset and needs to be changed once the production target for the vendor has been set (it almost always does), this need will have to be met through appropriate give-and-take in a mature vendor-user relationship. Once a production schedule is set, the vendors will do all in their power to meet it because they will be vulnerable if they cannot. But sometimes the cost of being on time is installing the wrong system. Unanticipated negative outcomes of justification such as this must be guarded against.

The last two categories are user *organizational culture* and user *size and structure,* which could have easily been combined to make one category. Culture was significantly ($p < .05$) more likely to be mentioned by suppliers than by users, but with the total number of mentions at only four (10 percent), this result has to be viewed with a great deal of caution. (Robert Lund has pointed out to me that it may be more than a coincidence that users are significantly more likely to report participation and top management support and suppliers significantly more likely to mention culture. Perhaps they are just seeing the same phenomenon from two different perspectives, and this is really the same variable.) Under this category, respondents discussed the personality of the user organization, the overall level of fear and resistance to change, and the attitude of the people involved—risk takers versus non-risk takers.

Organizational culture is a troublesome concept. It is not clear what the difference between organizational culture and organizational climate is, and whether it is the same as policy implementation (Broms and Gahmberg, 1983) or structural variables. Organizational climate is also a slippery concept (Schneider and Reichers, 1983), with some seductive aspects but with questionable usefulness in innovation research outside the research and development (R&D) laboratory. For example, in a number of studies (Ettlie and Vellenga, 1979; Ettlie and O'Keefe, 1982), we have rarely been able to obtain any significant correlations of risk-taking climate with other variables of interest. In addition, only a few dimensions of work-group climate are consistently and significantly correlated with R&D (Abbey and Dickson, 1983). It may be that the manifestations of culture, such as myths, rituals, stories, legends, and specialized language (Smircich, 1983), are correlated with the readiness stage of implementation. But typically, the whole organization is not involved with the adoption and implementation of these systems. Therefore, work-group climate might be a more useful concept to use (Schneider and Reichers, 1983).

Size and structure have already been hypothesized as key contextual or enabler variables (Ettlie, 1984), although it will be a challenge to capture the unique aspects of structure that distinguish successful implementation. The available questionnaire and institutional instruments that have been widely used

(Sathe, 1978; Ford, 1979; also see Chapter Five) will probably not be sufficient.

A fair share of comments from interviews went uncategorized in this content analysis. For example, managers mentioned technology concerns and aspects of the firm's environment such as economic stability. Many of these comments concern system-specific technical details of operation, justification, or control—for example, tooling performance, positioning accuracy, type of programmable control (PC) used, vendor analysis models, and measurement of flexibility.

Content of Category Versus Type of Participating Organization. Table 1 gives the correlations for the content categories, grouping the organizations first by user and supplier and then by technology area: robotics (supply or use) and machine tool (supply or use). As mentioned earlier, there are three significant correlations in the user-supplier column. Users are significantly more likely to report participation ($r = -.28, p < .05$) and general management support ($r = -.39, p < .01$). Suppliers are significantly more likely to mention organizational culture ($r = .28, p < .05$).

Interestingly enough, there were no significant differences in the likelihood of reporting comments in these categories when the sample of forty-one organizations was grouped by technology area (second column of Table 1). This result certainly gives some support to the notion that there is hope for a general theory of implementation—not only for these programmable technologies on the shop floor but also for convergence in the literature of implementation that includes other technologies like office automation (Bikson and Gutek, 1983; compare Chapter Two regarding a general theory of implementation).

Measures of Implementation Success

The second question on the interview schedule asks respondents to nominate valid measures that can be used across various organizational settings to gauge implementation success or utilization of programmable manufacturing systems. Table 2 gives the results of the content analysis of the responses to this

Table 2. Measures of Implementation Success.

Implementation Success Measure	Frequency (%)
1. Uptime (system reliability); time available for production	16 (39)
2. Cycle time met/parts per shift	14 (34)
3. Postaudit/account justification met	13 (32)
4. Utilization (cycle time, chip time)	12 (29)
5. Work-in-process inventory reduced	9 (22)
6. Payback period	8 (20)
7. Direct labor savings	7 (17)
8. Return on investment; simulation; quality (three-way tie)	6 (15)
9. Relieve bottleneck, work-flow integration; rework, scrap, yield (two-way tie)	4 (10)
10. Miscellaneous—time to install, time to fix, floor-space reduction, cost-per-part reduction, pallet utilization, flexibility, customer response	3 or less

question. As can be seen, there was no lack of ideas for valid measures, and certainly there was no consensus. The most frequently mentioned measure was uptime, or time available for production—sometimes called system reliability—which was mentioned in sixteen (39 percent) of the cases.

The balance of the list is also somewhat disappointing. If one had asked this same question ten years ago when programmable systems were just beginning to become available, the only measure that would probably not have made this hit parade would have been WIP inventory. All the other measures have been in common use for some time, both for the shop floor—utilization, cycle time, rework, scrap, yield—and for general purposes—postaudit method, payback, return on investment (ROI). An indication of the uniqueness of these systems appears only in the catchall category, which includes items like flexibility and customer response. Perhaps respondents take these measures for granted or do not think they are elements of distinctive competence. One respondent went to great lengths to explain the dimensions of flexibility* to me, but it is not

*These dimensions were (1) physical part size, (2) geometry, or part shape, (3) tolerance, (4) materials, and (5) amount of time for change-

clear that the concept of flexibility is widely understood in the industry yet—especially for the consequences of different technologies often combined into cells like robots, materials handling, and machine tools. If flexibility is not widely understood, it is not likely to be incorporated into a strategy. (See Chapter Nine.)

I concluded from these results that in order to adequately measure the success of these systems, multiple independent methods will be required, including unobtrusive measures and vendor assessments (Campbell and Fiske, 1959; Jick, 1979).

Major Problems

Respondents were asked in the third question to describe whether the problems encountered during implementation were major or minor. Major problems were the show stoppers. Minor problems tended to get resolved without too much difficulty.

The most frequently mentioned major problem was software and programming. A total of sixteen (39 percent) of the organizations mentioned this issue. System integration was next with fifteen mentions, or 37 percent of the sample. Design flaws were next with fourteen (34 percent) organizations mentioning reliability or functional problems of the new systems. The two problems mentioned next, goal not understood and training, both fit into implementation strategy, as discussed earlier. Then there is a long shopping list of barriers to successful implementation, including maintenance. These results are not surprising given that much of the flexibility of these systems is obtained through software control of the materials-handling-intensive design, and this control often involves the interfacing of several

---

over. The more flexible the system, the wider the variety and the quicker the changeover between variety input. Dr. Clay Whybark recently provided this investigator with a Swedish version of the flexibility concept that includes seven aspects: (1) volume flexibility, (2) programmed flexibility, (3) variant (on basic design) flexibility, (4) breakdown flexibility, (5) material flexibility, (6) design change flexibility, and (7) new products flexibility.

different types of technologies like computer numerical controls (CNC), programmable controls (PC), and hierarchical control. Additionally, much of this equipment is noncomparable. There is no standard operating system used by all.

Solutions to Major Problems

The fourth question on the interview schedule asks respondents to reflect and report on how these major problems were overcome. Two of the top three elements of implementation strategy emerged as the most frequently cited methods for problem solution. First was the supplier-user team, mentioned in thirteen (32 percent) of the cases, and second was user strategy, mentioned nine times (22 percent), as a way of overcoming these major problems. It is interesting to note here, as in the other data collected, how denial of the implementation is a problem in its own right: Managers deny that implementation is ever a problem. They believe that you simply buy technology, plug it in, and count your money. Their typical response is that a firm can plan in such a way as to avoid implementation problems. However, planning has to be linked to postadoption strategies for installation and integration of the system into the organization to ensure success. Some minimum amount of flexibility (mentioned six times) and fluidity will be needed to change the planned course as needed. In one case (not part of the data), operator job descriptions for an FMS were not specified until two years after installation began. (See Chapter Seven for application of sociotechnical systems principles to aid in this postadoption integration.)

Personnel assignment, cited previously as one of the major problems, is mentioned here as a possible solution seven times (17 percent); it is part of human-resource policy. An interesting question to be raised is whether the organization will acquire new personnel for the system or use existing staff. There is usually a strong bias for using existing staff, but it is not clear what the best approach is and for what positions and systems.

Relationship Between Reporting Tendency and Content

The ultimate purpose of the first phase of this study was to focus the theory of implementation for testing in the second phase. The goal was first to arrive at uncorrelated predictors of implementation success that managers can influence and then to explore alternative, causal model configurations of the process. Some help can be obtained from the literature (Ettlie, 1984). But a total of thirteen elements in an implementation strategy leaves a number of possibilities for overlap in the content categories that have already been commented on. For example, participation might be incorporated into the team-building aspects of the vendor-user relationship.

In a further effort to develop a parsimonious model of this process for subsequent test, the correlation matrix of categories of implementation strategy was produced to see whether any pattern in the reporting of these factors, regardless of source, emerged. Unfortunately, adequate data to establish convergent validity among the measures of success (Jick, 1979) of the various systems discussed by informants and actually examined in the field prevented any differentiation on that variable.

This exercise is not the same as correlating items for the purpose of building a scale to measure one variable or correlations among variables. Rather, it is an exercise to see whether any reporting patterns in these data can be exploited to form mutually exclusive categories of implementation strategy and to avoid correlation between the ultimate predictors that are adopted for further testing. The results of the analysis are presented in the correlation matrix in Table 3. There are ten statistically significant correlation coefficients (Pearson r) in this matrix. Recall that these coefficients do not represent relationships between levels of these variables per se but, rather, represent relationships between reports (score = 1 if mentioned, score = 0 if not mentioned).

Four of the ten significant coefficients involve user strategy. Respondents who report user strategy as a significant predictor of implementation success are also more likely to say that a process champion is important ($r = .28$, $p < .05$) and that

Table 3. Correlation (Pearson r) Matrix of Content Categories for Elements of Implementation Strategy ($N = 41$).

Content Category[a]	1	2	3	4	5	6	7	8	9	10	11	12	13
1. Supplier-customer relationship	1.0												
2. Product-process dependency	-.02	1.0											
3. Strategy (user)	-.31*	-.29*	1.0										
4. Training	.10	.21	-.02	1.0									
5. Computer-integrated manufacturing	-.16	.04	-.25	.16	1.0								
6. General management support	-.22	-.26	.03	-.16	-.30*	1.0							
7. Incremental adoption strategy	-.04	.04	-.02	.16	.21	.11	1.0						
8. Human-resource policy	-.10	-.14	.15	.09	.11	.29*	.25	1.0					
9. Champion	.16	-.16	.28*	.06	.04	-.08	.04	.23	1.0				
10. Participation	-.10	-.30*	.41**	-.08	.04	.07	.20	.23	.14	1.0			
11. Justification	.11	-.25	.07	-.17	.09	.28*	.09	-.05	-.19	.00	1.0		
12. Organizational culture	-.02	-.14	.06	.26*	.20	-.17	.00	.02	.07	.07	-.14	1.0	
13. Size, structure	-.11	.11	-.05	.18	.06	.08	.28*	.08	-.13	.12	-.12	-.09	1.0

[a] Interrater reliability for first four content categories averages $r = .47$ ($p < .001$).

*$p < .05$ (one-tail).

**$p < .01$ (one-tail).

participation is important (r = .41, p < .01), regardless of the type of organization—user or vendor—they represent. These same respondents were significantly less likely to report supplier-customer relationship (r = -.31, p < .05) and product-process dependency (r = -.29, p < .05). The tendency to report supplier-customer relationship and product-process dependency is not significantly correlated for this sample (r = -.02, n.s.), which suggests that the top three categories of implementation strategy (supplier-customer relationship, product-process dependency, and user strategy) ought to be kept intact for the model because the tendency to report them does not overlap.

The tendency to report general management support is significantly correlated with three other category reports. For human-resource policy (r = .29, p < .05) and justification (r = .28, p < .05), there is a common or shared tendency to report. Respondents who have concerns about CIM (r = -.30, p < .05) are not likely to report general management support. Whether this result indicates that these variables are substitutes for one another is difficult to determine.

The last three significant correlations involve reports of participation and product-process dependency (r = -.30, p < .05), reports of organizational culture and training (r = .26, p < .05), and reports of size or structure and incremental adoption strategy (r = .28, p < .05). The last two pairs of coefficients, however, involve the least frequently mentioned categories (culture, size or structure), and these results may be somewhat misleading.

A general pattern emerges from these correlations of reporting tendency. It is similar to the pattern—but perhaps not for the same reasons—reported previously concerning differences in user and vendor perspectives on the elements of successful implementation of programmable systems. The convergent reporting tendencies for the most important categories, as indicated by significant coefficients in Table 3, are user strategy with champion and with participation, and general management support with human-resource policy and with justification. The convergent reporting tendencies for the less important categories involve organizational culture with training and size or structure with incremental adoption strategy. The divergent reporting tendencies from Table 3 involve user strategy with supplier-customer relationship and with product-process dependency, product-process dependency with participation, and general management support with CIM.

With the exception of training, the first two categories, supplier-customer and product-process, are the only ones that place an emphasis on understanding both sides of the implementation process—that is, understanding from the perspective of both the supplier of the technology and the user of the technology simultaneously. The others emphasize the user's perspective. It appears from these results that this combined perspective is necessary to successfully implement these programmable process innovations; it may be a key ingredient in the team-building process for successful cases. The implication of these results is that these two variables—shared versus exclusive perspective—ought to be kept conceptually separate for subsequent testing.

Other Findings

In addition to the four major questions on the interview schedule, a number of other questions were included in the interviews when time permitted. These involved issues such as the factory of the future and the greenfield approach versus the existing-plant approach to adoption and implementation of advanced programmable manufacturing. Because of limited space, the findings are presented here without further elaboration.

Denial of implementation is a widespread problem in its own right. A common view is that "we could have planned" the installation better, rather than maintaining a controlled flexibility during implementation.

1. Regarding the factory of the future, only one respondent in fifty-five mentioned manufacturing in space. Most see only the advanced plant of today as the future.
2. Simulation is discussed but seldom used (appropriately) in justification and process control.

3. Greenfield plants are typically built for reasons independent of process technology—labor, suppliers' proximity, and other reasons.

4. At the outset of the study, the unit of analysis was the organization. Now it is the plant. There is virtually no technology sharing or influence across most multiple-plant manufacturing organizations.

5. Labor, management, government, and the man on the street are vulnerable and exposed on the issue of people displacement as the result of implementation of advanced manufacturing. In some cases, people are beginning to think and plan systematically for displacement, but it is only a beginning.

6. First installations are unique, especially of radical process change. The uniqueness is evident even from the beginning. The user purchasing department often requests a quotation for an FMS or cell and wants the vendors to respond in thirty days, the same way they would respond for a standard piece of equipment. Then, once the order is placed, it usually can't be changed—even if conditions change.

Summary and Conclusions

Profile of Success. Based on the data of the first phase of this study on the implementation of programmable manufacturing innovations, the profile of a successful implementation (rather than the successful firm) is as follows.

First, the successful implementation of programmable manufacturing innovation results from the combined efforts of the supplier(s) and the user of the system; they are representatives on a team that is committed to the success of the new manufacturing process. Team-building success within and across organizational boundaries predicts implementation success.

Second, many implementation attempts fail or are marginally successful because the process design as it is ultimately installed and integrated into the work flow of the organization is incorrectly matched to the product needs of the user organization. This disparity often results from an inflexibility of design, a premature rigidity of the process configuration, or an incomplete understanding of the product characteristics that are crucial for process capabilities—or all three.

Third, the absence of a strategy that does not balance the inputs of the production and design functions into planning for modernization is likely to lead to unsuccessful implementation. The new movement toward concurrent engineering supported by many professional societies (for example, SME) is likely to reduce this occurrence.

Fourth, training of properly selected participants in the implementation process is crucial for success. Training is probably the most common element of any successful implementation strategy, but it is often not properly integrated with other human-resource concerns (for example, job descriptions protecting against bumping, selection procedures, and long-term stability and growth of organization members). Turnover—even temporary turnover—can be damaging to an implementation team that may have to remain intact for several years to be successful.

This profile is incomplete and contains factors that are merely promising for further delineation and testing in the field; the most important conceptual issues raised by this study have to be resolved before additional data are collected. There are at least two outstanding issues: How do the categories of implementation strategy relate to one another—for example, should some of the categories be combined or relegated to other parts of the causal model of the process (causes and effects of implementation strategy)? And how can the results of this first data collection be reconciled with the theoretical model proposed for this study in Ettlie (1984)? These two issues are taken up separately now.

Redefined Elements of Implementation Strategy. Glaser and Strauss (1967, p. 242) recommend that "the conceptual level of categories should not be so abstract as to lose their sensitizing aspect but yet must be abstract enough to make theory a general guide to multiconditional, ever-changing daily situations." This approach places certain requirements on the person who applies the resulting grounded theory to translate, utilize, and even modify the theory as needed.

Several guidelines can be used to convert the results of

this study on implementation strategy for programmable manufacturing innovations into a parsimonious theory of implementation. First, conceptual overlap in definitions, which is often
manifested in ambiguity encountered by judges assigning data
to categories, can be exploited to make the categories more
compact and mutually exclusive than they now are. I have applied this guideline throughout the discussion where overlap was
present or absent in the categories. For example, the first four
categories (supplier-customer relationship, product-process dependency, user strategy, training) are indicated as strong con-
tenders for remaining intact because of reasonable interrater statistics of convergence without predetermined, agreed-upon
protocols.

A second approach that can be used is to examine reporting tendencies. The first three categories also appear to diverge
or are uncorrelated in reporting tendency, and there was a
strong suggestion in the interpretation of those results that simultaneous consideration of the user and vendor perspective is
a macrocategory for these elements of implementation strategy,
while the focused perspective of one or the other type of organization—for example, in user strategy—represents another
overarching macrocategory.

The question of combining or recasting the categories
reduces to what to do with the remaining ten of the thirteen
categories. I have noted that conceptually participation fits
nicely into the team-building aspect of the user-vendor relationship. Also, training fits nicely into the general concern for
human-resource policy, which includes selection, job descriptions, work rules, and so forth. Finally, justification comments
appear to fall rather neatly into the category of product-process
dependency.

The questions that remain in recasting these categories of
important variables appear to boil down to two issues. First,
how general ought the strategy category be? For example, should
it include human-resource policy, CIM, general management
support, and incremental adoption plans (Ettlie, 1973, calls this
combined category commitment)? Second, what should be
done with the last two categories: organizational culture and
size or structure?

The first recasting issue may be resolved by examining causal-model concerns and the original model developed for this study (Ettlie, 1984). In that model, as indicated later in this chapter, strategy was taken as exogenous to the elements of implementation strategy. One way of approaching this issue is to determine which aspects of strategy are temporally closer to the actual implementation or are likely to be construed as implementation variables or elements rather than long-range plans and strategy-formulation issues per se—for example, a business plan (Hambrick, 1983). If one uses this guideline, the strategy of the user becomes exogenous to the elements of implementation strategy and probably excludes most of the manifestations of strategy that emerge from the data in this phase of the study. That is, these data are primarily from middle managers. However, human-resource policy is likely to be subservient to overall strategy, but because it is a relatively complicated variable already—including training, for example—it would seem wise to keep it intact and not merge it with overall strategy.

One is left with general management support, CIM, and incremental adoption plans, which all are assumed to be functions of overall strategy. There is a significant shared reporting tendency for general management support and human-resource policy and justification. There is a significant divergent reporting tendency for general management support and integration (CIM), but it is difficult to tell whether this tendency is evidence of substitution or a common concept. One would think these two concepts might be shared by respondents in the overall tendency to report them, but, in the absence of good guidelines, these three strategy elements will be kept intact and dependent with the proviso that the intercorrelation matrix of items used to measure them be examined carefully during data analysis in the second phase because they may represent overlapping concepts.

The second general issue in recasting involves the last two categories of implementation strategy—organizational culture and organizational size or structure. I raised concerns earlier about the efficacy of the organizational-culture variable and its usefulness in organizational innovation research but held some hope that perhaps some of the indicators of culture, like shared special language, might be correlated with the readiness stage of implementation. The size-and-structure category is less of a conceptual or practical problem: Size has already been nominated as an indicator of slack resources (Ettlie, 1984); project management has been conceptually incorporated into the vendor-user relationship. All three variables—culture, size, and structure—are actually taken as exogenous to the elements of implementation strategy, so they are excluded from this list for now.

In summary, the recasting process discussed here has resulted in these recombined and redefined categories of implementation strategy: vendor-user relationship (includes project-management effectiveness, participation in decision making, and team building); product-process dependency (includes justification and flexibility of process design); human-resource policy (includes training, selection, work rules, job descriptions, and so forth); integration (CIM); general management support; incremental adoption plan; champion. Exogenous to these elements of implementation strategy are user strategy, organizational culture, size or structure, and unresolved technical (technology-specific) concerns.

Causal Model. How does this resulting configuration compare with the causal model proposed in Ettlie (1984)? In causal configuration, the new model is much simpler—the emphasis being on the constitution of implementation strategy, which is the prime causal determinant of implementation success and a function only of user strategy, as moderated by organizational size, structure, technology, and culture. Gone from the new model is the somewhat onerous implementation structure, which has become part of the vendor-user relationship under project management. Retained is the technology-policy variable —assuming that it is part of the ultimate, surviving constitution of the user-strategy variable. Slack resources that appeared in the Ettlie (1984) model are represented by organizational size but will be retained as the more general construct, which includes human and time resources.

Gone, explicitly, are the technology attributes, adoption history, economic conditions, and OEM service policy as moderators—which could be added as seen fit to the moderator list.

OEM service policy is probably adequately incorporated into the model in the vendor-user element of implementation strategy. Technology, measured at multiple levels (Gerwin, 1979), is retained as a moderator.

New is the comprehensive list of elements that are predicted to discriminate success and failure of implementation attempts—not only for advanced, programmable manufacturing, but for implementation of any innovation. Product-process dependency, in particular, is new and apparently important. Human-resource policy might have been part of the original implementation strategy, but the original model is somewhat vague on this point, with the exception of the first proposition in Ettlie (1984), which states that for radical-process implementation, human-resource deficiency is likely to predict failure. The familiar dimensions of organizational structure (complexity, formalization, decentralization) are now relegated to being moderators. They are usually significantly correlated with organizational size when institutional measures are used.

Glaser and Strauss (1967, pp. 36-37) warn against being too dependent on existing categories in deriving grounded theory. My attempt here is to have a healthy mix of respect for existing literature on the implementation in process and of enlightened interpretation of the qualitative findings of the first phase of the study. In particular, I emphasize the strong dependence on the simultaneous perspectives of supplier(s) and users of the technology. In the past, the exclusive study of users of new technologies has, perhaps, biased our models of the implementation process and limited our theory in this area.

References

Abbey, A., and Dickson, J. W. "R&D Work Climate and Innovation in Semiconductors." *Academy of Management Journal,* 1983, *26* (2), 362-368.

Alutto, J. A., and Belasco, J. A. "A Typology for Participation in Organizational Decision-Making." *Administrative Science Quarterly,* 1972, *17,* 117-125.

Bikson, T. K., and Gutek, B. A. *Advanced Office Systems: An*

Empirical Look at Utilization and Satisfaction. Santa Monica, Calif.: Rand Corporation, 1983.

Broms, H., and Gahmberg, H. "Communication to Self in Organizations and Cultures." *Administrative Science Quarterly,* 1983, *27* (3), 482-495.

Campbell, D. T., and Fiske, D. W. "Convergent and Discriminant Validation by the Multitrait-Multimethod Matrix." *Psychological Bulletin,* 1959, *56,* 91-105.

Czepiel, J. A. "Patterns of Interorganizational Communications and the Diffusion of a Major Technological Innovation in a Competitive Industrial Community." *Academy of Management Journal,* 1974, *18,* 6-24.

Das, T. H. "Qualitative Research in Organization Behavior." *Journal of Management Studies,* 1983, *20* (3), 301-314.

Ettlie, J. E. "Technology Transfer from Innovators to Users." *Industrial Engineering,* 1973, *5,* 16-23.

Ettlie, J. E. "Organizational Policy and Innovation Among Suppliers to the Food Processing Sector." *Academy of Management Journal,* 1983a, *26* (1), 27-44.

Ettlie, J. E. "Technology Policy and Innovation in Organization." Paper presented at the 43rd annual meeting of the Academy of Management, Dallas, Aug. 22-23, 1983b.

Ettlie, J. E. "Implementation Strategy for Discrete Parts Manufacturing Innovations." In M. Warner (Ed.), *Microelectronics, Manpower, and Society.* Brookfield, Vt.: Gower Press, 1984.

Ettlie, J. E., and O'Keefe, R. D. "Innovative Attitudes, Values and Intentions in Organizations." *Journal of Management Studies,* 1982, *19* (2), 153-162.

Ettlie, J. E., and Rubenstein, A. H. "Social Learning Theory and the Implementation of Production Innovation." *Decision Sciences,* 1980, *11,* 648-668.

Ettlie, J. E., and Vellenga, D. B. "The Adaption Time Period for Some Transportation Innovations." *Management Science,* 1979, *25* (5), 429-443.

Ford, J. "Institutional Versus Questionnaire Measures of Organization Structure: A Reexamination." *Academy of Management Journal,* 1979, *22,* 601-610.

Gerwin, D. "The Comparative Analysis of Structure and Technology: A Critical Appraisal." *Academy of Management Review*, 1979, *4*, 41-51.

Glaser, B. G., and Strauss, A. L. *The Discovery of Grounded Theory: Strategies for Qualitative Research.* Hawthorne, N.Y.: Aldine, 1967.

Gold, B. *Improving Managerial Evaluations of Computer-Aided Manufacturing.* Washington, D.C.: National Academy Press, 1981.

Hage, J. *Theories of Organization: Form, Process and Transformation.* New York: Wiley, 1980.

Hambrick, D. C. "Some Tests of the Effectiveness and Functional Attributes of Miles and Snow's Strategic Types." *Academy of Management Journal*, 1983, *26* (1), 5-26.

Jablonowski, J. "Aiming for Flexibility." *American Machinist,* Special Report 720, Mar. 1980, pp. 167-182.

Jick, D. "Mixing Qualitative and Quantitative Methods: Triangulation in Action." *Administrative Science Quarterly*, 1979, *24*, 602-611.

Jones, A. P., and others. "Apples and Oranges: An Empirical Comparison of Commonly Used Indices of Interrater Agreement." *Academy of Management Journal*, 1983, *26* (3), 507-519.

Kaplan, R. S. "Measuring Manufacturing Performance: A New Challenge for Managerial Accounting Research." *Accounting Review*, 1983, *58* (4), 686-705.

Mann, F. C., and Williams, L. K. "Observations on the Dynamics of a Change to Electronic Data Processing Equipment." *Administrative Science Quarterly*, 1960, *5* (2), 217-256.

Miller, D., and Friesen, P. H. "The Longitudinal Analysis of Organizations: A Methodological Perspective." *Management Science*, 1982, *28* (9), 1013-1034.

Miller, R. J. (Ed.). "Robotics: Future Factories, Future Workers." *Annals of the American Academy of Political and Social Science*, Nov. 1983, *470* (entire issue).

Sathe, V. "Institutional Versus Questionnaire Measures of Organizational Structure." *Academy of Management Journal*, 1978, *21* (2), 227-230.

Schneider, B., and Reichers, A. E. "On the Etiology of Climates." *Personnel Psychology,* 1983, *36,* 19-39.
Skinner, W. *Manufacturing in the Corporate Strategy.* New York: Wiley, 1978.
Smircich, L. "Concepts of Culture and Organizational Analysis." *Administrative Science Quarterly,* 1983, *28,* 339-358.
Williams, L. K., and Williams, C. B. "The Impact of Numerically Controlled Equipment on Factory Organization." *California Management Review,* 1964, *7,* 25-34.
Woodman, R. W., and Sherwood, J. J. "The Role of Team Development in Organizational Effectiveness: A Critical Review." *Psychological Bulletin,* 1980, *88* (1), 166-186.

FIVE

Adoption and Use of Computerized Manufacturing Technology: A National Survey

Ann Majchrzak
Veronica F. Nieva
Paul D. Newman

The factory of the future, characterized by the various applications of computer technology in the manufacturing process, is expected by many to improve sagging productivity in U.S. manufacturing. Proponents of computerized manufacturing emphasize its potential contribution to productivity and quality control. Frequently discussed under the generic term CAD/CAM (computer-aided design/computer-aided manufacturing), various technology applications are seen as fostering an array of benefits (for example, increased setting speed, flexibility, process precision, control consistency, and quality). CAD/CAM technologies are expected to reduce the long-standing trade-offs between the flexibility characterizing small-batch production and the efficiency characterizing mass production.

Elements of the factory of the future exist in today's factories, and there is widespread expectation that the diffusion of various CAD/CAM technologies will accelerate in the next few years. However, information on the nature and extent of cur-

Note: We would like to thank Paul Collins and N. Jeanne Argoff for comments on an earlier draft.

rently existing programmable manufacturing technology remains limited. Various sources of information provide pieces of
the puzzle. For example, the Robot Institute of America (1983)
estimates that by the end of 1982, the United States had 6,301
robot installations, or 13 percent of the total number of robots
internationally. The *American Machinist* (1983) shows over
100,000 numerically controlled machine tools in the United
States, representing about 4.7 percent of the total population of
machine tools.

Empirical data describing the factors facilitating CAD/
CAM adoption in manufacturing establishments are also limited,
although a number of reasons have been proposed to explain
the adoption or nonadoption of automation. These include, for
example, the size of investments required, the rate of capacity
utilization, and institutional arrangements (Riche, 1982). The
plant's predecision environment—that is, the firm's capital-plan-
ning horizon and organizational constraints—has been suggested
as an important determinant of technology adoption (Gold,
Rosegger, and Boylan, 1980). Other observers (for example,
Skinner, 1983) point to management reluctance and fear of new
technology as reasons for nonadoption.

This chapter assesses the current status of CAD/CAM
adoption and explores various factors that could explain the
level of adoption found in three manufacturing industries.
These three industries—transportation equipment, electric and
electronic equipment, and industrial and metal-working machinery—have been identified as the most likely beneficiaries of
CAD/CAM technology (Gunn, 1982). The potential payoff for
technological innovation in manufacturing is expected to be
particularly high in these industries, which involve a high proportion of small- to medium-batch production of machined
parts and assembled products.

Methods

The assessment of CAD/CAM adoption in this chapter is
based on a combination of data sources. One source is a national probability survey conducted in August 1982. We ran-

domly selected and contacted 303 manufacturing establishments in three industries—transportation equipment, electric and electronic equipment, and industrial and metal-working machinery. (The Standard Industrial Classification numbers for those industries are, respectively, SIC 37, SIC 36, SIC 35.) (For details of the sampling methodology, see Nieva, Majchrzak, and Huneycutt, 1982.) Plant representatives (including plant managers, human-resource directors, and chief executive officers) were interviewed by telephone concerning the use of various CAD/CAM technologies, company-supported education and training programs focused on computer-automated technology, and various characteristics of their firms. Data from this survey were weighted up to their representation in the population. The sample was used with the weights because the plants had been intentionally sampled to represent the population, rather than randomly and independently selected. In such situations, when the purpose is to make judgments about the population, weighting the sample is preferable (Frankel, 1971; Kish, 1965).

These survey data were combined with Census Bureau data on industrial characteristics for the period from 1960 to 1980. These industrial data included employment levels, wages, value added, and capital expenditures. Industry data were obtained at the four-digit SIC level, adjusted for constant dollars, and merged with the survey data for analyses.

Status of Computer Automation

Use of CAD/CAM Technology. The survey showed fairly low use of computer-automated equipment in the three industries studied. (In asking representatives about the status of their plant's automation, we used the following definition: "Computer-automated technology is any computerized hardware or software, either stand-alone or a system, which is used in the physical (not chemical) manufacturing process.") Most of the plants surveyed (56 percent) used no computer-automated equipment on the shop floor. Of the plants that possessed computerized equipment, most (71 percent) reported that a small proportion (1 percent to 15 percent) of their manufacturing equipment was computerized. Furthermore, about 40 percent of the computer-automated plants had only stand-alone equipment; none of their computerized equipment was integrated using computer-based links. Only 10 percent of the respondents indicated that most or all of their computerized equipment was integrated. The remaining 50 percent were moderately integrated.

These levels of computerized automation fall short of some optimistic projections made in the early 1970s. For example, an early forecast made by the Society of Manufacturing Engineers (Evans, 1973) had predicted that software for full automation in parts manufacturing would be widely used by 1980. This forecast also predicted that half to three fourths of all machine loading and scheduling would be done by computer in the mid-1980s. Although the survey found automation adoption levels at a somewhat higher level than expected from General Accounting Office (GAO) predictions in 1976—that is, the GAO predicted that by the mid-1980s the proportion of companies with CAM would not rise dramatically from the 17 percent level found ten years previously—we should keep in mind that the three industries studied were selected for their expected high adoption rates.

The low level of equipment integration is another important indicator that the factory of the future is not yet at hand. The survey suggests that computerized equipment is most often used in isolated islands of automation in the plants surveyed. Although stand-alone computerized equipment can result in productivity improvements, the full benefits of computerized automation can be realized only with equipment integration (Office of Technology Assessment, 1984). However, because integration often implies major changes in the product, production process, or organizational structure of the manufacturing plant—or all three—the transition to an integrated system tends to be slow and complex. Furthermore, the tools necessary to achieve integration—for example, common data bases, group technology, communication among different equipment—are still at early stages of development.

Of the three industries in the survey, metal-working machinery had the lowest levels of computerized automation. Only 40 percent of these plants—compared with 56 percent of the transportation-equipment plants and 46 percent of the electronic-equipment plants—had any computerized technology. In addition, metal-working plants also reported the lowest levels of equipment integration. The lag in the metal-working industry can probably be attributed to the generally small size and low product volume of metal-working shops, which make it relatively difficult to amass the capital necessary to invest in computerized equipment (compare Mansfield, 1975). Ayres and Miller (1983) suggest that the key for adoption of the relatively costly computerized technologies is the location of the indifference point between lower labor cost and greater efficiency on the one hand and higher capital cost on the other. The transportation-equipment plants, which have higher rates of adoption, tend to be larger and have more slack resources for investment than do the metal-working shops. A different rationale probably lies behind the relatively innovative, but small, electric and electronic plants. Chapter Three suggests that growing industries with diverse and emerging products—such as the electronic industry—tend to be more open to technological change than are industries without new products.

Types of Equipment Used. Plant respondents were asked about their use of six types of computer-automated equipment: robots, computer numerical control (CNC), direct (or distributed) numerical control (DNC), automated storage and retrieval, automated materials handling, and CAD. Definitions for these technologies were provided to the survey respondents. (Respondents could also indicate whether they had other types of computerized equipment not specifically identified in the survey. These might include computer-aided inspection and test equipment, programmable controllers, and electronic inserters.)

Table 1 shows the percentage of plants that used each type of technology. The most commonly used technology was CNC, which was used in over 60 percent of the computer-automated plants. The CNC dominance is not surprising, because numerical control is a mature technology, which began in the 1940s and 1950s. Furthermore, CNC machine tools are used by

Table 1. Use of Equipment Types, in Percentages.

	Total	Transpor-tation	Elec-tronics	Metal-Working
Equipment				
Robots	11.5	25.5	13.5	6.6
CNC	61.8	63.2	61.3	61.7
DNC	25.8	42.4	39.5	13.7
Storage	20.3	18.7	22.3	19.6
Materials handling	8.7	18.1	13.3	3.5
CAD	10.0	14.8	13.9	6.5
Unspecified	18.5	13.7	30.1	31.7
Percentage of total				
sample	100.0	14.9	30.2	54.9

human operators for discrete steps in the manufacturing process (for example, cutting metal into specified shapes) and thus do not involve major disruptions in the production process or the organization of manufacturing plants.

DNC was the second most prevalent technology overall, giving further support to the numerical-control dominance. Its use, however, tended to be more prevalent in the transportation-equipment industry (42 percent) and the electronic-equipment industry (40 percent) than in the metal-working industry (14 percent).

Automated storage and retrieval, found in 20 percent of the plants surveyed, followed numerical controls as the most prevalent equipment type. These automated warehousing systems, like CNC, can be adopted with relative ease—installation can be self-contained, and they do not usually require major changes in the entire manufacturing process.

Automated materials-handling equipment (conveyors, computerized carts or trucks guided by rails or tracks on the shop floor) was the technology least commonly found in the surveyed plants (8.7 percent). Materials-handling technology links large segments of the manufacturing process and thus is relatively more difficult to implement than contained technologies like CNC and automated storage.

Equipment Use and Automation Characteristics. Use of particular types of equipment was found to be related to the extent of shop-floor computerization and equipment integration. Most of the plants that used CNC, automated storage, CAD, and the specialized unspecified types of equipment tended to be less computerized (see Table 2), while most of the robot and materials-handling users were more computerized.

Table 2. Equipment Use and Extent of Computerization, in Percentages.

	Shop-Floor Computerization	
	1–15%	*Over 15%*
Equipment		
Robots	44.8[a]	55.2
CNC	60.4	39.6
DNC	49.8	50.2
Storage	53.0	47.0
Materials handling	39.6	60.4
CAD	51.4	48.6
Unspecified	91.6	8.4
Percentage of total sample	70.8	29.2

[a]Row percentages.

Equipment use also differed across levels of integration (Table 3). As noted before, the largest group was plants that were moderately integrated (50 percent); about 40 percent had no integration at all; and about 10 percent had most or all of

Table 3. Equipment Use and Level of Integration, in Percentages.

	Level of Integration		
	None	*Some*	*Most or All*
Equipment			
Robots	38.6[a]	50.0	11.4
CNC	40.0	44.8	15.2
DNC	29.0	38.0	33.0
Storage	40.7	32.8	26.5
Materials handling	14.5	77.1	8.4
CAD	15.4	42.5	42.1
Unspecified	31.9	66.6	1.6
Percentage of total sample	39.9	49.5	10.6

[a]Row percentages.
Note: 240 cases were missing on the integration variable.

their equipment integrated. This general pattern was mirrored among plants that used robots and CNC. In contrast, users of DNC, storage, and CAD tended to have higher levels of integration than might be expected from the overall pattern found among the plants surveyed.

Further examination of the various types of equipment combinations in these manufacturing establishments indicated that DNC use provides impetus for integration. (By far the most prevalent combinations are CNC and DNC—11 percent—and both forms of numerical control and storage—8.4 percent.) One fourth of the plants using both CNC and DNC reported that the shop floor was mostly integrated, while only 3 percent of plants that used only CNC responded this way (see Table 4). The addi-

Table 4. Equipment Profiles and Level of Integration, in Percentages.

	Level of Integration		
	None	Some	Most or All
Equipment			
CNC	48	49	3
CNC/DNC	37	38	25
Storage	84	16	0
CNC/Storage	61	39	0
CNC/DNC/Storage	52	13	35
Percentage of total sample	39.9	49.5	10.6

tion of DNC also appears to integrate the CNC-storage combination. Few plants (16 percent) using only automated-storage equipment reported any shop-floor integration, and about a third of the plants using CNC and storage were integrated to some degree. But when DNC, CNC, and storage were used, 35 percent indicated that most or all of the shop-floor technologies were integrated, and an additional 13 percent reported some integration.

Explanations for Variations in Automation

The results presented thus far describe a situation in which relatively few plants were using CAD/CAM technology.

Those manufacturing establishments with CAD/CAM varied substantially in the proportion of production-floor equipment with the computerized technology, the extent to which the equipment was integrated using computer-based links, and the combinations of CAD/CAM equipment used.

To describe the status of CAD/CAM in manufacturing plants today, explanations as to how or why certain patterns appear are needed. Our data allow us to explore such explanations. To undertake this exploration, we located data on twelve organizational and market variables that could be important determinants of a company's decision to adopt CAD/CAM. These variables were then used in a series of statistical analyses, such as regression and discriminant-function analysis, to determine how well they predicted a plant's decision to innovate. Furthermore, since our analysis thus far had indicated that extent and integration of automation were only mildly related, we were interested in predicting both extent and integration as different types of innovation decisions. Although previous studies have examined determinants of yes/no adoption decisions (for example, see the research reviewed by Tornatzky and others, 1983), our study was unique in considering more than one criterion of innovation. Furthermore, previous studies have neither included both organizational and market variables nor used a nationally representative sample of a large number of plants from more than one industry.

The inclusion of both organizational and market variables allowed for a comparison of their relative importance in innovation, a comparison that previous research had not made. The consideration of integration and extent as two different innovation criteria explicitly recognized the inherent complexity of CAD/CAM adoption decisions. Finally, the large representative sample meant our findings were more generalizable than studies done in the past. Therefore, for managers and researchers who want to predict why certain firms adopt CAD/CAM equipment, our findings have some credibility. Nevertheless, our study should be viewed as exploratory because it used only twelve of the thirty or forty variables that probably affect innovation. Comprehensive research should be done to expand on and verify our conclusions.

The twelve variables we used to predict CAD/CAM adoption included four characteristics of the plant: size (average of 1981 sales and personnel size), proportion of hourly workers at the time of the survey, founding year, and centrality of manufacturing operations to the plant (measured as the proportion of personnel directly involved in manufacturing). Research reviewed in Chapter Three indicates that size may be either positively related to innovation (because of slack resources) or negatively related (because of the lower flexibility inherent in large organizations). We thought that the proportion of hourly workers would be related to innovation either positively by creating a need to reduce labor costs or negatively because there would be fewer salaried professionals and managers to initiate new innovations (an argument used in Chapter Three to underscore the importance of specialists in the innovation process). Work by Utterback and Abernathy (1975) suggest that the older a firm, the more developed and rigid its production process—that is, the less innovative. Finally, we hypothesized that the more central manufacturing was to the operations of the plant, the greater the perceived need to innovate would be.

In addition to the organizational variables, characteristics of the plant's market environment were obtained from the Census Bureau Survey of Manufacturers at the four-digit SIC level. These market variables included wage rates for production workers, capital expenditures, and value added (in millions of dollars). Value added is the value of shipments in a year minus the total cost of materials adjusted for remaining inventory. Wages were used as a market demand variable because high labor costs have been predicted as a major incentive for investing in CAD/CAM technology (Mowery and Rosenberg, 1979; Myers and Marquis, 1969). Capital expenditures and value added were used to measure market supply factors because increases in these market variables mean that additional money is available for investing in CAD/CAM technology (Ettlie, 1973; Mansfield, 1975). Capital expenditures may be used for automation, while high value added generates the surplus needed for CAD/CAM investment. Furthermore, value added can be considered a proxy measure of industry productivity because increased output per employee is generally reflected by value added. Therefore, recent increases in productivity could provide the cushion to invest in high-cost equipment.

Market data were obtained for 1980 (two years before our survey) and as growth over two time periods: 1960-1970 and 1970-1980. All values were adjusted for inflation and then matched to the plant's four-digit SIC code. It is important to recognize that this procedure assumes that a market value describing a four-digit SIC industry is applicable to the concerns of individual plants within that industry. That is, we assume that when an industry has high labor costs, a plant within that industry is concerned about high labor costs. Although that plant may not actually have high costs, the aggregate total for the industry is likely to create a concern for high costs in that plant.

We matched the Census Bureau market data to the weighted survey data of the plants in our sample and then attempted to predict the extent of a firm's computerization as the proportion of equipment computerized (none, low, or some) and the extent to which computerized equipment was integrated using computer-based links (none, some, or high).

Extent of Computerization. To predict the extent of a firm's computerization, we used all twelve predictor variables. However, several of the predictor variables were not sufficiently different from each other to use in the same analysis; thus, several subsets of relatively unrelated predictor variables were identified. Results for one subset are presented in the top half of Table 5. Results of other subsets are not dramatically different. This analysis indicates several findings.

First, about 26 percent of the variation among plants in extent of computerization could be explained by subsets of organizational and market variables. Although three quarters of the variation is left unexplained by our variables, these variables at least contribute substantially if not completely to our understanding of adoption decisions.

Second, among the organizational variables, size and proportion of hourly workers were the most important predictors of extent. Furthermore, size was positively related and propor-

Table 5. Results of Stepwise Regressions of Automation with
Subsets of Organizational and Market Variables.

Variables	Standardized Beta	Change in R^2	Pearson r	Adjusted R^2 (Cumulative)
Extent of Computerization				
Proportion of hourly workers	−.41	.20	−.45	.20
Size	.23	.06	.31	.26
1980 wages	.04	.00	.13	.26
1970-1980 wage growth	.00	.00	.02	.26
Level of Integration				
1975-1980 growth in value added	.25	.08	.28	.08
Size	−.21	.02	−.16	.10
1980 value added	.21	.01	.09	.12
1970-1975 growth in value added	.12	.01	.03	.13
Proportion of hourly workers	−.09	.01	−.21	.13

tion of hourly workers was negatively related to extent; that is, the larger the plant's size, the more resources it had to invest in CAD/CAM, and the larger the proportion of hourly workers, the fewer technical professionals and managers there were to encourage adoption. This relationship of hourly workers to extent of computerization may also mean that firms with small proportions of hourly workers have less to automate and therefore find it easier to implement the equipment than do those with large proportions of hourly workers.

Third, market variables such as 1980 wage rates or growth in value added provided little explanation for why firms adopt the amount of computerized equipment they do.

Since data on the organizational variables were obtained at the same time as the data on innovation, inferences about causation are tentative at best. Nevertheless, this analysis indicates that markets with certain characteristics (that is, low versus high value added) are not more likely to adopt more computerized equipment. Therefore, market segmentation based on

past wage rates, capital expenditures, or value-added performance is not a useful basis on which CAD/CAM vendors should
base marketing strategies. Rather, vendors should look to characteristics of the individual plants: Those larger in size with
larger proportions of salaried workers are likely to be candidates
ripe for larger-scale adoptions.

These results also suggest that managers looking to convince corporate officers to adopt CAD/CAM need not turn to a
concern for high labor costs as the convincing evidence. Despite
a survey described by Ayres and Miller (1983) citing high labor
costs as the most frequent reason for adoption given by CAD/
CAM users, high labor costs were not found here to be the most
important reasons for adoption. Clearly, then, while adopters
may see high labor costs as important in their decision, they actually consider a number of other factors such as slack resources.

Integration Level. In addition to predicting the extent of
computerization, subsets of our variables were used to predict
the level of integration for those plants having adopted any
computerized equipment. These findings, for which one subset
is presented in the bottom half of Table 5, indicated that little
(8 percent) of the variation in plants' decisions to have integrated equipment was explained by the twelve organizational
and market variables. Therefore, while the extent of computerization depends primarily on a few organizational variables such
as size, level of integration depends on a much different set of
variables.

As has been discussed in several other chapters of this
book, a key feature that sets CAD/CAM apart from previous
technological improvements is the extent to which it promotes
integration with other operations in the organization. A stand-
alone CNC or robot involves only a few minor changes in programming, training, and maintenance. A flexible manufacturing
system (FMS) demands coordinating a series of scheduling,
work-flow, and distribution requirements throughout the entire
product line. Therefore, a plant decision to adopt a set of stand-
alone computerized equipment is inherently different from a
decision to adopt a set of integrated equipment. In our analysis,

those differences were upheld; that is, the variables that moderately predicted extent of computerization poorly predicted extent of integration. Furthermore, it is worth noting that for some predictor variables the relationship to extent of integration was the inverse of the relationship to extent of computerization. For example, smaller plants were more likely to have integrated equipment than larger plants, yet larger plants were more likely to have more computerized equipment than smaller plants. The implication from a CAD/CAM vendor's viewpoint, then, is that larger plants are likely to adopt more computerized equipment, but this equipment is not likely to be integrated. In contrast, the smaller firms, once having entered the ball game, tend to adopt the more integrated equipment. Clearly, then, the extent to which a vendor's product involves integratable equipment will in some sense determine the potential client base.

Combined Computerization and Integration. Because this analysis underscored the fact that a plant's decision to adopt computerized equipment is qualitatively different, with different predictors, from the same plant's decision to integrate through use of new equipment, both decisions must be considered in understanding variations among plants in CAD/CAM adoption. Therefore, a final set of analyses was conducted on plants grouped by both their extent of computerization and level of integration. Using the predictor variables, the analysis determined how well the variables could differentiate among the different groups of plants.

Plants were placed in one of six groups depending on the current status of automation on the shop floor: a little stand-alone equipment, some stand-alone equipment, a little moderately integrated equipment, some moderately integrated equipment, a little highly integrated equipment, and some highly integrated equipment. (There were no firms with more than "some" computerized equipment.) Taking these six groups two at a time (for example, little versus some stand-alone equipment), the extent to which the predictor variables could correctly classify plants was assessed (using discriminant analyses).

The results of this analysis were impressive: Subsets of the predictor variables were able to correctly classify 92 percent of the plants into those with little versus some stand-alone equipment, 83 percent into those with little versus some moderately integrated equipment, and 95 percent into those with little versus some highly integrated equipment. Clearly, then, our variables were able to correctly differentiate among firms choosing different levels of computerization and integration.

In addition, and most importantly for managers and vendors alike, our analysis indicated that the market and organizational characteristics that distinguish between firms varying in extent of computerization are very different across levels of integration. Table 6 presents the means of the variables for each level of integration. (Asterisks indicate variables that significantly contributed to differentiating among plants at the level —that is, variables that were significantly different between the groups.)

For plants with stand-alone equipment, increased extent of computerization was predicted by higher 1980 wages and value added, large and recent growth in value added, small-sized firms, and larger proportions of salaried workers. Therefore, for CAD/CAM vendors and for managers desiring nonintegrated computerized equipment, the smaller, more profitable firms with relatively more salaried workers are more likely to adopt more equipment. One explanation for this pattern may be that smaller profitable firms with large proportions of professionals and managers are more aware of and open to technological advances. Moreover, and perhaps most importantly, nonintegrated equipment such as robots and CNCs are relatively minor investments ($40,000 average cost for a robot versus $600,000 for an FMS) for which traditional economic analyses still apply and, when implemented, involve relatively small changes to the organization. As such, they constitute technological improvements manageable by smaller, more profitable plants.

In contrast to plants with stand-alone equipment, plants that adopted equipment allowing a moderate degree of integration showed a different pattern. Among these plants, those more likely to adopt more equipment were larger and had experienced substantial increases in wage rates over the last decade. Recent growth in value added and the proportion of hourly

Table 6. Means of Variables for Plants Making Different Decisions About Computerization and Integration.

	Low Computerization, No Integration	Some Computerization, No Integration	Low Computerization, Some Integration	Some Computerization, Some Integration	Low Computerization, High Integration	Some Computerization, High Integration
Market Demand						
1980 wages (in millions of dollars)	582*	763*	621*	888*	1647*	636*
1970-1980 wage growth	0.03	0.02	0.10*	0.49*	0.03	0.06
Market Supply						
1980 value added (in millions of dollars)	1689*	2039*	1870*	2612*	3986*	2020*
1970-1975 growth in value added	−.13	−.20	−.07*	.21*	−.13*	−.31*
1975-1980 growth in value added	.23*	.41*	.34	.32	.14*	.71*
Organizational Variables						
Size[a]	9.8*	7.1*	7.2*	11.7*	14.4*	7.2*
Proportion of hourly to total workers	78%*	52%*	68%	74%	65%*	52%*
Industry[b]						
Transportation	11%	22%	9%	24%	78%	17%
Electronics	20%	62%	25%	23%	20%	61%
Metal-Working	69%	16%	67%	53%	2%	22%

[a]Size is a composite index of sales and work force. Use for comparative purposes only.
[b]Proportion of firms in each two-digit SIC industry within each integration level is included for descriptive purposes only. This variable was not included in the discriminant analysis.
*Significant discriminating power.

workers did not differentiate among plants in the amount of equipment adopted. By implication, for equipment being used to moderately integrate a plant's shop-floor operations (such as a DNC), vendors should look toward larger plants wanting to reduce their labor costs. Smaller firms may not have the resources to obtain large numbers of such relatively costly equipment as DNCs and moderately integrated machining centers. And, without the high labor costs, sufficient impetus for the investment may be lacking.

Finally, for plants adopting highly integrated equipment, more computerization was found among smaller, more profitable firms with high proportions of salaried workers. Wage rates for these firms were generally low, without much change over time. This is a pattern generally similar to that found among plants adopting a greater amount of nonintegrated equipment. However, the reasons for adopting highly integrated equipment are probably different from those for adopting nonintegrated equipment. High integration implies the ability to conduct a large part of discrete-parts manufacturing via computer controls, materials-handling devices, electronic sensors, and automated machines. Because the costs to implement such a system are so high, only selected firms are willing to invest at this level of integration. Once they have this highly integrated equipment in place, the decision to extend it to additional work areas on their production floors is determined mostly by resources. As a result, small firms may computerize more of their equipment than larger firms simply because there is less to computerize. Furthermore, note that the small firms with such a high level of automation have either low labor costs coupled with increased recent rises or low value added coupled with recent value growth. The firms implement computerization, then, probably less out of a need to cut costs than out of a desire to take advantage of the opportunities that increased computerization will bring. By implication, then, vendors of highly integrated CAD/CAM equipment must recognize that it is not necessarily the larger plants that are willing to make a larger investment in such equipment. Although the table indicates that plants that invest in highly integrated equipment are generally larger than plants with nonintegrated equipment, among those adopting a highly integrated strategy, it is the smaller, more profitable plants willing to accept the risks that a heavy involvement in such a strategy entails.

Although this analysis has essentially ignored a plant's industrial classification, the table indicates that some industries are more likely to have certain automation strategies than others. Electronics firms are more likely to adopt a greater amount of both highly integrated and nonintegrated equipment, while transportation plants have adopted a little highly integrated equipment. These industry differences have been explained in Chapter Three as attributable to differences in the evolution of their product and process patterns. That is to say, because they historically give priority to efficiency over flexibility, transportation plants adopt fewer high-risk technological innovations than electronics plants. Nevertheless, industry differences do not explain the complete picture: Electronics plants adopt more of both highly integrated and nonintegrated equipment, while metal-working plants seem to have little to moderate integration and little to some computerization. Therefore, CAD/CAM vendors should not quickly segment their markets along obvious industrial boundaries. As Chapter Eight suggests, an emphasis among vendors on a sophisticated market-segmentation approach is necessary. Depending on the potential level of integration of the vendor's products, the results described here suggest some possible means for a more sophisticated segmentation than now exists.

Implications

The descriptive data presented here serve the important function of reporting on the recent status of CAD/CAM adoption in three American manufacturing industries. These data tell us that slightly less than half of the plants today have some computerized equipment on their shop floor. However, this computerization is dominated primarily by CNC, a relatively unsophisticated technology given current know-how and need. Technologies more advanced than CNC, such as CAD and computer-automated materials handling, have, as yet, reached few plants. Furthermore, these data tell us which types of CAD/ CAM equipment are most likely to be used by plants to integrate shop-floor operations.

These descriptive data have obvious implications for marketing strategies of CAD/CAM vendors, and several of these implications have already been discussed. However, the data go beyond that. They describe a situation in which integration and extent of computerization have little to do with the adoption of CNC. CNC may no longer be an important precursor to a plant's ability to meet the demands of a new sophisticated technology. Rather than progressing from CNC to robots to more advanced technologies, plants with just stand-alone CNCs and robots may not be prepared for the intricacies of integrated equipment. Therefore, although other authors recommend to vendors and users that past experience with CAD/CAM is an excellent predictor of success in implementing more CAD/CAM (see Gerwin, 1982), our data suggest caution in assessing the relevance of past experience. As Chapter Nine so aptly describes, the implications of integrated equipment for the strategy, structure, and process of the organization differ so dramatically from the implications of nonintegrated equipment that experience with nonintegrated equipment may be insufficient.

In accepting the qualitative differences between integrated and nonintegrated CAD/CAM equipment, our analysis proceeded one step further to predict which plants are likely to adopt which automation strategies. Vendors obviously need a complex market segmentation. Although larger firms may in general adopt more equipment than smaller firms, the amount of equipment they adopt at different levels of integration varies in predictable but not similar patterns.

Finally, managers in plants considering technological improvements need to be cognizant of these different patterns of adoption. The reasons people use to purchase several stand-alone machines are different from the reasons they use to adopt a single integratable machine—although the aggregate capital expenditure may be the same. When justifying a capital expenditure, managers may find that building into the rationale the dif-

ferences between integratable and nonintegratable equipment
will help to convince corporate decision makers.

These findings also have a message for academic researchers. Clearly, an innovation decision is a series of qualitatively
different decisions—the decision as to how many machines to
adopt is different from the decision regarding the degree of integration of the machines. Researchers may thus profit by con-
ceptualizing which decision to observe before jumping in.
Furthermore, we suggest that possibly the more interesting decision to observe is not the extent of computerization (the
amount of equipment) but the integration decision. To use a
conceptual paradigm for defining relative innovation offered by
Bigoness and Perreault (1981), the integration decision forces a
shift in defining innovativeness in both the referent group (from
past behavior of a firm to the plant's foreign competitors) and
content domain (from adoption of a new piece of equipment to
adoption of a new approach to manufacturing). Therefore, the
research question becomes not why firms choose to adopt
CAD/CAM equipment but rather which firms accept the risk of
changing their approach to manufacturing. It is this question
that may tell us something about the future of innovation in
manufacturing.

References

American Machinist. "The 13th American Machinist Inventory
    of Metal-Working Equipment." American Machinist, Nov.
    1983, pp. 113-114.
Ayres, R. U., and Miller, S. M. "Robotics, CAM, and Industrial
    Productivity." National Productivity Review, Winter 1981-
    1982, pp. 42-60.
Ayres, R. U., and Miller, S. M. Robotics: Applications and So-
    cial Implications. Cambridge, Mass.: Ballinger, 1983.
Bigoness, W. J., and Perreault, W. D. "A Conceptual Paradigm
    and Approach for the Study of Innovators." Academy of
    Management Journal, 1981, 24 (1), 68-82.
Ettlie, J. E. "Technology Transfer from Innovators to Users."
    Industrial Engineering, 1973, 5, 16-23.

Evans, L. L. "Delphi-Type Forecasts Regarding Discrete Parts Technology for the Period 1975-2000." Technical Paper MS73-981 presented at the 2nd Society of Manufacturing Engineers CAD/CAM Conference, Detroit, 1973.

Frankel, M. R. *Inferences from Survey Samples: An Empirical Investigation.* Ann Arbor: Institute for Social Research, University of Michigan, 1971.

General Accounting Office. *Report to the Congress: Manufacturing Technology—A Changing Challenge to Improved Productivity.* Washington, D.C.: General Accounting Office, 1976.

Gerwin, D. "Do's and Don't's of Computerized Manufacturing." *Harvard Business Review,* 1982, *60,* 107-116.

Gold, B., Rosegger, J., and Boylan, M. G. *Evaluating Technological Innovations.* Lexington, Mass.: Heath, 1980.

Gunn, T. G. "The Mechanization of Design and Manufacturing." *Scientific American,* Sept. 1982, pp. 115-130.

Kish, L. *Survey Sampling.* New York: Wiley, 1965.

Mansfield, E. "The Economics of Industrial Innovation." In P. Kelly and others (Eds.), *Technological Innovation: A Critical Review of Current Knowledge.* Document no. PB-242 551. Washington, D.C.: U.S. Government Printing Office, 1975.

Mowery, D., and Rosenberg, N. "The Influence of Market Demand upon Innovation: A Critical Review of Some Recent Empirical Studies." *Research Policy,* 1979, *8,* 102-153.

Myers, S., and Marquis, D. G. *Successful Industrial Innovations: A Study of Factors Underlying Innovation in Selected Forms.* Washington, D.C.: National Science Foundation, 1969.

Nieva, V. F., Majchrzak, A., and Huneycutt, M. *Education and Training in Computer-Aided Manufacturing.* Washington, D.C.: Office of Technology Assessment, 1982.

Office of Technology Assessment. *Computerized Manufacturing and Automation: Employment, Education and the Workplace.* Washington, D.C.: Office of Technology Assessment, 1984.

Riche, R. W. "Impact of New Electronic Technology." *Monthly Labor Review,* Mar. 1982, pp. 37-39.

Robot Institute of America. *Worldwide Robotics Survey and Directory.* Dearborn, Mich.: Society of Manufacturing Engineers, 1983.

Skinner, W. "Wanted: Managers for the Factory of the Future." *Annals of the American Academy of Political and Social Science, 470,* Nov. 1983, 102-114.

Tornatzky, L. D., and others. *The Process of Technological Innovation: Reviewing the Literature.* Washington, D.C.: National Science Foundation, 1983.

Utterback, J. M., and Abernathy, W. J. "A Dynamic Model of Process and Product Innovation." *Omega,* 1975, *3* (6), 639-656.

SIX

The Organizational Implications of Robotics

Linda Argote
Paul S. Goodman

Robots are being introduced in increasing numbers throughout the world. Although only a few hundred robots were used in the United States in 1970, 7,000 were in use in 1983 (Ayres and Miller, 1983; Hunt and Hunt, 1983). Forecasts of how many robots will be used in 1990 in the United States range between 75,000 and 150,000 (Hunt and Hunt, 1983). Little is known, however, about how individual employees react to the introduction of robots or about the changes needed in organizations to support robotics. Our research focuses on understanding the human side of robotics—how individuals react to robots, how and when organizations should be modified to support robotics, and what effective strategies can be used to implement robotics.

The Robot Institute of America (1982) defines a robot as a programmable, multifunctional manipulator designed to move objects through variable programmed motions to perform a variety of tasks. Two characteristics differentiate robots from most other forms of automation: multiple-task capability and programmability. The robots used most frequently in U.S. factories

Note: Support for this research was provided by grants from the Program on the Social Impacts of Information and Robotic Technology at Carnegie-Mellon University to both authors and by a grant from the National Science Foundation (No. RII-840991) to the first author. Parts of this chapter were written while the first author was on leave in the Department of Industrial Engineering and Engineering Management at Stanford University.

today, in jobs that involve moving material, welding, drilling, or spray painting, are called level I, or first-generation, robots. Researchers are now in the process of developing robots, known as level II, or second-generation, robots, with more sophisticated sensing and thinking capabilities. For example, a level II robot that is capable of identifying the location of parts of different shapes and sizes is currently being developed. Other examples of level II robots include those that mine underground coal seams, detect gas leaks, or perform sophisticated inspection tasks. Ayres and Miller (1983) provide a good description of the current and expected future capabilities of robotics.

In this chapter, we first develop a general framework for understanding the effects of robots on individuals and organizations. In this framework, we incorporate findings from our field studies on the implementation of robotics as well as findings from other field studies on this topic. The methodology and results of our field studies are described in detail in Argote, Goodman, and Schkade (1983) and Argote and Goodman (1984). We conclude the chapter with suggestions for researchers who are analyzing the implementation of robotics and with recommendations for managers who plan to utilize robotics in their organizations.

General Framework

The use of robotics may have a profound effect on the organization of work and on the productivity of organizations. Robots typically require new skills of both production and technical-support personnel and require close interactions among functional areas (Argote, Goodman, and Schkade, 1983). Robots may displace some employees and alter the jobs of those who are retained (Guest, 1984; Office of Technology Assessment, 1984). Robots may also enable organizations to be more flexible than they now are by decreasing set-up times associated with product changeovers. Moreover, robots may enable organizations to achieve increased consistency in the quality of their products (Ayres and Miller, 1983; Guest, 1984). In this section, we develop a general framework for anticipating these effects of robots on individuals and organizations as well as for predicting the conditions under which the use of robots will enhance organizational performance.

Organizational Performance. In order to present our general framework, we must first discuss the concept of organizational performance. Organizations can be thought of as consisting of three basic components—people, technology, and structure. The compatibility of these three basic components of organizations determines their performance (Leavitt, 1965; Emery and Trist, 1973). Organizational performance is thus a complex variable with multiple dimensions (Goodman and Pennings, 1977; Katz and Kahn, 1978). Examples of performance criteria that are critical in the manufacturing environment are productivity, product quality, manufacturing flexibility, absenteeism, turnover, and employee motivation and well-being. These criteria may vary in importance over time and to different constituencies. For example, sales and marketing departments may place a higher premium on manufacturing flexibility than other functional areas do because it enables the organization to adapt to customers' needs in a timely fashion. Similarly, manufacturing flexibility may be more important in the early than in the late stages of a product's life cycle (Kaplan, 1983).

Furthermore, these performance criteria are likely to be interrelated, sometimes in complex ways. For example, employee motivation may be positively related to work-unit productivity under the conditions of uncertainty that occur when a machine breaks down, but employee motivation may have little effect on the productivity of capital-intensive firms under routine or programmed conditions (see Goodman, 1979). Similarly, productivity, at least measured in the short run, may be negatively associated with manufacturing flexibility.

The complexity of the concept of organizational performance suggests that understanding the impact and effects of new technologies requires an appreciation of the interrelationships among the elements of organizations. It also suggests the need for examining multiple performance criteria and the trade-offs among them. Further research is needed to identify how the introduction of robots will affect the elements of an organization and the conditions under which these elements may be compatible. The few existing empirical studies of the introduction of robots (Argote, Goodman, and Schkade, 1983; Argote and Goodman, 1984; Office of Technology Assessment, 1984) and theoretical work on job design, organizational structure, organizational effectiveness, and the introduction of change enable us to suggest what these effects are likely to be and when the use of robots is likely to enhance manufacturing performance.

We want to emphasize that using robots does not automatically imply certain consequences for organizations, but rather the characteristics of the technology, the manner in which robots are introduced, the organization's structure, and the people who work in the organization determine the impact of robotics. For example, some companies provide little training for their robot operators and design the jobs of operators so that they have little autonomy and are dependent on technical-support staff. Other companies provide training for their operators, design autonomy into their jobs, and expect them to be actively involved in promoting the operation of the robots. Our sense is that involving operators in these ways results in more motivated operators and a speedier and smoother implementation than does not involving them. The technology in each approach is the same. The supporting organizational arrangements are different. Thus, the use of robots does not produce certain consequences for organizations. Instead the characteristics of the robots, the people who operate and maintain the robots, and the organizational arrangements that support the robots affect the performance of organizations.

Individual Employees. We now turn to what is known about how the introduction of robots typically affects individual employees in organizations. On one level, it usually changes the skills required of them and their job activities. In our study of a plant in the metal-working industry, the introduction of a robot that performed materials handling caused a shift in the robot operators' jobs from primarily manual to primarily mental activities (Argote, Goodman, and Schkade, 1983). The Office of Technology Assessment (OTA) reports a similar change in the automobile industry: The introduction of welding robots removed some of the physical demands from the jobs of human operators (1984). Thus, the introduction of robots in both studies had a positive effect on employees' work environments. The robots assumed some of the physically demanding tasks otherwise performed by humans.

At the same time, both studies found that the introduction of robots had certain negative effects on employees. Operators in our study reported that they experienced more stress and less control after the robot was introduced than before (Argote, Goodman, and Schkade, 1983). Similarly, the OTA report indicates that direct production employees felt less control with the introduction of the welding robots because their jobs were now tied to an assembly line (1984). Repair supervisors in the OTA report also experienced greater stress after the implementation of robots than before, apparently because of the pressures of maintaining a complex and highly integrated production system.

Based on previous research, we expect that if the introduction of robots leads employees to experience less control over their work environment than they previously did, they will be less satisfied, less motivated, and experience more stress (Blauner, 1964; Hackman and Lawler, 1971; Hackman and Oldham, 1975; Sutton and Kahn, in press). We also expect that systems that are complex or characterized by low reliability will be associated with increased stress (Bright, 1958; Office of Technology Assessment, 1984).

In addition, variety and feedback on the job promote employee well-being (Hackman and Oldham, 1975). If the use of robotics affects the variety and feedback employees experience, then we expect corresponding changes in their satisfaction and motivation. Along these lines, the OTA report indicates that maintenance workers experienced positive changes in their work environment after the introduction of welding robots because their jobs were characterized by greater variety and more challenge than they were previously (1984).

Another change that the introduction of robotics typically brings is in the skill requirements for both production and technical-support personnel. As noted earlier, the use of robots usually shifts operators' jobs from manually oriented to mentally oriented activities. If these changes are compatible with employees' skills and preferences, employees will feel more satisfied and less stress after the change than if the changes are not compatible with their skills and preferences. Strategies are suggested later in this chapter for maximizing the fit between employees and their jobs and for designing the jobs of employees, both direct and indirect, who must interact with robots.

The manner in which robots are implemented may also affect employee reactions to the change. Coch and French's (1948) classic study indicates that introducing change in a participative fashion increases the likelihood that employees will react positively. Other researchers have also stressed participation as a key variable in determining the extent to which employees react positively to change (Kotter and Schlesinger, 1979; Tornatzky and others, 1983).

Although employees in the two organizations we studied did not participate at all in any decisions surrounding the introduction of the robots, employees at both organizations desired more influence than they had (Argote, Goodman, and Schkade, 1983; Argote and Goodman, 1984). The discrepancy between how much influence they actually had and how much they desired was especially pronounced at the second organization we studied, possibly because the organization was unionized and had a tradition of employee participation. Although employees desired increased influence, they acknowledged that the implementation of robotics is a complex activity requiring technical expertise that they generally do not possess. Hence, employees did not expect a great deal of influence in decisions regarding robotics. They did feel, however, that they had some expertise, especially concerning work processes and machines in their department, and that they should be involved in decisions related to their areas of expertise.

Another dimension of the implementation process is the method organizations use to communicate with employees about the introduction of robotics. Organizations may use a variety of communication mechanisms, including talks by the plant manager, meetings with first-line supervisors, and demonstrations. In our research, we examined how effective employees rated the various communication techniques their organizations used to introduce robotics. Our results indicate that employees rate demonstrations of the operation of robots as the most effective means for increasing their understanding of robots (Argote, Goodman, and Schkade, 1983). This result is corroborated by the finding that the demonstration had a greater impact on employees' beliefs about and attitudes toward robotics than any other communication source the organization used (Argote and Goodman, 1985).

How employee motivation, satisfaction, and stress affect the performance of firms using robotics remains an open question. There is a growing sense in the business literature that these human-resource issues are critical to a firm's ability to compete effectively (Abernathy, Clark, and Kantrow, 1983). Some limited evidence also shows that using robotics and other programmable automation in ways that enhance employee well-being leads to increased organizational efficiency (Office of Technology Assessment, 1984). Consequently, we need to identify the conditions under which employee motivation, satisfaction, and stress affect the overall performance of firms using robotics. An interesting hypothesis developed from previous research is that these human-resource variables affect the overall performance of work units when unprogrammed situations occur—for example, when a machine breaks down or when a new product is introduced (see Goodman, 1979). Under routine operating conditions, human motivation and attitudes may have little effect on the performance of roboticized systems. That is, human-resource variables may matter more when technologies are first being implemented, when new products are being introduced, or when unexpected problems arise than when systems are operating routinely.

Organizational Structures. In addition to affecting individual employees, the introduction of robots may also change the basic structures of organizations—communication within and between departments, decision-making responsibilities, role relationships, and the like. In our study, we found that the introduction of a robot led to increased interactions between production and technical-support personnel from engineering and maintenance. Studies of other technologies similar to robots, such as numerically controlled machines, report similar increases in interaction among production, engineering, and maintenance groups (Williams and Williams, 1964; Office of Technology Assessment, 1984).

The use of robotics also has the potential to change relationships between production and marketing groups because robots may reduce the time it takes to change from one product to another. This potential could enable organizations both to accommodate a more varied product mix and to respond more easily to customer demands than they now do. Although we have not yet witnessed any empirical evidence of modified relationships between production and marketing because of the introduction of robots, these changes might occur as additional robots are put on line and linked in integrated systems.

According to some evidence, the use of advanced automation on the factory floor may enable organizations to centralize production-scheduling decisions (Office of Technology Assessment, 1984). Such centralization may reduce the need for technical experts who schedule production as well as eliminate scheduling tasks from supervisors' jobs. Similarly, intelligent robots that perform inspection tasks may reduce the requirement for special quality-control staff. Indeed, the use of intelligent robots may lead to fewer hierarchical levels within organizations as well as to a smaller number of direct production workers than now exist (Cyert and others, 1984). Intelligent systems are capable of performing many activities, both manual and mental, traditionally performed by supervisors and certain support staff as well as by direct production workers. In some cases already, the use of programmable automation has led to the elimination of one layer of supervisors (Chen and others, 1984). At the same time, the use of intelligent robots may require additional individuals with expertise in maintaining and programming robots.

Thus far, we have focused on describing how the use of robotics is likely to change the basic structures of organizations.

Now we seek to discover under what conditions these structural changes may be associated with improved manufacturing performance. As noted earlier, the use of robotics typically increases the interdependence of members of different functional groups. Hence, the use of robotics usually requires more rather than less interaction among these functional areas. We have observed companies where the increased interactions went extremely smoothly, and all groups were motivated to cooperate in the implementation of the new technology. We have also observed companies where the increased interaction was characterized by hostility, impeding the implementation. What differentiates these two situations? In their analysis of interdepartmental conflict in organizations, Walton and Dutton (1969) discuss the conditions under which interorganizational relationships are characterized by conflict. These conditions include a reward structure that emphasizes the performance of separate groups; asymmetric interdependence, in which one group is more dependent than the other; communication obstacles such as different locations or specialized languages; and aggressive individuals.

Applying these findings to the implementation of robotics helps us predict when the increased interactions required by the use of robotics are likely to be smooth and when they are likely to be conflictual. If a company's reward structure emphasizes the performance of separate groups, we expect the introduction of robotics to be characterized by conflict. For example, production groups might be rewarded on the basis of short-term efficiency figures while engineering groups are rewarded for the number of new equipment pieces they introduce.

Asymmetric interdependence characterizes most introductions of new technology where, at least in certain stages of the implementation, production is more dependent on engineering for hardware and software than engineering is dependent on production. The effect of asymmetric needs on conflict is moderated by the company's reward system. A reward system that emphasizes the performance of separate groups will only amplify the conflict potential of asymmetric interdependence. But a reward system that has a global and long-term orientation may foster cooperation and reduce the potential for conflict caused by asymmetric interdependence.

When the functional groups that must interact to implement new technology are located in different areas or use different terminologies, conflict is likely to surround the process. Conversely, if the different groups are located near each other, sit in on each other's meetings to understand each other's goals and constraints, and use a common language, then we expect the interactions required by the introduction of robotics to be graceful.

Finally, the nature of the people who play key roles in the introduction, such as the lead engineer, affects the level of conflict. When key positions are occupied by aggressive, authoritarian individuals concerned primarily with their own careers, the probability of conflict increases. The behavior of these individuals also will be affected, of course, by the company's reward system.

Another structural issue raised by the implementation of robotics is the balance between centralization and decentralization in an organization. Current thinking on this issue emphasizes the role of uncertainty. When uncertainty is high, decentralized structures are thought to be appropriate (Burns and Stalker, 1966; Lawrence and Lorsch, 1967; Argote, 1982). Centralized structures tend to function less effectively than decentralized structures under conditions of high uncertainty because the person or unit at the apex of the structure either becomes overloaded (Shaw, 1964) or lacks the information that people closer to the problem possess by virtue of their proximity (Perrow, 1984). More generally, the benefits of decentralized structures over centralized structures include greater sensing abilities as well as quicker processing and response times, which are especially critical when uncertainty is high. The advantages of centralized structures include enhanced opportunities for taking advantage of economies of scale and the ability to achieve coordination and control (Khandwalla, 1977).

The introduction of robotics and expert systems may challenge us to refine our thinking on the centralization question. On the one hand, intelligent robots and computer systems are able to provide us with increased processing capabilities. This feature may reduce the overload that people or units at the hub of centralized structures experience under high uncertainty. Hence, the introduction of intelligent systems may enable us to effectively centralize certain decisions previously made best on a decentralized basis. Evidence already indicates that the use of these systems facilitates the centralization of production-scheduling decisions (Office of Technology Assessment, 1984).

On the other hand, the use of robotics may reduce the set-up times required to change from one product to another. This feature may in turn reduce the benefits of long production runs. How these two forces—the increased processing capabilities of computerized manufacturing systems and the decreased benefits of long production runs—play out in affecting the centralization of roboticized systems is an empirical question. It appears that the use of computerized manufacturing systems may enable us to centralize decisions while at the same time enjoying fast response times and the ability to respond to change. Thus, robotics will perhaps increase the overall flexibility of organizational structures.

Technology. Finally, the third major component of an organization, its technology, may affect manufacturing performance. As noted already, robots have the capacity to provide consistency and quality as well as flexibility. Whether this potential is realized depends at least in part on the extent to which employees, both direct and indirect, understand the new technology and are motivated to utilize it to its full potential as well as on the organizational arrangements that support the technology. At the same time, the technology itself may have a direct effect on system performance. This effect is likely to be especially strong when the technology is highly reliable and does not require much human intervention. As the need for human intervention increases or the technology becomes less reliable or both, the effect of technology on performance depends on the motivation of employees and on supporting organizational arrangements.

Clearly, additional research is needed to increase our

understanding of the effects of robots on individuals and organizations. We now turn to a strategy for conducting research on robotics. We are following this strategy in our own work and believe it may be useful to others.

Suggestions for Research

Our suggestions for research on robotics fall into five areas: design, outcome variables, sources of data, levels of analysis and statistical analyses, and general methodological issues.

Design. Our strategy for studying the implementation of robotics is to conduct an integrated series of longitudinal studies in different organizations. It is important to examine how differences in organizational contexts (for example, union status, technological sophistication of the plant, relationships with other plants or corporate support groups, economic conditions in the industry) and in characteristics of the new technology (for example, its type, its integration with existing technology, its span or spread across production activities) affect the implementation of robotics.

It is also valuable at this early stage of theoretical development to do in-depth studies at each organization. Because these technologies are being introduced in different types of organizations, it is difficult to compare performance across organizations. Comparisons over time within each organization, however, are possible. Consequently, one may compare productivity data obtained before introducing the new technology with data obtained after its introduction. To make such comparisons, of course, requires a sufficiently lengthy period of time for data collection, before and after the introduction, to be able to adjust for seasonal and other shocks. Longitudinal studies also benefit from the use of a control group where possible. This approach to assessing the impact of a change on productivity and other outcomes is illustrated in Goodman (1979).

Longitudinal research also helps us understand the dynamics of the change process. Different organizational responses may be appropriate at different phases of the implementation. For example, the participation of direct production employees may be more appropriate in some phases (for example, designing the operator's job) than in other places (for example, deciding where to introduce robots). Collecting data at multiple points in time helps ensure that we capture these time-dependent phenomena.

Thus, we believe that a research program on the effects of new technologies requires not only in-depth studies but also studies at multiple sites. Our research strategy calls for drawing a sample of plants introducing new technologies, a sample that incorporates both union and nonunion plants, plants both high and low in existing technological sophistication, and so forth. Although our first study was conducted at a nonunion organization that forges and machines metal products, our second study is under way at a unionized organization with robots on line. The first plant's new technology is a robot that performs materials handling and the second plant's new installation is a manufacturing cell with multiple robots. Although employees' jobs at the first plant change, no one is required to move to a different job or shift; the second plant's installation, however, causes some employees to move to different jobs and changes the character of the jobs of other employees. The results of this sampling will be an integrated set of longitudinal studies involving different organizational contexts and different technological characteristics.

Outcome Variables. It is important to examine multiple criteria for the performance of roboticized systems. As noted previously, examples of particularly important criteria are productivity, product quality, manufacturing flexibility, absenteeism, turnover, and employee motivation and well-being. Inventory costs and the percentage of time the system is operating may also be useful criteria. These multiple criteria and their interrelationships should be examined to give us a complete picture of the costs and benefits of roboticized systems. For example, some evidence indicates that the introduction of robots causes employees to feel greater stress (Argote, Goodman, and Schkade, 1983; Office of Technology Assessment, 1984). We need to know more about this outcome of increased stress and how it relates to other outcomes. Will the increased stress have any effects on the long-term well-being of employees? If there are negative effects, would these costs be justified by other benefits, perhaps including the enhanced ability of the firm to survive and provide jobs for its employees? If the benefits outweigh the costs of increased stress, are there effective strategies for reducing the stress employees experience? Clearly, answering these questions requires an understanding of multiple-outcome variables and the trade-offs among them.

Furthermore, we should build models that predict each outcome variable. Previous research in the organizational sciences suggests that the variables that predict one outcome may be different from the variables that predict other outcomes. For example, research has shown that decentralized communication structures are associated with high member satisfaction but that the relationship between communication centralization and group performance depends on the uncertainty of the task (Shaw, 1981). Centralized structures are associated with better performance on certain or simple tasks, while decentralized structures are associated with better performance for uncertain or complex tasks. Similarly, the variables that predict manufacturing flexibility in roboticized systems may be different from the variables that are most associated with the productivity of the systems. If we are to increase certain outcomes such as productivity, we must understand the variables that lead to the outcomes. This goal calls for developing fine-grained models of variables that predict each outcome.

Sources of Data and Respondent Groups. To obtain valid and reliable information, we collect data within each organization through multiple methods and sources. Data are obtained through a combination of personal interviews, questionnaires, and observations. We also use company records or archival data on productivity, product mix, absenteeism, accidents, and turnover.

Previous research has shown that robots will have effects beyond the immediate departments where they are introduced. Capturing these effects requires interviewing many individuals at each organization. Key respondents within the plant include production workers from the departments where the new technology is introduced; individuals from other departments such as engineering, maintenance, quality control, production scheduling, marketing, and personnel relations; plus management and supervisory staff. In addition, key respondents outside the site include vendors (see Ettlie and Eder, 1984) and, if the plant is part of a corporation, members of corporate support groups. Because employees' positions and departmental affiliations affect their perceptions and beliefs (see Dearborn and Simon, 1958), collecting data from individuals in these different departments and at different hierarchical levels provides us with a balanced view of the implementation as well as with the perspectives of different constituencies.

Levels of Analysis and Statistical Analyses. Research on the effects of new technologies requires multiple levels of analysis, including the individual, the work group, and the organization. Variables that predict outcomes at one level may be different from variables that predict outcomes at another level (see Wagner, Pfeffer, and O'Reilly, 1984). Models should be built at the appropriate level of analysis. For example, understanding the effects of new technologies on employees requires analysis at the individual level. Because data are collected typically from about fifty individuals at each organization at multiple points in time, formal statistical techniques may be used to build models and to test hypotheses about the employee.

For other questions, such as the effect of the new technology on organizational structures, the department or plant is the appropriate unit of analysis. Although our sample size is presently too small to proceed with formal modeling at the departmental level, the intensive nature of these studies will provide insights into the process according to which and the conditions under which departmental structures change with the introduction of new technologies. Such insights can then be tested formally as data from additional sites are accumulated. Yin (1981) discusses issues surrounding comparisons across case studies.

Qualitative material is also extremely useful, particularly when it is combined with the results of quantitative analyses. Indeed, in our first study, some of the most interesting insights came from our respondents' answers to open-ended questions regarding their thoughts on what a robot was and how it affected them and their jobs. Chapters Four and Seven illustrate further the usefulness of qualitative material.

General Methodological Issues. Other methodological issues one encounters in studying the implementation of new technologies include attrition in one's sample over time, the nonindependence of data collected from the same individuals over time, the lack of an adequate conceptual scheme for representing the technology variable, the lack of instrumentation, problems in sampling technology users, and the nonequivalence of control groups in field research. These issues are discussed more fully in Goodman and Argote (1984).

Suggestions for Managerial Practice

Findings from our research and the research of others on the implementation of robotics are just beginning to accumulate. We will need additional field studies before we fully understand the consequences for individuals and organizations of using robotics. Yet many companies are now in the process of introducing robots into their factories. What is the best information currently available about effective implementation and utilization strategies? Our studies and previous studies of increased automation suggest strategies for managers to consider when introducing robots. These strategies are in five areas: managing job displacement, anticipating individuals' reactions to new technologies, anticipating organizational effects, implementing change, and being open to change.

Managing Job Displacement. The introduction of new technologies often raises the issue of displacement. To date, the amount of displacement directly attributable to robotics is low (Cyert and others, 1984). But this situation is likely to change if the adoption of robotics is accelerated.

Questions concerning job security and pay are important to employees; they may also worry about being bumped to a less desirable job or shift than they now have. Failure to deal with these concerns may slow down the speed of implementation and reduce the effectiveness of the change, as well as contribute to employee stress.

To deal with employees' concerns about job loss, many companies have successfully taken advantage of natural attrition to handle any reduction in the number of employees. In this way, although employees may have to change jobs, they are still working with the company. In-house training programs may be necessary to equip employees with the skills required by their new jobs. If shifting employees to different jobs is not feasible, the firm should be open with its employees and let them know as soon as possible who will lose their jobs as a result of the new technology. Ideally, the company should provide assistance with writing resumés, interviewing, and finding new jobs.

Anticipating Individuals' Reactions. New technologies often alter the job activities of individual employees. Therefore, it is important to analyze the requirements of the new job and to maximize the fit, or congruence, between job and employee characteristics. Research on job-person fit indicates that a lack of congruence may have dysfunctional effects on the person (for example, increased stress) and on the organization (for example, increased absenteeism and turnover). The question is not only whether the employee is able to perform the new activities but also whether the employee likes to perform the new activities. We have, for example, encountered factory workers who prefer manual to cognitive activities; for these employees, the fit between the job of robot operator and their preferences for manual work would not be a good one. Such incongruencies between the job and the person may be resolved by redesigning the job or by changing personnel-selection procedures.

Operators in our first study commented that they felt less control and experienced more stress after the robot was introduced than they had before. The possible sources of these perceptions could be their increased reliance on others (especially engineering and maintenance personnel) and the sense of having their work pace driven by the robot's cycle time. Because the experience of control has positive consequences for individuals, it is advantageous to design opportunities for control into the robot operator's job. This goal may be accomplished either through additional training or by providing the operators with some control, possibly through encouraging them to participate in designing the operator's job.

If introducing robotics changes the nature of employees' jobs from manual to cognitive, employees may experience boredom. Job rotation may be a mechanism to alleviate such boredom and to decrease stress. Job rotation would also increase variety for the individual employee, build up the skills of employees, and allow the company flexibility in staffing.

Moreover, evidence from the airline industry indicates that companies with more flexible work rules are more productive than their counterparts with less flexible rules (Bailey, Graham, and Kaplan, 1985). Many companies, both union and nonunion, are moving in the direction of flexible work rules. The benefits of increased flexibility are likely to be high, particularly for organizations operating in uncertain environments, where it is hard to plan in advance (Burns and Stalker, 1966; Argote, 1982). Because high uncertainty appears to characterize the introduction of robotics, flexible work rules may facilitate their implementation. Special care should be taken, however, to keep from exploiting the members of organizations with flexible work rules.

Anticipating Organizational Effects. The introduction of robotics usually leads to increased interaction between production employees and technical-support personnel from engineering and maintenance. New coordination mechanisms between these areas may need to be developed. These mechanisms are likely to be increasingly critical as the number of installations of the new technology increases.

High-technology firms, organizations in which the management of evolving technology is critical, require close coordination among marketing, engineering, and production (Chapter Eight; Riggs, 1983). For these firms, it is imperative that marketing, engineering, and production share information to ensure that there is a market for engineering developments, that products are designed for manufacturing, and that production capacity matches market demands. Arranging for members of different functional areas to sit in on each other's meetings is a step toward promoting coordination as well as cooperation. Riggs (1983) and Galbraith (1973) discuss additional strategies for promoting such coordination.

Previous studies of automation found that the increased automation of production tasks and the concomitant decrease in the number of people on the shop floor made employees feel isolated (Whyte, 1961). Operators in our first study also reported that they felt isolated and did not have as much opportunity to talk with their co-workers in the department because the operators did not want anyone breaking their concentration. We did not have the sense that this increased sense of isolation was severe. The possibility of isolation, however, does warrant managerial attention. Research has shown that social support from others can reduce stress (House, 1981). Hence, operators of new technologies who are likely to feel increased stress, at least in the short run, should not be deprived of a means for dealing with it. Management should consider strategies for building social support and opportunities for interaction into roboticized systems.

The introduction of robotics may also require changes in an organization's pay system. At a minimum, decisions will have to be made about the appropriate pay rate for robot operators. Such decisions will depend on how tasks are allocated between direct and indirect employees. More generally, the introduction of programmable automation such as robots typically increases the interdependence among members of organizations (Office of Technology Assessment, 1984). The quality of the output of roboticized systems depends not only on the performance of the operator and the equipment but also on the design and programming of the system. This increased interdependence makes it difficult to reward performance on the basis of the contribution of individuals; instead, rewarding performance at the level of the group of people who contribute to the system may be appropriate.

Implementing Change. When implementing new technologies, firms often find a discrepancy between the information employees desire about the new technology and the information they actually possess. This discrepancy occurs in part because employees do not always receive all the messages that management sends. Hence, management should monitor how much information employees receive from particular communication sources and how helpful employees perceive these sources to be. Establishing open, two-way communication, where employees feel comfortable raising questions and expressing their views, is critical for the success of the implementation of robotics.

Certain information sources appear more effective than others in introducing robotics. Based on our research, demonstrations of the operation of the new technology are an effective technique. In addition, communications that include a balance of both positive and negative messages are credible to employees. To the extent that the new technology has both positive and negative effects (and we believe that this is usually the case), such messages will give employees a realistic preview of what the new technology entails. Such a preview should contribute to smooth implementation. Finally, we have observed companies in which employees' first knowledge of the introduction of robotics occurs either with a crate appearing on the factory floor or on hearing from their friends that a robot has arrived. Clearly, this is not the most effective way to introduce employees to the new technology. Furthermore, employees who learn about the new technology from management rather than through informal sources are more likely to have a constructive attitude toward the change.

First-line supervisors should be given information about the new technology and receive support from upper management in dealing with employees' reactions to it. Studies have shown that during periods of threat, communication structures become more centralized than they previously were, with increased reliance on a leader (Staw, Sandelands, and Dutton, 1981). This result is consistent with our observation that employees approach their supervisors more often with questions during the introduction of robotics than they did before. Supervisors feel frustrated when they do not have adequate information to answer their subordinates' questions. Because supervisors' attitudes and behaviors are critical for the success of the change, they should be given adequate information.

Firms should also consider developing a strategy for employee involvement or participation in the introduction of new manufacturing technologies. There are many possible strategies for employee participation, such as the formation of a task force consisting of representatives from departments where robots are being introduced. In our two studies, management provided few opportunities for employee involvement when introducing the robots. Employees, especially employees at the second organization, desired more involvement than they had in decisions regarding robotics. Possible benefits of involvement include not only an understanding of the new technology but also a commitment to the change process.

In our current work we are examining whether the experience of employee involvement has positive effects on the individual or the organization. To this point, it is important that management's intentions regarding participation be translated into the experience of shop-floor employees. We have observed companies where management intended to introduce new technologies in a participative fashion but where shop-floor employees did not experience any involvement in the change. A task force was formed but it seldom met. Individuals who were not on the task force were unaware of the task force's activities. For participation to work, both the company and its employees need to work out in advance which decisions are going to be made jointly as well as what participation means to all involved. Does employee participation mean that management will consult employees and then decide what to do? Does participation imply that employees will have the final say over certain decisions? It is important that everyone understand what participation means for their organization and act accordingly. If they perceive that their recommendations have not been considered, employees may feel disillusioned. Similarly, management may become frustrated if it senses that its attempts to make changes participatively are not working.

Technical-support personnel should be involved early in the change process. We have observed companies who neglect to involve support personnel, particularly maintenance employees, in planning for the change. Stress and poor relationships usually result from this lack of involvement. Involving the support personnel early in the change process should facilitate a smooth implementation as well as reduce the stress they experience.

Being Open to Change. Many of the effects of robotics on individuals and organizations can be anticipated. The more a company is able to anticipate these effects, the more likely gains for individual employees and for the organization will result from the use of robots. Some of the effects of robotics, however, cannot be predicted because these technologies are just now coming into use. It is important therefore for management to create an open culture in which both the company and its employees can learn about robots and how to use them most effectively. Such a culture is most likely to evolve in organizations where trust already exists between management and employees, where it is legitimate for one to admit "I don't know," and where management and employees are willing to change and update policies and procedures as learning takes place. We believe that successful introductions will occur in companies with openness and responsiveness to change.

Conclusions

Changes in the organization of work, such as job enlargement, autonomous work groups, and quality-of-work-life programs, and changes in technology, such as robots and expert systems, appear to produce variable effects on individuals and organizations. For example, autonomous work groups typically result in employees having more control, learning more skills, performing more significant tasks, and interacting more often with members of their work group than they did before. Although autonomous work groups do not always lead to greater group effectiveness, on balance, members of autonomous work groups are more satisfied, less likely to be absent or to leave the group, and function at least as productively as their counterparts in traditional work groups (Katz and Kahn, 1978). Hence, many social scientists have advocated these types of changes in the organization of work as a way to increase the well-being of individual employees as well as the effectiveness of groups and organizations.

In contrast, many technological changes taking place on the factory floor today have an effect on individual employees that is antagonistic to the effects of these social changes. For example, the introduction of robotics often means that employees have less control and less opportunity to interact with others than they previously did. These employees perform smaller, less significant tasks, and, moreover, some of the discretion they once possessed is now embodied in the new technology.

This divergence between social and technological changes makes it imperative that we, as researchers and practitioners, get a perspective on the costs and benefits of the two types of changes and the trade-offs between them. When should employees have increased control and influence? When should decision-making rules be embedded in the technology rather than in the minds of employees? Under what conditions are interactions with co-workers beneficial for the individual or the organization? Are current social and technological changes in conflict with each another, or can they be orchestrated so that the strengths of one approach complement the weaknesses of the other? Clearly, we need a grasp of the costs and benefits of these two approaches to organizing. Once we gain an understanding of the trade-offs between these two different approaches, we can begin to design changes that truly allow for the optimization of both social and technological systems in the work place.

References

Abernathy, W. J., Clark, K. B., and Kantrow, A. M. *Industrial Renaissance: Producing a Competitive Future for America.* New York: Basic Books, 1983.

Argote, L. "Input Uncertainty and Organizational Coordination in Hospital Emergency Units." *Administrative Science Quarterly,* 1982, 27, 420-434.

Argote, L., and Goodman, P. S. "Human Dimensions of Robotics." In *Proceedings of the World Congress on the Human Aspects of Automation.* Dearborn, Mich.: Society of Manufacturing Engineers, 1984.

Argote, L., and Goodman, P. S. "Investigating the Implementation of Robotics." In D. D. Davis (Ed.), *Dissemination and Implementation of Advanced Manufacturing Processes.* Washington, D.C.: National Science Foundation, 1985.

Argote, L., Goodman, P. S., and Schkade, D. "The Human Side of Robotics: How Workers React to a Robot." *Sloan Management Review,* 1983, *24,* 31-41.

Ayres, R. U., and Miller, S. M. *Robotics: Applications and Social Implications.* Cambridge, Mass.: Ballinger, 1983.

Bailey, E. E., Graham, D. R., and Kaplan, D. P. *Deregulating the Airlines.* Cambridge, Mass.: MIT Press, 1985.

Blauner, R. *Alienation and Freedom.* Chicago: University of Chicago Press, 1964.

Bright, J. R. "Does Automation Raise Skill Requirements?" *Harvard Business Review,* 1958, *36* (4), 85-98.

Burns, T., and Stalker, G. M. *The Management of Innovation.* (2nd ed.) London: Tavistock, 1966.

Chen, K., and others. *Human Resource Development in New Technology in the Automobile Industry: A Case Study of Ford Motor Company's Dearborn Engine Plant.* Ann Arbor: Program in Urban Technological and Environmental Planning, University of Michigan, 1984.

Coch, L., and French, J. R. P. "Overcoming Resistance to Change." *Human Relations,* 1948, *1,* 512-532.

Cyert, R. M., and others. *The New Manufacturing: America's Race to Automate.* Washington, D.C.: Business Higher Education Forum, 1984.

Dearborn, D. C., and Simon, H. A. "Selective Perception: A Note on the Departmental Identification of Executives." *Sociometry,* 1958, *21,* 140-144.

Emery, F. E., and Trist, E. L. "Socio-Technical Systems." In F. Baker (Ed.), *General Systems Approaches to Complex Organizations.* Homewood, Ill.: Irwin, 1973.

Ettlie, J. E., and Eder, J. L. "The Vendor-User Relationship in

Successful vs. Unsuccessful Implementation of Process Innovation." Paper presented at the annual meeting of the Institute of Management Sciences/Operations Research Society of America, San Francisco, May 1984.

Galbraith, J. *Designing Complex Organizations.* Reading, Mass.: Addison-Wesley, 1973.

Goodman, P. S. *Assessing Organizational Change: The Rushton Quality of Work Experiment.* New York: Wiley-Interscience, 1979.

Goodman, P. S., and Argote, L. "Research on the Social Impacts of Robotics: Issues and Some Evidence." *Applied Social Psychology Annual,* 1984, *5,* 211-230.

Goodman, P. S., and Pennings, J. M. (Eds.) *New Perspectives on Organizational Effectiveness.* San Francisco: Jossey-Bass, 1977.

Guest, R. H. "Robotics: The Human Dimension." In *Work in America Institute Studies in Productivity.* Elmsford, N.Y.: Pergamon Press, 1984.

Hackman, J. R., and Lawler, E. E. "Employee Reactions to Job Characteristics." *Journal of Applied Psychology,* 1971, *55,* 259-286. (Monograph.)

Hackman, J. R., and Oldham, G. R. "Development of the Job Diagnostic Survey." *Journal of Applied Psychology,* 1975, *60,* 159-170.

House, J. S. *Work Stress and Social Support.* Reading, Mass.: Addison-Wesley, 1981.

Hunt, H. A., and Hunt, T. L. *Human Resource Implications of Robotics.* Kalamazoo, Mich.: Upjohn Institute, 1983.

Kaplan, R. S. "Measuring Manufacturing Performance: A New Challenge for Managerial Accounting Research." *Accounting Review,* 1983, *58* (4), 686-705.

Katz, D., and Kahn, R. L. *The Social Psychology of Organizations.* (2nd ed.) New York: Wiley, 1978.

Khandwalla, P. N. *The Design of Organizations.* New York: Harcourt Brace Jovanovich, 1977.

Kotter, J. P., and Schlesinger, L. A. "Choosing Strategies for Change." *Harvard Business Review,* 1979, *57* (2), 106-114.

Lawrence, P. R., and Lorsch, J. W. "Differentiation and Integration in Complex Organizations." *Administrative Science Quarterly,* 1967, *12,* 1–47.

Leavitt, H. J. "Applied Organizational Change in Industry: Structural, Technological, and Humanistic Approaches." In J. G. March (Ed.), *Handbook of Organizations.* Chicago: Rand McNally, 1965.

Office of Technology Assessment. *Computerized Manufacturing and Automation: Employment, Education and the Workplace.* Washington, D.C.: Office of Technology Assessment, 1984.

Perrow, C. *Normal Accidents.* New York: Basic Books, 1984.

Riggs, H. E. *Managing High Technology Companies.* Belmont, Calif.: Lifetime Learning, 1983.

Robot Institute of America. *Worldwide Robotics Survey and Directory.* Dearborn, Mich.: Society of Manufacturing Engineers, 1982.

Shaw, M. E. "Communication Networks." In L. Berkowitz (Ed.), *Advances in Experimental Social Psychology.* Vol. 1. New York: Academic Press, 1964.

Shaw, M. E. *Group Dynamics: The Psychology of Small Group Behavior.* (3rd ed.) New York: McGraw-Hill, 1981.

Staw, B. M., Sandelands, L. E., and Dutton, J. E. "Threat-Rigidity Effects in Organizational Behavior: A Multi-Level Analysis." *Administrative Science Quarterly,* 1981, *26,* 501–524.

Sutton, R. I., and Kahn, R. L. "Prediction, Understanding, and Control as Antidotes to Organizational Stress." In J. Lorsch (Ed.), *Handbook of Organizational Behavior.* Englewood Cliffs, N.J.: Prentice-Hall, in press.

Tornatzky, L. G., and others. *The Process of Technological Innovation: Reviewing the Literature.* Washington, D.C.: National Science Foundation, 1983.

Wagner, W. G., Pfeffer, J., and O'Reilly, C. A. "Organizational Demography and Turnover in Top-Management Groups." *Administrative Science Quarterly,* 1984, *29,* 74–92.

Walton, R. E., and Dutton, J. M. "The Management of Interdepartmental Conflict." *Administrative Science Quarterly,* 1969, *14,* 73–84.

Whyte, W. F. *Men at Work.* Homewood, Ill.: Irwin, 1961.

Williams, L. K., and Williams, C. B. "The Impact of Numerical-ly Controlled Equipment on Factory Organization." *California Management Review,* 1964, *7,* 25–34.

Yin, R. K. "The Case-Study Crisis: Some Answers." *Administrative Science Quarterly,* 1981, *26,* 58–65.

🔾 SEVEN 🔾

Integrating the Social
and Technical Systems
of Organizations

James C. Taylor
Paul W. Gustavson
William S. Carter

In 1978, Zilog, Inc., a California affiliate of Exxon Enterprises, built a new semiconductor (S/C) circuit plant in Nampa, Idaho. The manufacturing processes were designed using a sociotechnical systems (STS) approach, which resulted in product-related work groups rather than the technology-based or functional work groups typical for the industry. In other words, groups were arranged to produce an identifiable part of the completed S/C circuit chip (and to control technical variances associated with product quality), in contrast to merely being grouped around a type of machine or technical function. This work organization proved to be so successful that two years later the STS approach began to be used to redesign work in other areas of the company. The S/C product-design department (known hereafter as Component Design Engineering, or CDE) was one of the first.

CDE had been growing and changing as Zilog developed. Since Zilog was founded in 1975, CDE as a department had successfully provided the company with two generations of microprocessor devices (eight-bit and sixteen-bit) without paying much attention to how it was organized. But times were changing in the S/C industry. What had begun as a strictly high-tech industry was fast changing from being "engineering driven" to

154

being "marketing driven." Furthermore, for the company to remain competitive, the products CDE would be designing were much more complicated than those of the past and would require more than individual designers working alone to create them. This paradox, of engineering no longer being the sole arbiter of design but being expected to design ever more complicated S/C products, was apparent in late 1979 and early 1980 when the present project in CDE began. This chapter describes how CDE redesigned its organization to address its future—to cope with new process and product technologies, with dynamic competition, and with ever-changing markets.

This case is unique in several ways. To our knowledge it is the first application of the STS analysis and design technique to the computer-assisted design (CAD) technology of circuit-layout drafting. This case also addresses the place of professional engineers in the organization and how they are organized. Finally, and perhaps most importantly, the STS analysis described here places CAD technology within the total structure of the CDE department as an engineering system, and places CDE within the context of the other departments in the company and of its industry environment. The upper limit in capability of the CAD system (or any) technology is not achieved because of an exclusive focus on the technology itself but is placed as an extension of the organization that applies it, which is in turn dedicated to providing the company and its other departments with appropriate technical and social products. This case describes not only technological improvements but changes in management procedures and organization as well. These changes include the gradual dissolution of traditional separations between design and manufacturing, and between design and marketing.

Sociotechnical Systems Management

The STS analysis and design technique, as applied in this case, represents a purpose-oriented approach to organizational improvement. Efforts to improve organizations can be classified into three major types: problem-oriented approaches, solution-oriented approaches, and purpose-oriented approaches. There are many examples of the first two approaches, but, apart from open-systems planning and STS, there are few methods for applying the purpose-oriented approach. These methods approach organizational improvement by discovering "what business we're in" and "what we need to do to excel at that business." Thus, STS is not simply a managerial technique of applying group solutions, examples of which are quality work circles and computer-aided mechanization.

Since the first introduction of STS, a substantial body of evidence has accumulated to show that STS, as a purpose-oriented approach, can be applied to significantly improve organizational performance and quality of working life. It is established as a high-level management approach for improving any work process in a manufacturing or service organization. It has been developed over the past thirty years in Europe and the United States, and the results set new standards for white-collar and blue-collar effectiveness (Davis, 1981; Emery, Foster, and Wollard, 1978; Taylor, 1978; Trist, 1981). For example, Procter & Gamble began using the approach as early as 1969 and has continued to refine it. Other long-time users of STS include General Motors, Shell Oil, Best Foods, and Cummins Engine Company.

Why STS Management Works

There are three reasons for the success of STS management: joint optimization, purpose orientation, and structured process.

Joint Optimization. STS management gets its name from the way it integrates the production (technical) requirements of the work process with the organizational (social) functions of the people working in the process. We use the expression *work process* because STS management can be applied to any process in which work is being performed. These processes include manufacturing production, research and development, engineering, data-center operations, office automation, and clerical operations.

Many industrial-engineering (IE) techniques focus on the efficiency of the work performed, which is the technical part of the work process. Although IE practitioners consider social functions, they don't integrate them into the management of the process in any systemic way. The people portion of the process is usually organized around the technology on the basis of seat-of-the-pants opinions of how best to manage people. Organizational-development (OD) techniques focus on the social functions in the work process, but the OD practitioners tend to overlook the work that needs to be done.

STS uses many IE and OD principles, but the focus is on integrating them to obtain joint optimization of the social and technical functions in the work process. The overall effectiveness of a work process, however it is measured, can be thought of as the combined effect of the social and technical subsystems, each with its own optimal point. The work process that optimizes the technical functions is often not optimal for the social functions, and vice versa. What is best for the work process as a whole may not be optimal for one or the other subsystems.

Purpose Orientation. Because STS management focuses on the work process as a whole rather than on its parts, it is a systems approach. It starts with the particular mission or purpose of the organization and develops a design for and system of management tailored to that purpose. This purpose orientation is much more powerful than the more common problem-oriented approaches (for example, technical audits and questionnaire surveys) or solution-oriented approaches (for example, office automation and quality circles), which address only a part of the system and which often ignore strategic management issues and overall mission.

Structured Process. The third reason for the success of STS management is the structured approach it uses to analyze and implement the operational improvements. Many other management models are conceptually interesting but operationally soft. Most managers find it difficult to implement such approaches because there is too large a gap between the concepts in the models and actual day-to-day activities in the work process. The STS approach provides a process for data collection and analysis and thus makes the model operational.

Products of STS Analysis and Design

A lot of information has been developed on STS management. What we will focus on here are the products of the approach as used in successful cases in North America and how these were used to make important improvements in the work process. These products are:

> Systems scan
>> Management mission and philosophy
>> System inputs and outputs
>> Boundaries of the organizational system
>> Important environments for the system
> Technical analysis
>> Unit-operations flow chart
>> Key-variance matrix
>> Variance-control table
> Social analysis
>> Social-system grid
>> Focal-role-network chart
>> Quality-of-working-life evaluation
> Design recommendations for improved organizational outcomes

This is an iterative process. The analysis continues after improvements are implemented, resulting in a continuous process of analysis and change.

Scan. Any organization or part of an organization or parts of more than one organization can be considered a sociotechnical system if it contains a purposive transformation process (a technical system) and people working together over time in stable relationships (a social system). A purposive sociotechnical work system can be considered part of a larger organization, from which it is analytically separated, if its mission and philosophy are aligned with, and contribute to, those of the larger body. Scanning involves the fairly brief but extensive overview of the system to be examined—purpose (technical mission and social philosophy), boundaries, inputs, products, staff, relationship to its environments, and the presenting problem, if any.

Technical Analysis. Once the boundaries of input into the system and output from the system have been defined, it is possible to identify the unit operations in the technical process. The output of each unit operation is the result of the transformation of input, where that input is either physical or informational. The output can be physical or informational also. It can be a product or a service, but it must express in measurable terms the tangible results of the system's mission or purpose.

The STS analysis has the advantage of defining technology by its input and product rather than by its tools, processes, or techniques. This focus ensures that the technical system will be analyzed separately from the jobs and work of people on the one hand, and from the supervisory and control system on the other. In identifying these unit operations, STS managers frequently find that they can establish fewer unit operations for their system than they at first thought because many of the operations performed on the input are checking, verification, or inspection activities rather than fundamental changes in the state of the input.

Identification of key variances is the second part of technical analysis. Once unit operations have been determined for the system, there follow the important tasks of identifying the many technical requirements, stated in terms descriptive of the output, and, from among those factors, of selecting the most important ones.

The actual process of identifying key variances involves first the listing of all known variances (aspects and conditions) of the product for each unit operation. Variances representing human failure or breakdowns in the technical process itself are not included in this listing. The next step is preliminarily to identify as key variances those that are most direct or important in their impact on quantity, quality, or costs of the system output.

The key-variance matrix is the final step in identifying key variances. It is an interaction table that includes all the variances, grouped within their unit operations, arrayed along both sides. Cell entries in this square table represent the relationships between each pair of variances throughout the work process. Once this interaction table is constructed, informal rules are applied that define a factor as key if it has an impact on one or more of the key factors identified in the preceding step or several other factors in unit operations downstream.

Variance control forms a bridge between the technical and social analyses; it is central to the design process. In it, key variances are examined one at a time to determine the manner in which they are currently controlled (for existing work processes) or are usually controlled in conventional plants (for designing a new work process). The analysis is accomplished through the use of a table of variance control, which lists the unit operations in which each key variance originates, is observed, and is controlled. The table also lists who or what controls the key variance, what actions are used to control it, and the source of information used in control. Tables of variance control frequently reveal that variances are not controlled where they originate and that much of the control is undertaken by management or support staff long after the variance limits are exceeded. The completion of this table provides the transition to the social analysis.

Social Analysis. The social system comprises the work-related interactions among people. These interactions include vertical (superior-subordinate) relationships, either internal to the work process or across its boundaries, and horizontal relationships among persons within the same class (for example, nonsupervisory, supervisory, managerial) or, more specifically, among persons at the same pay or status grade. As with vertical relationships, horizontal relationships may be internal to the work process or may cross its boundaries. The initial boundaries of the social system are the same as the boundaries of the technical system: the points of entry of raw material and the output of results or product. In addition to relationships among people, social interactions are driven by the role expectations that people face. Our positions as parent, spouse, friend, supervisor, and subordinate create many and sometimes conflicting role expectations for us.

The social analysis essentially involves examination of the roles and relationships within the whole work process. This activity includes mapping both the persons who have work-related interactions in the system and the reasons for that contact. Because a comprehensive analysis of all positions would be too time consuming, the social analysis focuses on those most involved in the control of key variances, based on the assumption that every organization exists in order to meet the short-term goal of producing its product. We refer to this process as the focal-role analysis; it maps the cooperation of and coordination between those with focal roles and others within and outside the work process.

Defined this way, the social system is not mere friendship or recreation but rather the coordinating and integrating buffer between the technical-transformation process and the demands and constraints of a turbulent environment. The demands of this environment go beyond merely satisfying a consumer market or coping with supplies of raw materials or the other tasks directly affecting the technical system. The environment is actually many environments—legal, legislative, labor, cultural, climatic, and so forth.

Any social organization, if it is to survive in those environments, must perform four basic functions: goal attainment in controlling key variances (G), adaptation to the external environment (A), integration of the activities of people within the system (I), and long-term development (L). Every organization exists in order to meet the short-term goal of producing its product (G). However, in doing so, it must not adversely affect its capacity to survive as an organization. It must adapt to, and be protected from, short-term changes and pressures in its immediate environment (A). It must also combine or integrate activities to manage internal conflict and to promote smooth interactions among people (I). Finally, it must ensure the long-term development of knowledge, skills, and motivation to cope with goal-related, environmental, and systems requirements in the future (L). In the social analysis, the letters G, A, I, L are used to indicate what types of functions are affected in contacts among people.

Many organizations have departments to perform these functions. For example, IE, planning, personnel, and training departments can have the main responsibilities for one or another of the four basic functions. Yet we know from experience that not all such activities are handled by special departments. Indeed, informal activities at the level of the focal role are often more frequent and more influential in affecting functional behavior than are formal methods and policies. For instance, the informal initiation that production operators receive often contradicts formal instructions from training classes. The task at hand for the social analysis is to describe the ways that these necessary social-system functions actually get carried out and to evaluate how effective these methods are for satisfying the human and technical requirements of the organization.

The examination of the presence or absence of a fixed set of functional relationships in a social system is aided by charting them in a way that combines both the four functional requirements (G, A, I, L) and the particular relationships (vertical, horizontal, internal, and cross-boundary) describing the work process. This combination is charted on a 4 X 4 *grid of social relations.*

From the behaviors noted in the social grid, the patterns of interaction with the focal role can be mapped according to frequency and direction of contact, and these contacts can be identified by the social function(s) served. Mapping these patterns produces a *focal-role network.*

Finally, incorporating human preferences into the design of organizational systems is vital to STS management. In part, human preferences are assessed through discussion and development of the design principles and management philosophy. Assessing preferences, however, must also consist of identifying those aspects of work that are seen as desirable by members of the organization. These aspects are the elements in the *evaluation of quality of working life* (QWL).

QWL is more than merely wages, hours, and working conditions. Those are important, but QWL also includes dignity and respect, social support, prospects for advancement, and challenging work. Recent research into comprehensive employee-generated lists of QWL reveal that employees also value a job that is central to the essential business of the enterprise, and that this centrality is an important contributor to employee attitudes when jobs are enhanced. It has been found with STS management that high QWL is the result of competence in creating a meaningful product. Furthermore, competence and centrality are greatly enhanced by designing work so that employees consciously control key technical variances as close to their source as possible.

Design Recommendations. The social analysis builds on the technical analysis to identify ways that key variances can be controlled by improving the fit between the technical functions and the social functions. With the information developed in the analysis, managers and employees can implement improvements in the work process that identify and control variances at their source, place coordination of the work at the lowest organizational level compatible with the technical and social systems, and develop organizational structures that fit the structure of the unit operations.

STS is thus a continuous management process involving four steps, and it is an iterative process. The analysis continues after improvements are implemented, resulting in an ongoing process of analysis and change.

Case Study

Once Zilog realized that the Nampa, Idaho, manufacturing facility was not merely organized differently from other plants but was much more productive, the company widened its application of the process introduced in the Idaho plant design. In fact, the 1983 recruitment brochure described Zilog's management style as a "sociotechnical one." This diffusion of results is an important sign that the STS efforts were supported by others in the company apart from those directly using them. The STS project was extended next to CDE, one of the first de-

partments at Zilog's California headquarters to show interest in
the STS experiment at the Idaho plant as an improvement
process.

The Idaho STS organization, begun in 1978, proved to be
a success in two ways. Quality results (die/wafer yield) exceeded by 15 to 20 percent the results of other organizations in
the United States that build similar products, and the employee
turnover of 10 percent or less was drastically lower than industry figures, which range from 50 to 100 percent annually. The
questions that remained by 1980 were: Can this STS process be
used in Silicon Valley, where competitive pressures are higher
and loyalties lower than in Idaho? Can it deal with the high
turnover and high entrepreneurial spirit of high-tech engineering, an atmosphere in which people are rewarded for being specialists? Can it work in the design industry, in a place other than
a manufacturing plant? Can it work in engineering?

Those issues were important to the founder and first
president of Zilog, Federico Faggin. In conversation with one of
the authors, late in 1979, Faggin said, "You know, those STS
results in Idaho are great for an S/C manufacturing area of the
company; that's our life blood, we have to produce high-quality
product. But where this sociotechnical process would have even
greater value is with the people who design and create the new
devices." He had two reasons for wanting to extend the STS
process to design. First, engineers will typically create just to
create; Faggin wanted to help them create something that was
useful to other people and therefore matched the market need.
Second, if the people who were designing the new generation
of microprocessors could be sensitive to what the key manufacturing variances were, the company could build a product
less expensively with higher yields than before. Sensitivity to
manufacturing would allow the manufacturing organization
building the product to begin feeding back data to the design
people.

At this time, Zilog's director of CDE was faced with a
series of challenges. He saw that the company was changing
from eight- and sixteen-bit microprocessors and moving into
the design of thirty-two-bit products. The complexity of the

thirty-two-bit microprocessor is much greater than that of the sixteen-bit. A thirty-two-bit chip has over 100,000 transistors, which is more than five times the 17,000 transistors on one sixteen-bit microprocessor. Complex chips used to have only a single function. It is not uncommon now for a complex chip to integrate the functions of what used to be three chips. The length of time needed to design and develop the eight- and sixteen-bit microprocessors was typically a year or a year and a half. The new thirty-two-bit processors require three or four years of product development. The CDE director realized that a chip-development project that used to require only a design engineer, a layout designer, and an architect was now going to require a dozen to fifteen people.

The other problem he faced was his organization. In late 1979, CDE was organized functionally with fewer than a hundred employees. There were separate groups for architecture, logic and circuit design, layout design, product planning, applications, and documentation. More than 80 percent of the people had college degrees. Of those people who had degrees, at least two thirds had an advanced degree—an M.S. or a Ph.D. The special qualifications of these employees had shaped the functional nature of the CDE organization. This functional division was marked by conflict and friction among the various groups in CDE.

Functional specialization among design workers is widespread in Silicon Valley companies. Engineers are an elite caste with individual star performers. Layout specialists, although not an elite group, have high wages. This division of individual engineering stars and a clannish underclass of layout designers does not encourage commitment to the organization or cooperation in the design of integrated circuits (ICs). Most of the companies in the Silicon Valley have been organized in this functional way to recognize and support both types of design specialists because demand for design people is high. On any Sunday, Bay Area newspapers carry full sections of ads for design engineers, test engineers, and system architects. There is high turnover in these jobs, consistent with the number of start-up companies in the Valley. People leave one company for another in quest of becoming millionaires. People in these design specialties are often hired like players in professional sports—a whole company can be built around one of them.

Differences in background and training distinguish design engineers from layout designers. Design engineers are a sensitive group—they know how good they are, and they know what they are worth. Many of them do not mind saying exactly what they feel. Throughout their education and training, they have been rewarded for being the best specialists. Layout designers, however, generally do not have a college education. They produce in graphic form the specific circuits created by the design engineers. Because they work in the last step of the design process, they often take the blame for the engineers' inattention as well as their own mistakes. Layout people often feel like second-class citizens. To counteract high turnover, layout people are highly paid; in this way, they are rewarded for being specialists in their particular field.

In early 1980, when the sociotechnical analysis in CDE began, the circuit-layout function was overlooked by management planners. Figure 1 shows the original organization chart. Although the circuit-layout group consisted of fifteen designers reporting to a supervisor, who in turn reported to a senior manager in charge of IC design, it was not shown on Zilog's rudimentary organization charts.

CAD Technology and Layout Design. The layout function in Zilog had recently undergone some mechanization through the introduction of CAD. CAD technology was developed for application in the S/C industry during the 1970s, and these efforts to standardize the layout process were successful. Using CAD technology, simple, low-performance, standardized chips can be laid out for masks in regular, repeatable arrays easily and efficiently. The two best-known CAD packages for layout are the Applicon and the Calma. Both are widely used in S/C layout processes in Silicon Valley. The two systems are essentially similar in that they permit the layout designer to sketch the arrangement of devices and interconnecting lines on the screen of a video-display terminal (VDT) instead of on a drafting board or light table. As with other

Figure 1. Original Organization.

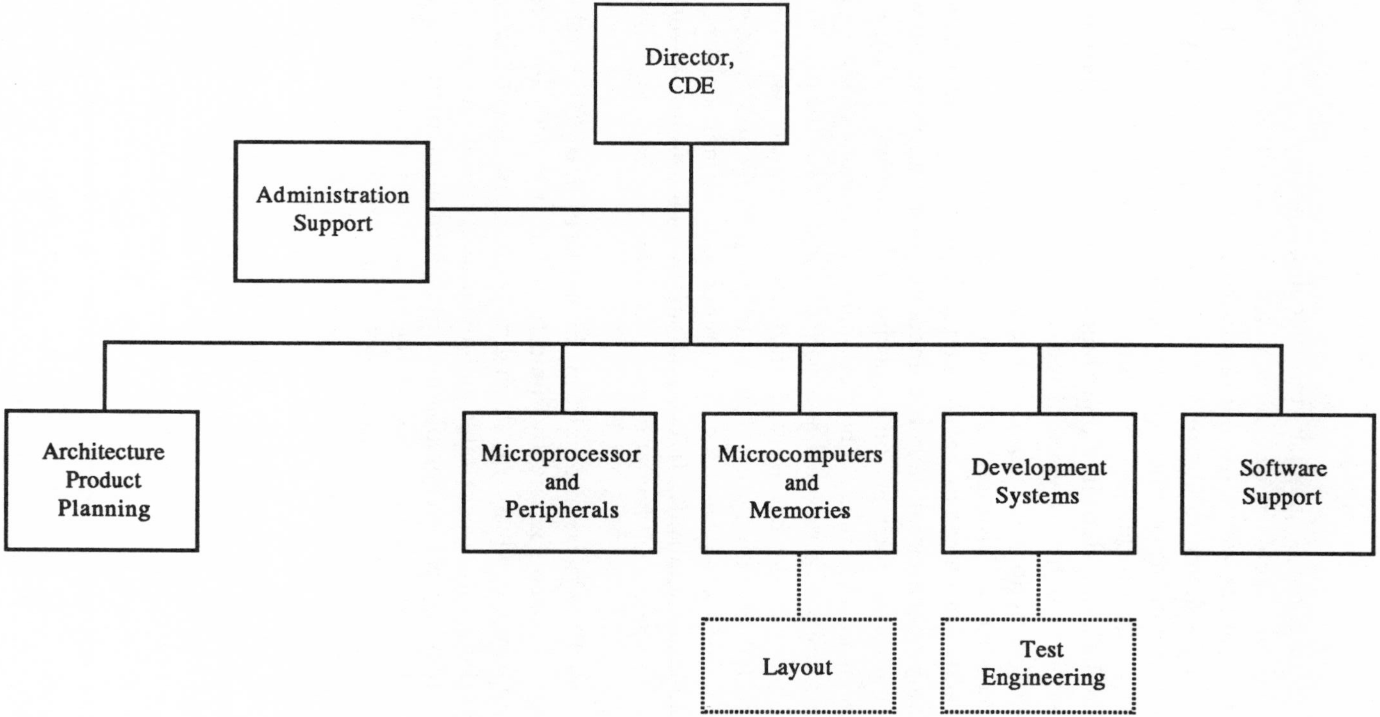

computer-based graphics technologies, the layout lines electronically sketched can be adjusted, moved, tilted, and erased easily and at will. CAD packages also permit copying or reproducing a sketch (a line or a whole subcircuit) in any other location and in any numbers elsewhere on the chip.

CAD technology has three primary benefits: It eliminates the digitizing step; it allows comparison of several solutions, to permit a tighter layout in less time; it permits faster editing and correction of layout drawings. In addition, Applicon will recognize as distinctive the set of hand-drawn symbol commands introduced by each operator. Thus, all operators can customize their circuit-layout commands to the machine, allowing retention of their personal drawing style (the way they use the stylus on the tablet). The dictionary of commands for each layout designer is retained as a part of the data for the part of the chip he or she has worked on. Should operators use the data created by others, they can load their own dictionary of command strokes over those of a predecessor without deleting the original commands. It takes about two months for an otherwise experienced layout designer to develop a working skill with Applicon.

Drawbacks also exist in the application of CAD technology. Applicon is said by some to reduce the need for careful preplanning, which was the hallmark of a good layout designer working with a light table and mylar drawings. With that earlier technology, patient preplanning prevented much correcting and erasing. Also, some layout designers report that by using CAD packages they have had to give up some of the artistic control that was possible by working with pencil on paper or mylar. They report feeling less identified with the results of their work (the drawings) when they design layouts with CAD. Applicon's unique dictionary of command strokes allows the designer to have some control over the work process, but it apparently does not replace the direct identification that designers associate with their own drawings. The net effect of CAD in S/C circuit layout therefore is a mechanization of tasks without extension of the designer's individual commitment to the product. STS was considered by Zilog management as a way of understanding the needed integration of CAD technology into the design of complex products that required more designer commitment than ever before.

At first, the CAD required a shake-down. System crashes were frequent, and with the reliance of all VDTs on a single CAD central processing unit (CPU), a crash would bring all operators to a standstill. The earliest CAD system installed at Zilog was not only unreliable but also too small for the work to be done. If additional VDTs were installed so that operators could be added to work on a design project, the response times were annoyingly slow to the layout designers. And if large segments of an IC product were called for, the memory available to the CAD CPU was often insufficient, which caused additional frustration. Finally, with this initial version of Applicon, a pattern-generator (PG) tape had to be created on the CAD CPU, which converted the Applicon data to a form used to manufacture masks. Because this conversion required considerable CPU time to complete, the tapes were generated once a week, usually late at night or on weekends, in order to maximize the time during which layout designers could use the CAD system. The design engineers complained about the bottleneck caused by this batch-mode processing of CAD data. Once these initial problems were identified and technical solutions (including the replacement of the early CPU with an improved one) were implemented, the problems of the organization of the CAD system became clear.

The layout supervisor was the person in the group most knowledgeable about Applicon, and she trained the layout designers in its use. She controlled the assignment of work to CAD and the assignment of layout designers to terminals. She also operated the CAD CPU for departmental work (such as creating PG tapes) after hours. The supervisor, and her later replacements, attempted to act as a buffer between the layout group and the design engineers. The supervisor would request engineers to route their layout-requiring work though her. She, in turn, assigned CAD work to her subordinates, usually according to their skills and their availability. Layout designers could thus be assigned to a different project each day, and they might have no connection with or understanding of the progress being made on a given project.

This arrangement proved unsatisfactory for the engineers, who complained that layout provided poor support. Engineers reported having more contact with layout than with any other group except for their own, yet these contacts were often frustrating. Engineers saw layout designers as unwilling to take direction from them and as being reluctant or perhaps unable to complete their work within the schedule.

Half of the layout designers reported frequent contact with engineers and half reported no contact with them at all. From the layout designers' point of view, many (but not all) of the engineers created an adversarial climate by considering layout people as merely the implementors of their designs and not the independent contributors that the layout people felt they were. Engineers were seen as blaming layout for slipping schedules when the fault often lay in the circuit designs that the engineers created. Turnover of layout designers at 50 percent was high at that time, especially among the new employees who knew nothing of the days before the introduction of CAD. The company and its layout group began to earn a poor reputation among potential layout recruits because of the stressful working climate and poor and inadequate CAD equipment.

The STS Process. The director for CDE felt that the whole organization rested on his shoulders. He took pride in calling himself a benevolent dictator. He liked getting in and doing the coordination and making the decisions. But he said, "I'm not going to be able to handle this in the future. If we do take on more projects, I'm never going to be able to leave here. I'm going to have all the integrating and coordinating mechanisms among all of these guys at the same time. . . . I'll be coming in at seven in the morning and going home at seven at night." He had been doing some reading on matrix management and felt that he might consider some form of that approach. Another Zilog manager had strong views about project management and had discussed that approach with the CDE director. The director also knew about the good results in the Idaho manufacturing plant, and the company's president had talked to him about what was happening there. The president had done the right kind of encouragement, but which course to take was now the director's responsibility.

The director was given an overview of STS analysis and design by an external consultant (Taylor). He and his staff asked questions, particularly whether STS analysis had ever been done in an engineering organization. The consultant did not think so but mentioned that it had been done in a number of organizations other than manufacturing plants—specifically, offices and hospitals. Two of the director's key engineering managers attended an STS seminar presented by UCLA. These two managers, after returning from the course, felt good about this approach. In the meantime, the director of CDE spent time with the manager of the Idaho plant, talking through philosophically and conceptually what STS analysis was. By July 1980, the CDE director had decided to use STS analysis to aid in the development of an appropriate organizational design.

After that, events followed in quick succession. A project consultant was hired. A steering committee of Zilog top management people was selected to make certain that the project was supported. Volunteers for an STS design team composed of CDE employees from each level of the hierarchy and from each functional group were requested by CDE management, who selected ten people from among the volunteers. The design team's charter was to complete the STS analysis while meeting periodically with the steering committee to report on current progress and what they had learned and to identify the support they needed to continue with the process. The STS design team worked under the guidance of the internal consultant (Gustavson) with advice from the external consultant (Taylor).

Each person on the STS design team was a representative of a group within the organization and was expected to take information back to that group. The STS group also called general meetings of CDE at which they explained their activities. Minutes of the STS design group were always published. Small group meetings were the responsibility of each member of the STS design team. Both analysis and feedback to co-workers became an educational process to help those people (especially layout designers) understand their role in the larger process. The members of the design group were excited because they were experiencing something new. They wanted to share it with other people. But, in retrospect, this communication was not as effective or as complete as intended. Considerable skepticism that anything could or would improve was voiced by those outside the STS group. The STS jargon ("mission," "variance") used by the group also alienated some co-workers.

The STS process that the team followed was divided into five phases: systems scan, technical analysis, social analysis, design recommendations, and implementation of design.

The first things the STS design team worked on in *the systems scan* were the mission statement and the philosophy statement. The idea of the scan was to state clearly the organization's purpose, its product, what was outside the organization, what was inside, and its boundaries (both physical and technological). They also created a statement of the values held throughout the organization. The scan of CDE was begun early and continued over the life of the STS design project. From the scan process, the team developed an understanding of both the external and the internal environment. If the UCLA training is counted, this process took one and a half years before implementation.

The scanning phase did not always go smoothly. The mission statement changed many times; coming to a consensus regarding the mission of CDE was a difficult task. The mission statement finally agreed on for CDE was "to be the leader at developing and supporting IC products." There were also a lot of battles over the philosophy. Originally the design team arrived fairly readily at what it felt was a meaningful list of value statements. When this list was taken to the steering committee, it was readily approved. The design group soon discovered, however, that the committee's value system was different from its own, which caused some problems. For instance, one value on the list was open communications; yet, within a week of steering committee approval, the layout designers pointed out that their supervisor had been replaced in a single evening without any advance warning to them. Such differences were resolved as the steering committee began to live seriously by the values they expressed or approved.

CDE viewed Zilog as being driven by technology and not markets. This research and development (R&D) emphasis was a reflection of competition in product development industrywide. CDE did not see itself coming out with someone else's product later or being a manufacturing producer as such. The CDE group wanted to be able to do with subsequent products what they had done with their first major product. That first product (the Z-80 microprocessor) had become an industry standard, and CDE wanted to repeat that performance. They were hungry for that success. Through the new plant in Idaho, this company had a manufacturing organization that was willing to work with and support R&D. CDE saw that the interfaces were there and hoped the marketing support was also there. Many managers in the larger organization, however, did not share this view. The dominant management view emphasized the importance of markets and customer preference. But CDE saw Zilog not as a marketing company or as a manufacturing company but as a design company. In this view, marketing would go out and try to find a place for products that CDE invented and manufacturing would make them.

In reality, therefore, the company had three different views of itself. When the STS design team came up with its mission statement and went to the steering committee (which was made up of representatives from marketing, manufacturing, and upper management), the response was "You guys go back and work on it." Although the STS group felt that the members of the steering committee were not clear about what the mission was themselves, they worked on the mission statement sporadically throughout the course of the project. A mission statement that addressed state-of-the-art products and emphasized the market was finally drafted in late 1981, after the technical analysis and social analysis were completed. To write this draft, the design team and top CDE management, as well as representatives of the marketing and manufacturing divisions, went on a three-day retreat near Monterey, California, during which they developed the mission statement and philosophy. Off-site meetings such as this one are useful for resolving differences among groups.

For the engineers on the STS team, the *technical-system analysis* was clearly a valuable part of the STS process. They liked to analyze and to discuss the ideas among themselves, as well as to examine the technical variances that had to be controlled. In the technical analysis they began assessing how the current system was operating. The twelve key variances they identified were clustered as follows:

> Quality of product
>> Quality/organization of engineering specification varies
>> Quality of logic/circuit schematics information varies
>> Quality of composite plan varies
>> Quality of composite layout information varies
> Timeliness of product
>> Quality of project schedule varies
>> Time to complete logic/circuit design varies
>> Timeliness of composite layout information varies
>> Timeliness of samples varies
>> Timeliness of finished document varies
> Other factors (such as market acceptance)
>> Customer needs incorrectly/inadequately defined
>> Quality of concept in terms of manufacturability varies
>> Extent and number of features affecting constraints on chip size varies

In examining the current control of these key variances, the STS team became interested in receiving information from outside their closed system and in understanding what was going on in the rest of the company. Although they said that marketing did not provide any information to them and they felt that marketing had an exaggerated view of its own importance to the company, they also began to realize the importance of having marketing accept whatever they were doing. They concluded that "if a product is conceived and what we do develop is different [from] what the marketplace wants three years from now, . . . we aren't going to succeed or survive. How do we get that market data? How do we do it now?" They decided that CDE did need to work with marketing people. The STS design team also began to realize that in designing a product they had to understand the manufacturability of that product. A representative of the test engineers (who write test programs and design test hardware that manufacturing must use) sat on the STS design team. His people were obviously interested in manufacturability. In addition, the layout people on the design team began to say to the engineers, "If I had known what you wanted earlier in the work process, I would have been able to do a lot better. My frustration has been that I really don't know what this product is supposed to look like in the end." The layout designers in the CDE department were no different from the operators on an assembly line who do not know where the product is coming from or where it is going. The members of the STS team also began to see the value of product engineers in helping the manufacturing people to increase yields.

In summary, the STS team identified the key variances of customer needs, market needs, the timeliness of getting new designs to the marketplace, manufacturability, and quality considerations. The nonengineering members of the team also began to understand that the number of features designed into an IC were going to affect the size of the chip, which was also going to affect whether it could be tested and whether it could be economically manufactured.

Benefits of the technical analysis were clarifying the product of the design system and the key variances (and how those variances were controlled); giving people a common language, the language of the product, to unify their communication and to bridge the gaps between their separate languages of specialization; using specialists to educate the design team about other technical functions; and beginning to remember and use the analysis because it was written down.

The *social-system analysis* focused on the logic and circuit designers because they were the ones who lived with the IC project for the longest period of time and were most involved with control of the key variances. The STS team collected data on who talked to whom about what kinds of issues from every employee in the CDE organization. Several findings emerged. Significantly, manufacturing was hardly mentioned. This omission can be explained in part because new chips usually involve new manufacturing processes that are also under development, but nevertheless it remains that designers are often too busy to look at future products with manufacturing. Product engineers in the manufacturing area were also not mentioned in the interviews. Product engineers were trying to increase the product yield, and they were also supposed to know the most about what was going wrong with the product. Product engineers were an organizational invention, intended to span the boundaries between design engineering and manufacturing, yet they were never reported to be in touch with the group of design engineers. In general, respondents reported that managers were genuinely concerned about people and were accessible. All groups interviewed reported a high degree of social contact with peers in their own and other CDE units. Most individuals said they received positive support from their own units, but engineers said that layout provided poor support. Many respondents mentioned that most people talked about setting schedules but that few talked about meeting them. Little contact was reported with corporate staff. Company policy in the areas of compensation, performance evaluation, and career planning was criticized. The STS team began to realize that the social system was not just a group of people who liked one another. The analysis helped them to understand how they could control key variances (particularly those dealing with timeliness) and how members of CDE could keep one another informed about factors that were important in improving the results of their work.

In the meantime, the CDE organization had grown from about 60 to 150 people, including new people and new managers brought in for technical reasons. Many of these people, who were not philosophically aligned with the design values in that they agreed with blurring of caste and functional differences, felt somewhat threatened about what their positions would be after the recommendations were developed.

In fact, as recommendations did begin to emerge, other individuals and groups began to feel threatened. The CDE director himself realized that his management style was at odds with the emerging recommendations. As noted above, he jokingly referred to himself as a "benevolent dictator," which meant that he knew that he wanted the best for his employees while producing the best for the company. The theory of STS joint optimization was therefore an acceptable way to approach organizational improvement. However, although the proposed organization failed to meet his individual needs, he was willing to support the recommendations his STS design team was producing. Meanwhile, the layout group, with its third supervisor in a year, was hearing from its two STS team representatives that some changes were likely within their organization. Yet the layout manager told the same group that he did not know of any likely changes. In part, he must have been trying to deal with poor morale by assuring them that things were stable and becoming better rather than that things were becoming even more turbulent. He was also reflecting the anxieties of several members of his layout group who felt that they would miss the security of their own group if they were permanently assigned to work with a design engineer—one of the recommendations made by the STS team.

The social analysis was completed by the end of the summer in 1981. It then took four to five months before *recommendations for change* were presented to CDE. After the STS design team generated its first, second, and third choices for a design, the consultants often met off site with the top management of CDE, working on the implications of the recommendations. In the recommendation finally chosen, four design teams were formed, each of which included people who possessed all of the skills required for the production of one major IC product. Each team had responsibility for both the design and the support (with marketing and manufacturing) of their product. Figure 2 shows this new organization.

In the new CDE organization, layout designers and engineers, with most of the skills required to create a manufacturable IC design, constituted a product team. The physical move of

Figure 2. STS Management Organization.

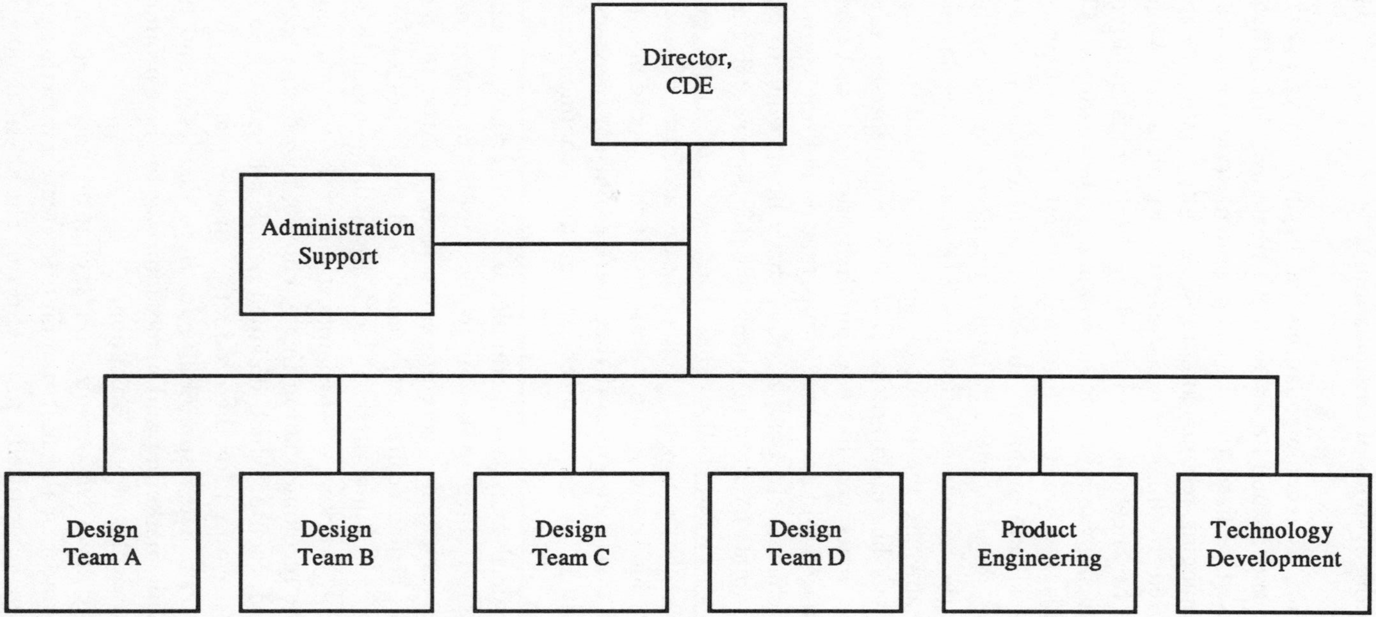

Skills on each design team include architecture, logic design, circuit design, layout design, test engineering, leadership.

most of the company, including CDE, to a new location in January 1982 provided the "unfreezing" necessary for the new organization of CDE to be implemented. With this new approach, most of the drawbacks of CAD technology and its use were expected to be eliminated. In this design, CAD technology had been adapted for the purposes of the CDE system and not merely for maximizing use of the technology itself. Layout designers and engineers now worked closely together, and their adversarial relationship became a thing of the past. Layout designers could understand the whole process, and they could identify with a single product or family of related products. Additionally, engineers were hired to learn CAD-based layout techniques, which further improved relations within the product-design teams and improved layout effectiveness by shortening the communication links between circuit design and layout. Design engineers often acted as quality inspectors on the layouts of their circuits, and, by doing some of their own layout and circuit design, they inspected their own work. The Applicon hardware and software were operated and maintained by an organizational unit separate from layout design, which, in addition, had responsibility for the creation of simulation programs (called CAD programs) for testing or confirming the logic and circuit designs prior to layout.

The layout designers were expected to develop a set of ground rules for using Applicon during prime time. As this plan was to be implemented, one layout designer would create the mask design, and a colleague would correct and update it later that day. In this way, the layout designers were able to control the CPU space available for the most urgent jobs. Layout designers had their own individual work space and desks away from the Applicon terminals, but within the area dedicated to their product team. This space was to be used as either a quiet area to plan subsequent tasks or as a place to meet and discuss the work with their colleagues. In this way, the flextime arrangement used by the layout designers permitted a substantial overlap in their work hours without a conflict over using the Applicon VDT assigned to them. A layout designer could, for example, come in at 8:00 in the morning and work at the VDT until 2:30. The layout colleague assigned to that same terminal could come to work at noon and spend those two and a half hours until the VDT became available in his or her individual work space, planning the work to be done with the Applicon that afternoon and evening.

Each product team was to have the skills in architecture, logic and circuit design, layout design, test engineering, and leadership that it needed to bring a design to manufacturing. In actual practice, each of the four teams has an architect on it, and several teams include test engineers. Six months before the completion of the design transfer to manufacturing, a product engineer or two joins each of these product-design teams and becomes part of it. When the product moves into manufacturing, the team moves into manufacturing and stays until the manufacturing people have the information and knowledge to begin testing out and manufacturing the product. As a new chip begins to be manufactured, a test engineer stays in manufacturing while the rest of the design group goes back and starts work on a new product. Unlike the usual design team in the S/C and computer industries, these teams do not break up. Instead, there is a continuity in team process for supporting past ICs and developing new ones.

This organization is based on the realization that the product of CDE is information—information that manufacturing uses to manufacture and test the product and that marketing uses to sell the product. The technical writers are supposed to be part of this organization, although they are not yet. As the product is being produced, the role of technical writers is to obtain information from the engineers and to train new customers in use of the product. In addition, a separate strategic marketing group was created in the marketing department to perform two functions: helping to create the original concepts for future projects and helping to introduce those products into the marketplace.

The difference between specialists and generalists was a major issue with which the new unit design contended. Some people thought that one of the drawbacks of this proposed organization was that it would reduce the depth of technical-skill specialties, forcing all team members to become multiskilled. They also thought that when the specialty-based work groups were disbanded, the lack of proximity and regular group meetings would drastically reduce (if not eliminate) the passing of hints and tricks among peers. This problem was addressed by forming technical-affinity teams, which formalized a structure for each of the technical-skill categories: test engineering, product engineering, logic and circuit design, and layout. Each affinity team was expected to hold a meeting at least once a month during which the members would upgrade one another's skills. People could share information and stay up to date. The affinity-group solution has not been going as well as desired, mainly because of an absence of interest on the part of layout designers in meeting with layout designers from other teams. Most prefer working in teams with engineers after they make the change rather than in a centralized organization.

The teams in CDE, averaging about ten people each, have leaders. Team leaders have responsibility for work-group processes, selection of group members, feedback on group performance, and group planning. Team leaders negotiate resources on behalf of the team, lead product development, provide direction and integration, manage external boundaries, and facilitate activities within the team. Team leadership can be a rotating task; the same people do not have to continue to be team leaders or team administrators, although in actuality they have done so. Members and leaders are evaluated on skill and direct contribution to design tasks. Leadership and other social skills are not linked to the appraisal system.

The company has provided team-skills training sessions that anyone can attend. In the beginning, the team members and leaders needed skills for working in groups, and a half day of training each month for a year to acquire skills was planned —not only for those people assigned as team leaders but for members as well. Despite this dedication to the idea of training, both leadership and group-process skills have not come up to their required levels.

Impact on Organizational Effectiveness. The performance measures used by CDE prior to the STS study included employee turnover, schedules (sometimes but not always set by engineers for layout designers) met, product-release dates met, self-assessment of engineering quality (especially innovation), and market acceptance of products designed. Such measures as turnover are often contaminated by multiple but undefined effects (for example, being attributed both to dissatisfaction within the company and to the many attractions outside the company) and are thus suspect as indicators of organizational change. Other traditional measures such as product release or product acceptance are too long term or coarse to provide help for self-correction as the changes unfold.

Following the STS study, the managers in CDE have begun to use additional measures. These include tracking the unit performance to schedule on a weekly basis; tracking product schedules on a finer, more detailed basis than before; and measuring initial product performance.

Turnover is also used even though it remains an indicator of external attractions and internal frustrations. Since the new organization was introduced, turnover has been about 10 percent for layout designers, which is lower than for similar organizations in the Valley. Layout designers are feeling committed to their group, and they are more concerned than they were previously with when the products come out and whether they can be manufactured the first time around. Evidently for layout designers the internal attractions in CDE are outweighing the external ones. Engineers, however, do not present such a sanguine picture. Nearly one third of the design engineers in CDE left the company within six months after the STS reorganization. The reasons given in exit interviews were varied. Some wanted to join start-up companies as the economy turned up. Often these engineers left the S/C industry and IC design to enter the computer industry, leaving IC design to younger colleagues. Others who left said that they did so because they did not enjoy the managerial responsibilities of working with others. Many have been replaced with engineers who do enjoy close working relationships.

Meeting schedules is a measure that is taken more seriously by CDE employees now than in the past. In particular, people in the design teams note and discuss the short-term scheduled releases from one design step to another. Because layout designers are involved in decisions affecting their schedules, they are more likely than before to "own" those decisions and are more willing to act in new ways to meet schedules. Despite this realistic view of timeliness, the schedules are slipping. It seems that the complex nature of the current IC products is such that even the CDE managers do not know enough to accurately estimate completion times. This poor ability to schedule is even more frustrating now that schedules are important to employees.

Measurement of layout productivity has been introduced in an attempt to create some short-term schedule goals. This measure is a daily count, by designer, of the number of transistors drawn. Layout designers say that although this transistor count is a precise measure, readily available from the Applicon technology, it may prove to be merely a measure of average Applicon output rather than an accurate indicator of the work done by a designer on a given day. Despite voicing this reservation, the layout designers are motivated to achieve good schedule performance and are thus interested in measures that may help them do so.

Product performance at "first silicon" is a new end-result measure that CDE intends to use. This measure will evaluate whether the product works as expected when it is manufactured or fails this first test. This indicator is important for assessing the care taken in checking the internal logic of IC circuit and layout design as well as for assessing the manufacturability of the resulting chips. It will determine whether the design needs substantial rework or if up to six months can be saved by avoiding that usual but onerous task. The product teams are oriented to design with this goal of "first silicon" in mind.

CDE management undertook an informal assessment of the new product-team organization in June 1983, more than a year after its implementation. Ten of the forty members constituting the CDE design staff and most of the CDE managers met to review their experience with the new unit organization. They discussed the communications within teams, both in informal and formal meetings; communications between teams; and communications among people with the same skills. They commented on the time and quality aspects of the CDE style of decision making by consensus. They also listed issues affecting morale in the teams and their own feelings about these issues.

Nearly all those involved in this informal assessment expressed strong positive feelings. Only one of the sixteen people had little to say. Fully three quarters reported that morale was higher because of increased communication and understanding within the teams. Among the factors mentioned as enhancing team morale were member support for one another, increased ownership of decisions made by the group (especially by layout designers), and increased awareness of and learning about the total design process and its progress.

Half of the respondents also expressed mixed feelings and, in some cases, frustration with some of the effects of the new structure. Managers complained, for example, that decision making by consensus removed the ability to simply dictate decisions to subordinates or that it took too long (in an industry where time is always short), even though it led to the ownership of decisions as a positive aspect. Some engineers questioned the quality of decisions made by a group because the "best" idea might not always be the one accepted. Engineering specialists commented that they had difficulty obtaining layout support from other design teams when they needed it. Meetings that lasted too long or that did not concern them were mentioned as drawbacks by some layout designers. Managers, engineers, and layout designers all commented that the product-team structure interfered with close professional relationships among people with similar skills and formal training and that the affinity teams had not worked out as well as they wanted.

A telling comment by a manager outside CDE was that despite the fact that the STS analysis and design process took a long time and many man-hours to complete, its usefulness is more essential for the current design projects (such as the thirty-two-bit microprocessor), which require a team structure, than for the more simplified projects of the past. He continued that the one-person (or master-slave) organization that worked for earlier generations of products would simply not be appropriate today. He concluded that it was unfair to compare the performance of the new organization, with its multiperson, multiskilled, product orientation, to past arrangements over a time during which IC products have changed so much.

What Was Learned? The change in structure from a functional, specialty-based organization to a product-oriented, multiskilled organization has been a powerful educational experience. The relationships among people have changed to fit the form, and the old, adversarial relationships between specialties have been greatly reduced. At the same time, however, the relationships among people with the same specialty background have deteriorated because of the structural change. An important activity, therefore, is to constantly reinforce the supporting structures, such as the affinity teams, to make certain they continue and succeed.

What could be done differently? If the project could be repeated, training in leadership and team skills would be more strongly emphasized earlier in implementation and continued as a part of doing business. In addition, CDE would attend to short-term performance measurement, based on the key variances identified in the technical analysis, as well as to the long-range measures based on goals and mission. Planning for measurement would include consideration of formal indicators of social performance within and between teams. Team members would be involved in the creation of these measures as well as in their use. Finally, the values stated in the mission and philosophy of CDE would be tested and shaped early in the process to assure the department that these were living guidelines and CDE's real focus.

Would CDE implement the same technologies and structures for the creation of the current generation of IC products? CAD technology has proved to be useful and would be retained. Applicon has features, in the version currently used by CDE, that provide advantages over other systems. The multiskilled, product-oriented teams permit the creation of complex and large IC products. The use of permanent teams rather than the temporary task forces of the more usual matrix-type organization permits an identification with products and their follow-through and would be continued. Finally, the inclusion of both layout designers and design engineers in these teams has proved to be an appropriate structure within which to apply the Applicon technology. The CDE decision to recruit young engineers for the teams to learn to design layout on CAD technology in addition to designing the circuits themselves has been a powerful initial validation of this approach in CDE. This team orientation is also used strategically to recruit new employees. The company's description of this organizational feature in its recruitment brochure is proof of its commitment to this idea.

References

Davis, L. E. "Organization Design." In G. Salvendy (Ed.), *Handbook of Industrial Engineering.* New York: Wiley, 1981.

Emery, F. E., Foster, M., and Wollard, W. "Analytical Model for Socio-Technical Systems." In F. Emery (Ed.), *The Emergence of a New Paradigm of Work.* Canberra: Centre for Continuing Education, Australian National University, 1978.

Taylor, J. C. "The Socio-Technical Approach to Work Design." In K. Legge and E. Mumford (Eds.), *Designing Organizations for Satisfaction and Efficiency.* Westmead, England: Gower Press, 1978.

Trist, E. *The Evolution of Socio-Technical Systems: A Conceptual Framework and an Action Research Program.* Occasional Paper No. 2. Toronto: Ontario Quality of Working Life Center, 1981.

Marketing Advanced Manufacturing Processes

Dorothy Leonard-Barton
Janis Gogan

"A company's manufacturing function typically is either a competitive weapon or a corporate millstone." Since Skinner (1969) wrote those words, many U.S. corporations have set about the task of converting their millstones into guided missiles. Manufacturing, once considered merely the logical antecedent of product design and the minion of marketing, is now discussed in many board rooms as a strategic corporate function. (See Jelinek and Goldhar, 1983; Hayes and Wheelwright, 1984).

Thanks largely to Japanese competition, there is a more receptive market for advanced manufacturing technologies today than ever before, and the need for advances in manufacturing practices is widely acknowledged. However, although the technologies are new, many of the individuals involved in both marketing and purchasing are veterans. Thus, old suppliers are forced to learn totally new technologies, and new suppliers have to learn about—and educate—old markets. (See Chapter Four.)

Between 1981 and 1983, shipments of U.S.-made machine tools fell two thirds, partly because of the recession but also because of foreign competition and old technology. Many companies were forced to change their businesses entirely. For example, Acme-Cleveland has gone from traditional machine tools to computer controlled flexible manufacturing systems

Note: We are grateful to Dean LaCoe, manager of marketing programs, Visage, Inc., for comments on an earlier draft.

(FMS). B. Charles Ames, Acme-Cleveland's chairman and chief executive officer, has noted: "This company was geared to a business world that no longer exists" (Winter, 1984).

The same two decades that have witnessed a growing realization of manufacturing's strategic importance have seen a maturing of marketing practice. In this chapter, we trace some main themes in the industrial-marketing literature that are particularly relevant for the diffusion of advanced manufacturing processes, and we refer to critical issues that suppliers of the new technologies must address.

To begin, however, it is important to briefly consider the changing environment in which suppliers of advanced manufacturing technologies must operate. The past few years have witnessed changes in the technologies available to manufacturers, the types of benefits to be derived from advanced processes, and the nature of the vendor-customer relationship.

Manufacturing Environment

To many people, the term *advanced manufacturing processes* conjures up pictures of large computers controlling high-volume manufacturing lines. The picture is accurate in only some cases. Although it is true that most advanced manufacturing technologies are computer driven, the computers involved may well be micros. By mid-1983, over one million personal computers were being used in American industry, over 12 percent of which were in manufacturing companies. Although many of these micros have been used for passive applications such as tracking daily product work orders, worker bonuses, and so forth, at the end of the line, increasingly they are evolving into interactive systems used by the foremen to control production in real time (see, for example, Zerkis, 1984). Therefore, advanced manufacturing processes can involve quite small-scale computers.

The term can also refer to mid- or even low-volume batch processing. Although historically automation has been linked with standardization and hence with high-volume production, FMSs are changing this picture. Using a host computer to coordinate machine tools and materials-handling equipment for the processing of a variety of work pieces, such systems can transform mid-volume discrete-batch production lines into an approximation of continuous flow. The market for FMSs was approximately $53 million in 1982; by 1986, some sources estimate current industry spending on these systems to be $265 million and predict that as much as $1.3 billion will be spent by 1990 (Yankee Group Factory Systems Planning Service, 1983). Therefore, computerized manufacturing processes are no longer the exclusive province of high-volume commodity producers.

Another changing aspect of the manufacturing environment is that the significant savings are not to be found in reducing labor costs, which typically constitute only 15 to 20 percent of total production costs (Gold, 1982a). Manufacturers are increasingly concerned with reducing inventory levels and with controlling for quality as the work progresses, not just at the end of the line. (Ironically, some evidence indicates that quality control may be more, not less, difficult with CIM; see Blumberg and Gerwin, 1984.) Thus, the bases for investment in capital are changing in many firms.

Furthermore, in their drive to control inventory and materials-handling costs, manufacturers are realizing the desirability, even necessity, of long-term relationships with their vendors. In this important manufacturing trend, as in so many others, they are influenced by the Japanese example. Many Japanese suppliers function almost as part of the corporation they furnish. In the United States, a recent sign of changing times was General Motors's August 1984 purchase of stock in three companies producing artificial-vision products for use in manufacturing: Automatix, Difracto, and View Engineering. As researchers in marketing are beginning to recognize, the skills required to build and maintain the new, long-term vendor-customer relationships are different from those required in a less stable market situation (Arndt, 1979).

These extensive changes in the environment make it difficult for any vendor to survive without a highly developed concept of marketing.

Concept of Marketing

Selling and *marketing* are not synonymous terms. In 1960, Levitt's famous article "Marketing Myopia" opened many eyes to the limitations of selling: "Selling focuses on the needs of the seller, marketing on the needs of the buyer. Selling is pre-occupied with the seller's need to convert his product into cash; marketing with the idea of satisfying the needs of the customer by means of the product and the whole cluster of things associated with creating, delivering, and finally consuming it" (p. 50).

Customer orientation is thus a key tenet in marketing theory. Yet, although many marketers pay lip service to defining their offerings as solutions to customer problems, the temptation remains for sellers of high-technology products to present their products as bits, bytes, and hardware instead of as contributors to added control or productivity (Balakrisha, 1978; Cooper, 1975). One reason for this failure to carry out Levitt's ideas is that it is easier to provide the technical specifications of input and capacity than to describe the output: solutions to customer needs (Page and Siemplenski, 1983). Communicating solutions requires an intimate knowledge of the customers' business needs and how one's products meet those needs. A successful marketing endeavor begins with the development of a needed product.

Product Design

New and Schlacter (1979) argue that "the marketing concept in technology-based firms is often applied too late in the product-development cycle to prevent costly marketplace failure." That is, vendors of technical products generally understand Levitt's theme but too often fail during the early stages of product development to consider the potential impact of the marketplace. In one study, nearly half of the product failures were not eliminated until costly test marketing or even full production had been implemented (Myers and Sweezy, 1978).

Does this finding suggest that adequate information about

market preferences does not exist or merely that such information is difficult to access? In many cases, neither is true. Rather, technically sophisticated and creative people often find it difficult to believe that potential users will fail to see the obvious benefits to be derived from the new product—or that users will make unexpected trade-offs, between efficiency and cost, for example.

Two sources of information exist against which to check new concepts even at an early stage in their development: colleagues within the firm who are close to the market and the potential users themselves. New and Schlacter (1979) argue that increased communication within the firm will augment the opportunities for vendors to understand their products' potential in the marketplace. As designs move from idea development to product development, early communication between key parties in research and development (R&D), marketing, and manufacturing will increase the odds of eliminating unsuccessful products before heavy commitments of resources have been made.

Yet communication within the firm across functional boundaries is not without cost. Allen (1977) has demonstrated that informal communication between co-workers drops off sharply when they are separated more than thirty meters; moreover, he found that technical people are loath to seek help from colleagues within their own firm. The difference between the goals, education, and work patterns of new-product developers and those of marketing personnel lead members of the two groups to avoid contact and often to distrust each other (Souder, 1980). Early incorporation of market information into the product-development process from other areas within the company, like any other intrafirm boundary spanning, requires a great deal of organizational forethought and management. (See Graham and Leonard-Barton, 1984, for a discussion of intrafirm technology-transfer issues.)

The other valuable backboard against which to bounce ideas is, of course, the members of the user community themselves. Von Hippel (1983) suggests that one source of already market-tested but highly innovative new-product ideas is today's *lead users,* defined as "individuals or firms who have needs which are not now general among users of a given product—but which can be predicted to become general and provide a commercially interesting marketplace in the future" (p. 12). Lead-user segments need not themselves be members of the marketplace whose needs they represent. For example, products such as highly reliable fasteners have been developed for the aerospace industry, yet tomorrow's automobile manufacturers may have need for similar products. As von Hippel himself notes, such lead-user groups probably will not precisely simulate the needs and skill base of the majority of the potential users in the predicted marketplace because innovators generally differ from the rest of the population. However, such groups can provide clues to desirable products and product attributes that can be tested on a representative sample of the general population.

Empirical evidence to support this notion was found in a number of studies of industrial innovation conducted by von Hippel and his students. In several industries (notably, scientific instrumentation and semiconductor and electronic subassembly manufacturing equipment), the primary source of innovation was the manufacturers or other users themselves, not the suppliers. In these firms, customers defined their own needs, designed a prototype to meet those needs, and encouraged vendors to manufacture the product and sell it back to them.

Von Hippel also suggests that many novel product ideas can be gained by identifying high-need users, individuals or firms "who have a significantly stronger unmet need for a given novel or familiar product attribute or product concept than does the average user" (1983, p. 19). These are presumably potential lead users who do not have the resources or initiative to conduct the actual innovative activity themselves but who have an untapped wealth of data on those needs. Empirical evidence to support the usefulness of this idea is scanty. Moreover, although it seems logical to seek information about the marketability of one's possible technological solution from those who have an acute need for such a solution and may have some ideas about what will and will not work, the same cautions hold here as in the case of lead users. Such an extreme population is not exactly comparable to the rest of the potential marketplace. Nevertheless, product ideas from such users may well be more radical and potentially more profitable than those gained from the more usual approaches to market research.

Product developers working in the field of management of information systems (MIS) have found that the best way to communicate with users about a new product and incorporate user insights into the design early is to prototype. Today's MIS literature emphasizes the benefits of an evolutionary approach to product design over the highly structured, systematic, and frequently protracted design processes advocated in the 1970s.

Prototyping offers the marketer three important advantages. First, customers are much better able to specify their requirements when given a tangible product to which they may react than when simply having it described. Second, although a systems focus is a rational long-term strategy, marketers may find they are more effective trying to sell a system piece by piece than all at once. This practice reduces the buyer's perceived risk, may help the vendor manage user expectations effectively, and also lowers the vendor's investment. Third, an evolutionary design is never complete. Users continually identify enhancements; technology enables features today that were not possible yesterday; and so on. This evolutionary approach to design is a natural way to nurture long-term relationships with customers.

Suppliers who are responsive to potentially high-volume customers sometimes find that they have unintentionally followed the prototype-and-revise strategy. A young robotics firm was rather taken aback when one of their first customers said they would be happy to buy more—if the vendor could make several dozen changes in the product. Although these demands necessitated a back-to-the-drawing-board rehaul of the product, they were extremely helpful for the company in designing a second model. Engineers who have never designed for manufacturing before (as many involved in building computerized systems have not) often underestimate the demands that environment places on machinery—for instance, because of particles in the air. In the case of proprietary processes, of course, it is difficult for security reasons to involve the users in the design. However, especially as the balance in manufacturing-process innovation swings more toward software than hardware, the development process will increasingly become a joint effort between vendor and user; prototyping is likely to become an ever more respectable communication mechanism.

One of the primary tenets guiding product development is to "know thyself"—that is, to build on the distinctive capabilities of the firm. As Corey (1975) has written: "Market selection . . . is influenced considerably by the manufacturer's assessment of his own strengths and weaknesses. He may count his product design, possibly protected by patents, as an important asset. . . . He may perceive his established position and reputation with existing customers as his critical strength. He may regard his size, financial strength, and production resources as his strong suit. Limitations in any of these areas must be counted as weaknesses" (p. 123). Meyer and Roberts (1983) present preliminary evidence of the importance for small firms of maintaining a strategic focus in their development of new products. Firms that build off their core technologies are hypothesized to fare better in the marketplace than those who stray farther from what they know well. Large corporations entering new markets have similar limitations. (See "Changing a Corporate Culture," 1984, for a discussion of Johnson & Johnson's moves into high tech.) Yet, as noted previously in this chapter, today's competition often forces manufacturing suppliers to shift gears. Even when they move into new technologies, however, firms can still take stock of those distinctive capabilities that might be applied to the new field. The question "What do we do well?" is simple; the answers may be somewhat complex. Bitondo and Frohman (1981) provide some guidance in assessing a firm's distinctive technical capabilities.

Corey (1975, p. 123) suggests using this assessment of strengths and weaknesses as a background against which "should be posited a list of feasible product/market opportunities, with an evaluation of buying behavior, market needs, and the competitive environment for each one." This process could be particularly useful if those market needs and opportunities are expressed as critical success factors (CSFs) guiding product choice by firms in a targeted market segment.

The CSF concept has been presented under different names (for example, key variables) and has been used extensively in the literatures of management control and marketing. Anthony and Dearden (1980) list the following characteristics of a key variable: "(1) It is important in explaining the success or failure of the organization. (2) It is volatile; . . . it can change quickly, often for reasons . . . not controllable by the manager. (3) Prompt action is required when a significant change occurs. (4) The variable can be measured, either directly or via a surrogate. For example, customer satisfaction cannot be measured directly, but its surrogate, number of returns, can be a key variable" (p. 89). In short, a key variable is one on which the marketplace success of the company depends.

Rockart (1979) translates these CSFs into a practical technique for identifying strategic applications of information technology in organizations. The process begins with interviews with general management and MIS managers, utilizing a structured process to clearly define the broad corporate CSFs, the keys to success at the departmental level, and specific information required to support those critical needs. The understanding thus gained of corporate strategy, competitive weapons, and distinctive capabilities is translated into information-technology products designed to support those important organizational needs.

In itself, analysis of CSFs helps identify needed product dimensions. The technique would seem well suited to the development of computerized manufacturing technologies. However, as our previous discussion suggests, this technique might be most useful to manufacturing suppliers if the CSF analysis were combined with an examination of in-house capabilities to see where product opportunities lie. (See Table 1 for hypothetical examples.)

Market Segmentation

Market segmentation is a concept more widely used in consumer than in industrial marketing. The task of selecting a logical marketing strategy is complicated by the chaotic mass of

Table 1. Matching Customer Requirements with Vendor Capabilities.

Critical Success Factor for Customer	Distinctive Vendor Capability
Customizing scientific test equipment	Design sophisticated, powerful hardware; no in-house software
Just-in-time inventory management	Reliable delivery; convenient location
Higher quality product than competitors	Thorough quality assurance

potential customers out in the marketplace. These customers can be segmented in many different ways, but some targeting approaches are far more successful than others. Yet how does the vendor of manufacturing-process technologies choose an effective segmentation approach?

Again, one solution is to segment according to customer CSFs. It may be possible to select companies with particular operating strengths or weaknesses that make them especially appropriate customers. For example, Digital Equipment Corporation for years targeted customers with enough computer sophistication to develop their own software.

Bonoma and Shapiro (1983) present a nested approach to segmenting industrial markets, which serves as a useful guide. Their hierarchy, summarized here, progresses from relatively simple, observable market characteristics to more specific and considerably more subtle ones.

1. Demographics
   Industry, company size, location
2. Operating variables
   Technology
   User-nonuser status
   Customer capabilities
3. Purchasing approaches
4. Situational factors
   Urgency
   Order size
   Specific application
5. Personal characteristics of decision makers

Bonoma and Shapiro suggest choosing the most general approach that will be effective. For instance, although it is unlikely that one could adequately segment one's market on the criterion of size alone, certainly a first cut by size would make sense for vendors selling a product costing several million dollars.

The operating level of the hierarchy is perhaps most useful to marketers of high-technology products. It is often possible to segment industrial customers by the production technologies they employ. Plants using copper-based resistors, for example, need different controls than do those producing silver palladium resistors on the boards because copper is subject to oxidation.

Segmenting by user and nonuser is an approach often overlooked. The best market for robotics in the immediate future consists of companies that have already invested in one, not only because these are high-need users, in von Hippel's (1983) terms, but also because the economics of installation and use favor adding robot capacity. At the end of 1980, almost 30 percent of the U.S. robot population was owned by only six firms. As of January 1983, twenty-six firms owned about one half of all the industrial robots in the United States (Ayres and Miller, 1983).

Some vendors seem to pour a disproportionate share of their marketing resources into building new markets because the market they already own is often far more valuable to them than new ones. There can be more than one possible application for a given product. We find it useful to extend von Hippel's (1983) lead-user concept to include unanticipated benefits being derived from one's product by current customers. One can sometimes identify new market segments this way. A case in point is that of a company selling a software package intended for use by an electronics firm's test operations. In one company, salespeople observed their package being used by circuit designers because of its superior simulation capabilities. This observation led them to realize they could segment their marketplace according to derived benefits rather than according to strict organizational functions. They actually had more than one target market within each company. By segmenting according to product benefits rather than user function, they not only enhanced the number of potential sales per company visit but discovered a new selling point—compatibility of design data across product-development functions.

The three inner nests of the Bonoma-Shapiro segmentation approach represent successively more specific, situational, individualized levels. We would speculate that the higher the ticket price of a product and the greater the complexity of the sell, the more appropriate it would be to segment on these much more specific and subtle criteria. This approach is often applicable to the sorts of product discussed in this chapter. For example, a vendor of computer-aided design (CAD) technology might want to segment at the specific-application level. One possible breakdown of the CAD market at this level is: mechanical (43 percent); electrical/electronics (26 percent); architectural/engineering/construction (16 percent); mapping (10 percent); and other (5 percent) (Yankee Group Factory Systems Planning Service, 1983).

The innermost nest, personal characteristics of decision makers, is the most difficult basis for market segmentation and requires the most intimate knowledge of the firm. Bonoma and Shapiro include buyer-seller similarity, buyer motivation, individual perceptions, and risk-management strategies in this category.

A good deal of evidence from the psychological literature supports the idea that individuals who perceive themselves to be similar are attracted to each other and that a homogeneous information source is more trusted than a heterogeneous one (Rogers, 1983). In the marketing literature, these concepts have been expanded to hypotheses about the seller-buyer relationship. Not surprisingly, perceived similarity to the salesperson biases the buyer favorably toward the sale (Evans, 1963; Gadel, 1964). Yet this concept is sometimes ignored by purveyors of advanced technology (Page and Siemplenski, 1983). Too often the salesperson, in an attempt to demonstrate technical credentials, overwhelms the customer with foreign-sounding jargon about ROM, RAM, bits, and bytes.

A lesson can be learned from the experiences of MIS managers through the 1960s and 1970s. Their systems analysts and programmers were perceived by users as a breed apart, speaking an incomprehensible language and unable to understand the business needs of the firm. Although users pleaded for systems professionals who could talk the language of management, they had little success. Programmers held the key to understanding computers, hence they wielded power. The lack of communication resulted in many large systems fiascoes; massive systems representing hundreds of man-years of development effort had to be shelved. Today's nontechnical managers are more computer literate than their predecessors, thanks in part to personal computers. Systems professionals can no longer function as information priests, speaking an exotic language; they must meet users more than half way. The same is true in the manufacturing environment. Some vendors may have to hire different kinds of salespeople.

Another approach is to retool the sales force with extensive training in effective listening, business strategy, and so on. For instance, IBM sales representatives rarely talk bits and bytes. They are taught to focus on what the customer says, not on the pitch they want to make. Only when a salesperson thoroughly understands the customers' business objectives and the benefits the customer might be seeking from a computer system does the salesperson begin to discuss specific IBM solutions.

Once a segmentation approach is decided on, management must convey it clearly to the sales force. Salespeople should be rewarded not merely for selling units but for selling units to the right customers. A key part of sales training is teaching the sales force when to say, "We don't have the right product for your company today."

Marketers have also studied the psychology of motivation as a basis for segmentation. Bonoma (1982) suggests identifying the major decision makers, finding out what motivates them, and working with those motivations. But first, he warns, learn who is doing the buying. We discuss approaches to this topic next.

Making the Purchase Decision

One might imagine that a purchase decision for a product as important and complex as computer-based manufacturing technology would be made in a highly structured, rational manner, with all the possible costs and benefits objectively weighed. In fact, of course, the decision-making process is far from straightforward and rational.

There are three key reasons for the complexity of decisions about major capital investments. First, product purchases represent different levels of risk, and the decision-making process therefore varies according to the perceived risk. Second, although buyers may wish to make their decision in a totally rational fashion, our rationality is generally bounded by nonrational factors. Third, a purchase decision of this magnitude is rarely made by one person alone; usually, it is a complex, political process involving many individuals.

The major dimensions contributing to perceived risk are the size or cost of the project and the familiarity of the buyers with the problem or the technology. So many manufacturing technologies constitute systemwide innovations that the sale can have an impact on a corporation's procedures, policies, and profits for years to come. Buyers are correct in perceiving these capital investments as high risk.

One of the reasons that vision systems for quality assurance have sold more readily than have robots integrated into a production line is that the inspection systems constitute less of a risk to profit if they fail temporarily. Visual inspection is more easily reversed to a manual procedure than are many automated production tasks. Also, interrupting the production line even for a few minutes is extremely costly. Manufacturers might be wise to take a careful look at the need for comprehensive solutions. Is it really necessary to package the process-technology product in a large, high-risk bundle?

Again, a look at the MIS experience may be instructive. The early days of data processing were characterized by highly dispersed, fragmented computer operations. As use of the computer resource expanded, managements began to bring data processing under centralized control. The late 1960s, early 1970s were the heyday of long-range data-processing planning. Many corporations underwent lengthy investigations of their total data-processing needs. IBM's business systems planning was one example of thorough data-processing planning that could take two or more years and then result in comprehensive systems proposals. But these highly rational, comprehensive solutions tend to solve yesterday's rather than today's problems. Some companies that undertook these lengthy planning sessions in order to reduce risk found that they increased risk because they designed highly interdependent systems. The trend today in MIS, because of rapidly changing technology and business environments, is to balance distributed processing power with centralization of a few key aspects of the data resource.

A piece-by-piece approach is advantageous to the customer because it reduces risk. It is useful to the marketers in two ways. First, it is much easier for the customer to say "yes" to many small decisions than to take one giant step forward. Second, the vendor can incorporate future technological innovations into the higher-payoff modules rather than having to completely redesign the system.

However, manufacturing technologies appear to be moving increasingly in the direction of large systems, so perceptions of risk are increasing, not decreasing. One analysis of the robotics industry states: "The robot business is no longer the business of robots, but of robot systems. The end user wants solutions to application and manufacturing problems, not simply devices. No industry or user, with the possible exception of the automobile industry, is presently knowledgeable enough about robotic applications to drive a market in just 'robots.' The key to expanding the robotics market is systems. . . . The marketing effort by the manufacturers must become more aggressive as the focus moves towards 'systems integration' in the production process. At the high end, robots with advanced sensors that will be a part of a totally integrated manufacturing system will attract an expanding target market" (Yankee Group Factory Systems Planning Service, 1984, p. 8).

As this quotation suggests, vendors are under considerable pressure to supply systems. But because users also fear to take big risks, vendors may be able to achieve success by building systems that users can grow into. An example of this technology is provided by Automatix, which has stressed a systems approach from the beginning. Robots are treated as peripherals, potential parts for an inspection or an assembly system. Automatix has not hesitated to purchase hardware parts from other vendors (for example, arms from Hitachi) because management believes that the firm's competitive advantage lies in the software tying computers together, not in the hardware. The Automatix controller can integrate vision as well as other sensor options, can control several robots (including those built by competitors, if necessary), and has off-line programming capabilities that make links to CAD systems feasible. This systems approach was an important contributor to the firm's early market success.

It is apparent, then, that the drive to systems is both a potential liability and a possible benefit for vendors. On the one hand, suppliers who produce stand-alone units, incompatible with other systems, present one kind of risk to buyers—the threat of inability to tie all operating systems together into a system. On the one hand, vendors who sell huge systems raise the cost and therefore the risk of the purchase. The key to reducing risk on both counts would appear to be attention to flexibility and compatibility. In a survey of fifty-seven firms using computer-aided manufacturing (CAM) equipment of various kinds, Rosenthal and Vossoughi (1983) found that the two factors most frequently considered in the selection of the current system were interface requirements and future add-on capabilities. It is not surprising, then, that vendors that produce products that constitute systems in and of themselves but that also are designed to tie into other functions and systems are doing well in the marketplace.

Computervision, which dominated the early CAD market and which persisted in basing system upgrades on internally developed hardware, changed its basic marketing and product-development strategies, moving toward much more compatibility with competitors' products than it had previously. The firm signed a joint marketing agreement with IBM, providing them access to IBM's expertise in data-base management, data communications, and decision-support software. As part of the agreement, Computervision agreed to adapt its software to run on the IBM 4300. In addition, Computervision acquired several software companies (for example, Cambridge Interactive Systems of the United Kingdom; SUN Microsystems; the Organization for Industrial Research). All these moves were intended to push the company toward manufacturing systems technology products rather than stand-alone, proprietary, CAD equipment. Such moves increase the competitive advantage of a supplier and are in fact essential for survival, although in some cases they may increase the size of the investment and the scope of the purchase decision. As we imply later in this chapter, the ability of a purchasing firm to trade off different kinds of risk and to deal with benefits such as the potential for system integration (which are not immediately recoverable in cost reductions) depends on the constitution of the buying center.

The second dimension of risk, as we noted previously, is lack of familiarity with the technology. Probably not since the Industrial Revolution have vendors faced such a necessity to educate their customers. In interviews with thirty-eight suppliers of CAM processes, Rosenthal and Vossoughi (1983) found that only 24 percent of their respondents felt their potential customers had a "good understanding" of what their technology does and does not do with regard to their incremental factory-automation needs. When the same question was asked relative to the integrated factory-automation needs of the customers, that figure fell to 3 percent. In that same survey, 60 percent of the vendors said that their customers were offered or requested (or both) guidance in how to assess their needs; 55 percent found it necessary to provide general assistance in helping customers ask the right questions; and 73 percent provided general education in technology to their customers.

One of the most ironic aspects of this education is that suppliers often need to reduce, not enhance, their customers' expectations about the new technology. This is a key difference between the hard sell of the apocryphal used-car salesperson and the needs-oriented marketer in manufacturing today. Salespeople today have to manage customer expectations so that they are perceived as a reliable information source in the future. Prospective customers have been exposed to such media hype as the 1980 cover of *Time* magazine, which implied robots were already capable of many activities they could not yet perform, and the 1983 cover of *U.S. News and World Report,* which overstated the case for artificial intelligence by announcing: "Machines That Think—They Are Brewing a Revolution."

Even sober, knowledgeable engineers (possibly under the influence of such magazine headlines or Star Wars) sometimes attribute degrees of sophistication and reasoning power to robots that far exceed the current state of the art. As one vendor observes bluntly, "A robot cannot, by itself, be expected to substitute as a worker and monitor" (Hinson, 1984). When expectations are pared down to reality, the customer response initially is likely to be negative. In one of the few marketing studies examining the effect of additional information on initial high expectations about technology, Lilien and Johnston (1980) found that prospective purchasers' intentions to purchase residential solar equipment dropped after they began to appreciate the difficulties of installation and some of the trade-offs in economic terms. Hayes and Wheelwright (1984) note a similar phenomenon. When management's knowledge about a manufacturing technology is low, the perception of risk is high. As managers gain more knowledge about the technology, "surprisingly, their perception of the risks . . . may actually increase because they can identify specific problems that have no apparent solutions" (p. 312). However, "once a certain threshold of familiarity is reached . . . the magnitude of the perceived risks associated with pursuing changes in the technology begins to decrease" (p. 313). Educating the consumer, therefore, constitutes less of a liability than selling to one who buys on the basis of inflated expectations.

The second reason mentioned for the difficulty of controlling the purchase decision is that such decisions are rarely as rational as one might expect them to be. Simon (1947, 1952) noted that a truly rational decision would involve careful appraisal of all feasible alternatives and choice of the alternative with the highest expected value. However, he said, individuals cannot absorb all the information about every feasible alternative; that task is beyond the capacity of human information processing. Hence, human rationality is bounded. Although a manager may intend to behave rationally, he or she tends to "satisfice" on a solution that is adequate for the task at hand and represents a reasonable review of a subset of the alternatives. Simon further hypothesized that individuals seek solutions in a more or less sequential fashion, stopping at the first satisfactory solution identified.

As we discuss later in this chapter, purchase decisions are also frequently affected negatively by the strict application of financial rationales that were designed for different, earlier manufacturing technologies. However, vendors also run into the problem of purchases based on whim or fad. An able salesman of robots recently remarked: "It's hard to understand. Here's an experienced engineer, who has been responsible over the years for countless important equipment-purchase decisions. Always before, he's had a careful plan about exactly how he intended to use that equipment and what cost efficiencies he expected. He knew precisely how it fit in with all the other equipment. But show that man a robot, and he's like a kid. Maybe he's just been to a trade show, or he's seen one in another plant. But he's just got to have one!"

Another astute observer of the industrial robot market observed that mention of a robot installation in corporations' annual reports probably peaked about 1982 and since has begun to fall off. Such observations suggest that many companies have purchased robots on an experimental basis. However, few seem to acknowledge that rationale. In Rosenthal and Vossoughi's (1983) survey of vendors, only 11 percent said that over a fourth of their customers were clearly installing their product as an experiment, and only 11 percent of the users surveyed said that the installation they had chosen to describe in response to the questionnaire was an experiment. Usually a vendor whose customer buys for nonrational (and nonexperimental) reasons winds up helping the customer analyze exactly what tasks the robot is best equipped to handle and advising on potential system integration—or, at least, the vendor who wants repeat sales does. Vendors of personal computers (PC) for business managers, especially IBM, have done this effectively. Vendors help PC users organize into user groups to share tips and experiences. They publish newsletters with case histories of successful user applications. Basically, they are capitalizing—successfully—on the power of word-of-mouth advertising.

The third reason that the buying decision relative to manufacturing technologies is complex is that it is difficult to precisely identify the person who has the most say in the final decision from among the many people in various positions who are involved. Marketers in consumer goods sometimes refer to multiple decision makers as the *decision-making unit*; industrial marketers use the term *buying center* (Robinson, Farris, and Wind, 1967). Categorizing the purchase decision as a routine fully rebuy, a partial rebuy, or a new purchase, Robinson, Farris, and Wind found that two phenomena occur as the decision moves toward the new-purchase end of the spectrum. First, more stages in the decision process are involved—that is, there is a more protracted search and evaluation period—and, second, more people are involved in the ultimate decision. These findings were later confirmed in a Norwegian setting (Gronhaug, 1975).

Johnston and Bonoma (1981) not only confirmed the Robinson, Farris, and Wind theory that a new purchase (in contrast to rebuys) involves more people but also found that those people represent more functions in the organizational structure, vertically and horizontally. In the most exhaustive studies of complex decisions, the average number of individuals involved has been five to seven (Moriarty and Bateson, 1982).

The questions of concern to vendors are: Who really makes the decision among all these people, and on what bases? Knowledge of the customer is important not only for product-design and market-segmentation purposes but also so that one can target the influential people in the firm. But apparently those people are moving targets. Different individuals tend to be involved in major purchase decisions at different stages of the process (Brand, 1972), and even the participants themselves cannot agree as to which individuals wield the greatest influence in the purchase decision (Silk and Kalwani, 1981). In their supplier survey, Rosenthal and Vossoughi (1983) found that suppliers felt caught in a classic dilemma: "Decisions to adopt expensive factory-automation technologies are often made by managers who lack the background to assess technological options, while staff familiar with the new technologies are less able to appreciate associated strategic dimensions" (p. vi).

Even if vendors are able to determine the power bases and influence of the individuals involved, the strategic manufacturing environment is changing faster than are the financial reckoning mechanisms used to judge the worth of innovations. As Jelinek and Goldhar (1983) point out, the cost of the new integrated manufacturing "is often of the 'you bet your company' magnitude. Perhaps even more important than the cost, however, are the strategic implications—often unrealized by management until after the fact. You 'bet your company' here, too" (p. 33). (See also Chapter Nine.)

It is not always easy to persuade the financial analysts of these strategic advantages, yet financial people are part of the buying center. Research on the introduction of stand-alone numerically controlled machine tools shows that the majority of nonusers rejected the new equipment because they could not evaluate it and hence justify the investment (Putnam, 1978). A study of the adoption of CAM equipment in five companies showed that the firms had trouble deciding on financial grounds whether to make the purchase. The firms found that "analytical financial tools such as discounted cash flow are of limited utility" (Blumberg and Gerwin, 1984, p. 117). Vendors of advanced manufacturing technologies therefore have to lead, rather than follow, their customers in financial evaluation techniques.

In recent years, the limitations of conventional cost accounting have been explored by a number of researchers. As early as 1969, Dearden enumerated the problems with using return on investment (ROI) across the board in decentralized companies. Gold (1982a) states that although CAM evaluations should "conform to a company's normal framework for deciding on equipment proposals, . . . CAM does require a broadening of these criteria, a lengthening of the relevant time horizon, and a consideration of the long-term implications of saying no" (p. 93). The same author elsewhere observes (1982b) that firms continue to rely on capital-budgeting models for evaluating manufacturing technologies—models that worked reasonably well for incremental improvements in established technologies in the past but that have serious shortcomings in generating and evaluating proposals for major advances in technology like programmable automation (p. 144).

In this same article, Gold makes the point that the usual characterizations of capital as a fixed cost and labor as a variable cost may be outdated because unions resist reductions in labor in response to reduced output; therefore labor costs have become increasingly fixed. Meanwhile, the recent trend toward adjusting depreciation rates in response to changing levels of capacity utilization enhances the variability of total capital charges. Gold is not alone in seeing the need for changes in the way capital investments are evaluated. A well-known accounting expert, Robert Kaplan (1984), has called for innovations in accounting procedures to match the march of new technology in the other fields that are critical to corporations.

Robots provide an illustrative case of an innovation that on its own merits can rarely be justified in direct labor savings alone. As several authors have noted (Gold, 1982b; Ayres and Miller, 1983), direct wage and benefit payments to production workers constitute less than 20 percent of the total value of output on average. Therefore, labor reductions may not have that much impact on profit. The positive impact of robots and CAM on costs may come through better utilization of machinery and equipment. Given incomplete use of second or third shifts, time off for operator breaks and vacations, plus normal downtime, most machines are actually utilized only a fraction of the time theoretically possible. Ayres and Miller (1983) estimate that manually operated metal-cutting machines are in use 13 percent of the time. These authors write: "We believe the major quantifiable economic impact of robotics and CAM will be to expand sharply the effective capacity of production facilities by increasing both the amount of time per year the plant is operating and the throughput per shift" (p. 40). From this line of reasoning, they go on to conclude: "Assuming that there is a market for additional goods, an increase in output can be viewed as a reduction in unit cost. . . . Increased machine utilization resulting from the adoption of robotics can be viewed as recouping some of the capacity that was lost as a result of capital sharing" (pp. 45-46).

Other writers have suggested similarly expanded cost-analysis techniques for evaluating CAD. In addition to the fairly traditional productivity ratio (manual labor as a ratio to labor conducted with CAD), the author of a Klein newsletter suggests turnaround-time ratio, error-reduction ratio, cost of office space, operational cost, and payout period as a percentage of CAD net savings per month (Bakey, n.d.). Another example of creative ROI is offered by Votapka (1980), who suggests that CAD significantly reduces the product-development cycle and that these savings can be quantified: Each week saved has the potential of returning a given additional percentage or profit. As he comments wryly after presenting this argument: "Cost accountants may not allow this subjective evaluation in an ROI analysis, but it certainly is a way to sell a product-line manager on the concept of CAD" (p. 2).

Rosenthal and Vossoughi (1983) found that most of the users in their survey used traditional investment techniques in assessing payback on their automated manufacturing processes. However, asked about capabilities enhanced by the new system, 60 percent cited the ability to react more quickly than before to product-design changes; only 26 percent said their ability to offer competitive prices by holding costs down was improved. In the survey of manufacturing-technology suppliers conducted by these same authors, vendors reported that the prime reason for a decision against purchase was that the "proposed project did not meet investment criteria or that the expected returns could not be quantified adequately." It would seem that "suppliers . . . have an incentive to educate users on appropriate criteria for evaluating specific factory-automation options" (Rosenthal and Vossoughi, 1983, p. 20). Understanding the customer's business environment and CSFs will enable the vendor to help the customer develop a strong financial rationale.

Implementing the Purchase Decision

As the Rosenthal and Vossoughi (1983) survey of vendors showed, purchasers of computer-based manufacturing technologies rely heavily on their vendors for consulting, training,
and trouble shooting after the sale. Of the suppliers surveyed,
only one third felt their customers had "a realistic sense of the
time and other resources required to get [their] product operating smoothly" (p. 23). Thus, during and after the purchase decision, vendors are often responsible for the continued education
of their customers.

Education—not just training. Customers may look to suppliers for training in the use of new technologies, but in fact
good vendors are providing a good deal more than training. We
have already discussed the need for new ways of evaluating capital investments. Customers have to adjust many other operating
routines as well. People have a tendency to learn new things by
analogy and to allow their creativity to be blocked by previous
experience (Birch and Rabinowitz, 1951). Therefore, managers
and operators often fail to see the implications of the new technology for old practices.

Recounting General Motors's early experience in the
1970s with CAD/CAM, Ruff (1972) notes the tendency of an
organization to generate problem solutions that would have
been entirely appropriate with the old technology but that do
not match the characteristics of the new. "Sometimes these
[solutions] completely violate the integrity of the new process
and cascade a local problem into a global one. For example,
changes made to a die model with no comparable change to the
stored mathematical model result in a corrected checking fix-
ture but the subsequent machining of an incorrect die" (p. 8).

Users often need to establish entirely new operating performance measures. In the design department of General Motors, supervisors used to chart the progress and rate of work according to the releases of finished drawings. However, when
CAD was introduced, progress became invisible to the supervisors. Suddenly one day, a single computer run could generate
a drawing tape and a drafting machine could complete the work

at a rate measured in hundreds of inches per minute. Supervisors felt powerless to monitor or control the flow of work because hard copies of design no longer represented stages in the process. Instead, supervisors had to learn to measure progress by the growth of the mathematical data base for the designs. A wise salesperson knows the current practices of the company well enough to educate supervisors in the need for new performance measures to complement the new technologies. (See Chapter Seven for an example of revised performance measures.)

Today's vendors of computer-related technologies sometimes also find themselves in a peculiar role during implementation of a new system—that of negotiator between factions within the customer organization. Because new systems almost always require some development within the user corporation, vendors frequently have at least three sets of clients to satisfy: the technology-development group, the plant (manufacturing), and higher management. Vendors cannot just hand off the technology to the development group and leave. If manufacturing is not satisfied with the product, there will be no future sales. Therefore suppliers have to shepherd their product through the process of tailoring it to a particular customer's needs. When there is disagreement between development and manufacturing over who has responsibility for that customizing, the vendor may have to negotiate agreement between the parties. This rather nontraditional role exemplifies the kind of vendor involvement in implementation that is required in developing long-term relationships between suppliers and customers.

Other issues of new-technology implementation are covered amply elsewhere in this book. Many do not directly concern vendors; however, one theme that echoes throughout all the literature on new technologies is deserving of note here because it clearly delineates success from failure in many cases (Byham, 1984; Margulies and Colflesh, 1982): involvement of users in the choice of technology and the implementation plan. As one consultant study of robot installations concluded: "Failures seem to occur primarily when the workers, supervisors, and middle managers are not appropriately involved in the installation decision" (Byham, 1984, p. 62). A review of case studies in the literature on implementing new technologies came to a similar conclusion: lack of user participation in the decision process was associated with failures in implementation (Margulies and Colflesh, 1982). One of the significant findings for vendors in a number of recent studies is that the bottleneck for technology acceptance is often not at the top of the bottle or at the bottom but in the middle. That is, workers and top management may not be the chief sources of resistance, but supervisors and middle managers are (Zuboff, 1982; Foulkes and Hirsch, 1984). Vendors helping their customers plan the introduction of new technology would do well to keep this often-overlooked segment of the user population in mind during discussions of education plans.

Similarly, vendors may be able to help their customers avoid a subtle but important pitfall in managing the transition to automated processes. The software and hardware that make up a robot or an expert system cannot fully capture all the skills embodied by the operators whose functions they automate. The human skills that remain unembodied are therefore often lost to the organization when the operators leave. Not until the new system has been up and running for a while is the criticalness or unimportance of those skills evident. Because the environment and application for each system are unique in some way, vendors cannot guarantee that the skills being automated are captured completely by the computerized system.

Customers who assume that all the subtleties of their particular production process can be completely machine embodied are naive. Yet, because the workers whose functions are automated frequently remain to operate the new equipment, it is not immediately apparent whether some critical judgments based on long experience with this production process are still embodied only in the human operators. When these experienced workers leave, managers may expect that virtually anyone in a new wave of operators can run the equipment; that expectation can be disastrously untrue. At least part of the problem at the Three Mile Island nuclear-power-plant accident was that the operators of the heavily automated system did not understand the operations they were controlling. When the system failed, their responses were totally inappropriate (Stephens, 1980). In a plant, the disaster may be on a smaller scale—a line shut down instead of power plant shut down—but the problem is costly nevertheless. Again, the best deterrent to such problems is the involvement of users in the implementation phases, with some attention focused specifically on analyzing the extent to which important skills have been captured. Knowledgeable engineers working on expert systems are accustomed to this kind of analysis. Designers and vendors of other computerized processes are often not.

We have noted that the trend today is toward piecing together components sale by sale into systems. We have observed that the rebuy decision is a much easier sell than the new-buy decision. These observations add up to the conclusion that marketers of manufacturing innovations need to develop a commitment to continuing customer service and long relationships.

Conclusions

In this chapter we have attempted to summarize some of the key themes that emerge from a review of the industrial-marketing literature as it applies to the marketing of advanced manufacturing processes and to suggest ways in which marketing of these new systems is particularly challenging. The manufacturing environment is changing so rapidly that suppliers have greater need than ever to dog the footsteps of their customers, matching their own distinctive capabilities with the CSFs of their users to produce the needed products.

The role of vendors today extends beyond the traditional one in that they must not just train but must educate their customers. That task is complicated by the fact that the workings and benefits of these advanced technologies are much less accessible to prospective customers than similar investments have been in the past. Customers can rely neither on their own mechanical-engineering skills as a basis for technical judgments nor on previous experience with capital-budgeting decisions as a basis for financial evaluations of the new equipment. This lack of comparability to previous production-innovation situations makes the purchase decision difficult for users. The forces to change the bases for investment decisions must come not only from the users but from the suppliers. Vendors have a tremendous stake in seeing new and imaginative accounting procedures brought to bear on both the purchase decision and post-purchase cost and performance measurement.

The necessity for long-term, close relationships between suppliers and customers to meet world competition will probably force many of these changes. However, those vendors who are first to recognize the new climate will undoubtedly profit, much as vendors who foresaw the need for systems instead of stand-alone units have.

What are the implications for future research? Just as the concept of selling was expanded into the broader idea of marketing, so now marketing is being stretched at its conceptual boundaries to include the interface with product development upstream and with customer implementation of new processes downstream. The management of neither interface is well understood.

Vendors struggling with the necessity of bringing products to market quickly and with a high success ratio may believe that part of the solution to their problems lies in somehow involving marketing sooner or more effectively in new-product development than they now do. However, a crucial set of unresolved questions lies between the decision to integrate market-based information into development and the operationalization of that decision. How does one involve marketing soon enough in the development process to enhance the chances of market success, yet at the same time minimize the risk of stifling technological innovation? How does one nurture understanding of and respect for the different points of view held by marketing and R&D organizations so that product development moves smoothly? Remarkably little research is available on this important management issue, probably because of the same discipline-based biases that provoke the issue to begin with. We need to understand the mechanisms (for example, development of multiskilled people who move across functional boundaries), the organizational policies, and the cultural values that foster increased cooperation between marketing and other company functions. Cross-cultural comparisons would be useful. The Japanese, for example, organize rather differently, and some evidence indicates that they may bring products to market more rapidly than their counterpart U.S. firms (Inai, Nonaka, Takeuchi, 1984; Sasser and Wasserman, 1984).

The second interface requiring study is that between vendor and customer after the sale. As noted in this chapter, vendors have an increasing responsibility for implementation of their innovations. This trend toward extensive technical support after the sale, coupled with the new emphasis on long-term vendor-user relationships, again creates new managerial problems that are neither well understood nor researched.

We would hope that, without dismissing the traditional issues of industrial marketing, marketing practitioners and academics may turn some of their attention to the boundary-spanning issues raised in this chapter. Research on these topics will require a multidisciplinary approach and perhaps some action research, in which academics join with practitioners to produce learning through experimentation.

References

Allen, T. J. *Managing the Flow of Technology: Technology Transfer and the Dissemination of Technological Information Within the R&D Organization.* Cambridge, Mass.: MIT Press, 1977.

Anthony, R., and Dearden, J. *Management Control Systems.* (4th ed.) Homewood, Ill.: Irwin, 1980.

Arndt, J. "Toward a Concept of Domesticated Markets." *Journal of Marketing,* 1979, *43* (4), 69-75.

Ayres, R. U., and Miller, S. M. "Industrial Robots on the Line." *Technology Review,* 1983, *85* (4), 35-45.

Ayres, R. U., and Miller, S. M. "Robotic Realities: Near-Term Prospects and Problems." *Annals of the American Academy of Political and Social Science,* 1983, *470,* 28-55.

Bakey, T. "Economics of CAD." *S. Klein Newsletter on Computer Graphics.* Sudbury, Mass., n.d.

Balakrisha, G. "Better Use of the Industrial Marketing Concept." *Industrial Marketing Management*, 1978, *7*, 71–76.

Birch, H. G., and Rabinowitz, H. J. "The Negative Effect of Previous Experience on Productive Thinking." *Journal of Experimental Psychology*, 1951, *41*, 121–126.

Bitondo, D., and Frohman, A. "Linking Technological and Business Planning." *Research Management*, 1981, *24*, 19–23.

Blumberg, M., and Gerwin, D. "Coping with Advanced Manufacturing Technology." *Journal of Occupational Behavior*, 1984, *5*, 113–130.

Bonoma, T. V. "Major Sales: Who Really Does the Buying?" *Harvard Business Review*, 1982, *60* (3), 111–119.

Bonoma, T. V., and Shapiro, B. *Segmenting the Industrial Market*. Lexington, Mass.: Heath, 1983.

Brand, G. T. *The Industrial Buying Decision*. New York: Wiley, 1972.

Byham, W. C. "HRD and the Steel-Collar Worker." *Training*, 1984, *21* (1), 59–64.

"Changing a Corporate Culture: Can Johnson & Johnson Go from Band-Aids to High Tech?" *Business Week*, May 14, 1984, pp. 130–138.

Cooper, R. "Why New Industrial Products Fail." *Industrial Marketing Management*, 1975, *4*, 315–326.

Corey, E. R. "Key Options in Market Selection and Product Planning." *Harvard Business Review*, 1975, *53* (5), 119–128.

Dearden, J. "The Case Against ROI Control." *Harvard Business Review*, 1969, *47* (3), 124–135.

Evans, F. B. "Selling as a Dyadic Relationship—A New Approach." *American Behavioral Scientist*, 1963, *7* (9), 76–79. Cited in Bonoma and Shapiro.

Foulkes, F. K., and Hirsch, J. L. "People Make Robots Work." *Harvard Business Review*, 1984, *62* (1), 94–102.

Gadel, M. S. "Concentration by Salesmen on Congenial Prospects." *Journal of Marketing*, 1964, *28*, 64–66. Cited in Bonoma and Shapiro.

Gold, B. "CAM Sets New Rules for Production." *Harvard Business Review*, 1982a, *60* (6), 88–94.

Gold, B. "Robotics, Programmable Automation, and International Competitiveness." *IEEE Transactions on Engineering Management,* 1982b, *EM-29* (4), 135-146.

Graham, M., and Leonard-Barton, D. "Technology Transfer Within the Firm: A Framework for R&D Implementation." Paper presented at American Production and Inventory Control Society/Computer and Automated Systems Association/ Society of Manufacturing Engineers Synergy Conference, Chicago, Nov. 13-15, 1984.

Gronhaug, K. "Autonomous vs. Joint Decisions in Organizational Buying." *Industrial Marketing Management,* 1975, *4,* 265-271.

Hayes, R. H., and Wheelwright, S. C. *Restoring Our Competitive Edge: Competing Through Manufacturing.* New York: Wiley, 1984.

Hinson, R. "Robots Provide Improved Quality in Manufacturing." *Industrial Engineering,* 1984, *16* (1), 45-46.

Inai, K., Nonaka, I., and Takeuchi, H. "Managing New Production Development: Lessons from Japan." Paper presented at the Harvard Business School 75th Anniversary Colloquium on Productivity and Technology, Boston, 1984.

Jelinek, M., and Goldhar, J. D. "The Interface Between Strategy and Manufacturing Technology." *Columbia Journal of World Business,* 1983, *28* (1), 26-36.

Johnston, W. J., and Bonoma, T. V. "The Buying Center: Structure and Interaction Patterns." *Journal of Marketing,* 1981, *45,* 143-156.

Kaplan, R. S. "The Evolution of Management Accounting." *Accounting Review,* 1984, *59* (3), 390-418.

Levitt, T. "Marketing Myopia." *Harvard Business Review,* 1960, *38* (4), 45-56.

Lilien, G., and Johnston, P. *A Market Assessment for Active Solar Heating and Cooling Products.* Washington, D.C.: Active Buildings Systems Branch, Office of Solar Application for Buildings, Department of Energy, 1980.

Margulies, N., and Colflesh, L. "A Socio-Technical Approach to Planning and Implementing New Technology." *Training and Development Journal,* 1982, *36* (12), 16-29.

Meyer, M., and Roberts, E. *New Product Strategy in Small High*

Technology Firms. Sloan School of Management Working Paper No. 1428. Cambridge, Mass.: Massachusetts Institute of Technology, 1983.

Moriarty, R. T., and Bateson, J. E. G. "Exploring Complex Decision Making Units: A New Approach." *Journal of Marketing Research,* 1982, *19* (2), 182-191.

Myers, S., and Sweezy, E. E. "Why Innovations Fail." *Technology Review,* 1978, *80,* 40-46.

New, D. E., and Schlacter, J. L. "Abandon Bad R&D Projects with Earlier Marketing Appraisals." *Industrial Marketing Management,* 1979, *8,* 274-280.

Page, A. L., and Siemplenski, M. "Product Systems Marketing." *Industrial Marketing Management,* 1983, *12,* 89-99.

Putnam, G. P. "Why More NC Isn't Being Used." *Machine and Tool Blue Book,* 1978, 98-107. Cited in Blumberg and Gerwin.

Robinson, P. J., Farris, C. W., and Wind, Y. *Industrial Buying and Creative Marketing.* Boston: Allyn & Bacon, 1967.

Rockart, J. F. "Chief Executives Define Their Own Data Needs." *Harvard Business Review,* 1979, *57* (2), 81-93.

Rogers, E. M. *Diffusion of Innovations.* (3rd ed.) New York: Free Press, 1983.

Rosenthal, S. R., and Vossoughi, H. *Factory Automation in the U.S.: Summary of Survey Responses and Initial Commentaries.* Boston: School of Management, Boston University, 1983.

Ruff, K. *Managing the CAD/CAM Revolution.* Technical Paper MS72-910. Dearborn, Mich.: Society of Manufacturing Engineers, 1972.

Sasser, W. E., and Wasserman, N. *From Design to Market: The New Competitive Pressures.* Cambridge, Mass.: Harvard Graduate School of Business, 1984.

Silk, A. J., and Kalwani, M. U. *Measuring Influence in Organizational Purchase Decisions.* Sloan School of Management Working Paper 1077-79. Cambridge, Mass.: Massachusetts Institute of Technology, 1981.

Simon, H. A. *Administrative Behavior.* New York: Macmillan, 1947.

Simon, H. A. "A Behavioral Model of Rational Choice." *Quarterly Journal of Economics,* 1952, *69,* 99-118.

Skinner, W. "Manufacturing—Missing Link in Corporate Strategy." *Harvard Business Review,* 1969, *47* (3), 136-145.

Souder, W. E. "Promoting an Effective R&D/Marketing Interface." *Research Management,* 1980, *23* (4), 10-15.

Stephens, M. *Three Mile Island.* New York: Random House, 1980.

von Hippel, E. *Novel Product Concepts from Lead Users: Segmenting Users by Experience.* Sloan School of Management Working Paper No. 1476-83. Cambridge, Mass.: Massachusetts Institute of Technology, 1983.

Votapka, R. E. "A Practical Guide to the Selection and Implementation of a CAD System for Printed Circuits." Paper presented at the 2nd annual International Printed Circuit Conference, New York, Apr. 10, 1980.

Winter, R. E. "Acme-Cleveland is Making Risky Changes to Survive in New Machine-Tool Industry." *Wall Street Journal,* May 17, 1984, p. 1.

Yankee Group Factory Systems Planning Service. *Convergent Strategies.* Vol. 1: *CAD/CAM: From Design to Production.* Boston: Yankee Group Factory Systems Planning Service, 1983.

Yankee Group Factory Systems Planning Service. *The Next Generation of Robots.* Boston: Yankee Group Factory Systems Planning Service, 1984.

Zerkis, S. W. "MRP: A Micro Model." *Micro Manager,* Apr. 1984, pp. 9ff.

Zuboff, S. "New Worlds of Computer-Mediated Work." *Harvard Business Review,* 1982, *62* (5), 142-152.

❉ NINE ❉

Maximizing Strategic Opportunities in Implementing Advanced Manufacturing Systems

Mariann Jelinek
Joel D. Goldhar

The opportunities and the threats posed by the new technologies —computer-aided design, computer-aided manufacturing, computer-aided engineering, robotics, automated sensors, expert systems, and ultimately computer-integrated manufacturing— are widely discussed, but all too often discussion has been the end of the matter. Amid widespread calls for new public policy and reindustrialization, many perfectly practical, available advances are often ignored. All too often, either the new technologies are not acquired at all or they are acquired but sit unused. Even worse, failed implementation can produce bitterness, resentment, and lingering resistance. Effective implementation is still often problematical. The thesis of this chapter is that although there is no simple technological fix, effective implementation is both urgent and possible.

To achieve effective implementation, barriers at two levels must be overcome. First, at the strategic level, we must appreciate the true nature of the challenge facing us and the real opportunity it presents for business—not in any vague, abstract sense, but in concrete terms. The mission and purpose of the firm and its relation to its chosen market must be reconsidered in light of the new technologies. Second, at the operating level,

effective implementation requires a new emphasis on the human aspects of the situation: learning, potential resistance, the
displacement of human beings by machines, the changed role
of human beings in manufacturing, and new relationships
among functional departments, among others. Effective implementation can pay enormous dividends to individual companies
and, in the aggregate, to society as a whole. Without attention
to the strategic and operational problems, however, the technology will fail.

   We will begin with a brief survey of the state of the art in
technology, especially in manufacturing. A look at market
trends and their implications for manufacturing will follow.
These two lines of discussion lead to the inescapable conclusion
that advanced manufacturing technologies are not optional
luxuries but necessities. Next, we will turn to the difficulties impeding effective implementation of the new technologies. At
the strategic level, a new understanding of technology in the
firm is needed. At the operational level, new understanding
must focus on the relationship between technology and human
beings. We will close with recommendations for successful implementation.

State of the Art and Trends in Technology

   Manufacturing and Electronics. The application of electronics to manufacturing technology is widespread and growing
daily. At the simplest level, electronic controls are now routinely used to govern the operation of manufacturing processes
—virtually any process. For instance, machines supervised by
numerical control or programmable logic controllers routinely
execute programmed sets of instructions. Although programs
can be input by keyboard or tape or read electronically from
local memory, instructions can also be sent automatically from
a controlling computer. The computer can be programmed to
send new instructions after the old set is finished, to coordinate
the activities of many machines, and to stop in the event of difficulties (such as running out of materials, tool-point tempera-
tures beyond a specified range, broken tools) or for routine main-

tenance. Computers coordinate both action sequences among machines over time and contingent responses. In some cases, expert systems allow sophisticated computer judgment and analysis. Such controls offer significant advantages over previous ones: increased reliability of process, lower operating costs, increased machine usage (and thus increased productivity), smoother operations, better scheduling of maintenance, less waste, and, typically, better quality. Instructions, monitoring, corrections, and coordination can be provided automatically, once programmed (Bright, 1958; Faunce, 1965; *IEEE Spectrum,* 1983).

The same advantages are also available in other areas besides manufacturing. Computer-aided design (CAD) makes use of electronics and software to ensure that designs are completely accurate and within specified constraints (such as materials strength or desired physical geometry). Because of large-scale memory, computers can facilitate the design of highly complex equipment such as large steam turbines for generating electricity. General Electric routinely designs turbines using computers to keep track of the 350,000 parts and their placement. Because design constraints can be programmed, the designer need not consciously take them into account. General Electric can ensure that limits on strength of materials, weight, or dimensions are attained, and that two designers do not choose the same place for different parts of the equipment, according to General Electric managers (Jelinek, 1983). St. Gobain, the glassmaker, uses CAD to achieve precise volume control, while designers concentrate on elegant designs for perfume or liquor bottles. Similarly, General Motors used CAD to downsize the Cadillac Seville, and in 1978 CAD was credited with cutting a year from the time needed to design the X-body car. Boeing used CAD to design its 757 and 767 aircraft simultaneously—a feat possible only because computers provided vastly increased design productivity and reliable records of all the details (Goldhar and Jelinek, 1983). Lockheed used CAD extensively for the C-5, C-130, and C-141 transports, with productivity improvements of from 33 to 97 percent (Barnette, 1982). Ensuring timely updating of engineering drawings to reflect changes is itself a significant recording process with an important impact on quality assurance, delivery dates, and costs. In addition, computers can automatically detect flaws or inadequacies in design long before the commitment to prototypes or production tooling makes correction expensive. Connecting CAD with simulation programs to test design adequacy is an area of high interest.

Integration of various computer controlled functions promises a still larger impact. What is new here is the automation of a portion of the knowledge governing machine use and, importantly, the connection of all this information into a system. Computers assist both design and actual manufacturing processes. They can also control loading and unloading of work pieces, delivery of raw materials, and the transfer of work pieces from one stage in the process to another, as well as the accounting and record keeping associated with these functions (Hughes and Hegland, 1983). In addition, order entry, packaging, shipping, procurement, and inventory control are susceptible to computer management. Each individual function gains the advantages of accuracy, speed, quality, and reliability, but connections among them significantly multiply the benefits of automating individual machines, functions, or systems (*American Machinist,* 1985; Goldhar and Jelinek, 1983; *IEEE Spectrum,* 1983). Without such integration the maximum potential of advanced technologies will not be achieved (Salzman, 1981).

Trends. Many of the examples given here are drawn from metal working, discrete-parts manufacturing, and heavy manufacturing. However, a variety of other industries and operations are also amenable to computer controls, including semiconductor manufacture; design, manufacture, assembly, and test of electronic components or equipment, automobiles, aircraft, and appliances; printing and publishing, and information transfer and processing generally; and inventory, order, materials-control, and shipping operations. These examples suggest some important trends in technology, with applications well beyond metal machining or heavy manufacturing. Among the advantages of advanced technology presently available are increased scientific knowledge, improved process controls, new materials, new processes, increased product complexity, programmable "just about everything," increased integration, and the multiple use of information (Goldhar and Jelinek, 1983; National Research Council, 1984).

In short, the factory of the future exists now. Production technology is not a barrier to accomplishing wholesale improvements in process, control, reliability, productivity, and flexibility. Yet, despite all this technology at hand and all the potential it promises, implementation has been slow. Yes, there are many examples of advanced manufacturing plants, planning and control systems, and the like; but they are limited typically to the largest, most sophisticated users, despite compelling economic arguments and increasingly reasonable price (see Chapter Five). In any case, application of the new knowledge is not as widespread as it could be. Thus many opportunities for improvement are missed, while competitors (often from abroad) make steady inroads by utilizing the sort of knowledge we ignore.

A look at some of the consequences of using advanced technology will underline both the urgent need to adopt them and some of the difficulties impeding implementation.

Consequences of Advanced Technology. Advanced manufacturing technologies radically shift production economics, principally by streamlining the transfer and use of information: Advanced systems are information driven. Because electronic information can be economically accessed and transferred and repeatedly used again in identical or varied form, change at the production stage is low in cost. As a result, variable costs per unit decline, and there is a relatively flat learning curve. The equipment does not learn anything through repetitions, as a human operator would; it merely replicates its program. Short-run average costs approach long-run average costs, and learning advances are pushed back into the design phase, where, typically, CAD systems assist in developing the most effective designs, the most economical pattern layout, and the like (General Electric's reported tripling of productivity underlines the point; General Electric, 1985).

As with process production systems, automated technology creates highly integrated systems with little room for error and little opportunity for error (because much operation is computer controlled). When design changes occur or improved methods are developed for production, they can be swiftly adopted. These new systems require a substantial investment in software as well as hardware, but often the software itself produces substantial savings. For instance, one General Electric unit reported labor savings of 3:1 to 5:1 in comparison with manual methods but 6:1 to 10:1 for updating drawings already on the software system (Cheeseman, 1983); Lockheed-Georgia experienced a 97 percent productivity increase for inking final drawings (Barnette, 1982).

Operating characteristics of the computer-integrated factory reflect the underlying technology and emphasize accuracy, reliability, cost control, and product variability. The economic order quantity approaches one because variety has little or no penalty at the production stage. Indeed, the potential for variety may well be engineered into products, along with manufacturability. Costs per unit are quite insensitive to production volumes for individual designs because the equipment does not "care" whether it makes an extended run of many units or an extended run of a wide range of units. The changeover costs are small because tool changes are typically automatic, and program change electronic. Production scheduling too is electronic and thus changeable in response to changing priorities, materials availability, season, and the like. Response to changes in product design, market demand, or production mix is also easy.

Joint cost economics and economies of scope, reflecting the benefits of equipment range and adaptability, will be the norm (Baumol and Braunstein, 1977; Braunstein, 1976; Goldhar and Jelinek, 1983). The value of a new-technology manufacturing system is a function of the bundle of products (or activities) it produces, and they are limited more by imagination and design creativity than by the technology itself. Thus, extensive and expensive preproduction support activities like engineering, process design, software engineering and marketing, in various combinations, will be quite important. Emphasis will shift from management responsibilities traditionally considered line toward staff and engineering support activities; much of the routine line activity will be automated, leaving managers actively engaged in planning, creative problem solving, and personnel management. Because much operation will be unmanned, shop personnel will typically supervise machine operation rather than perform operations themselves. Fewer, higher skilled, better paid, and more autonomous people will be required than now are, and, to manage them, new policies for training, motivation, and reward will be needed.

The new technologies open possibilities for control and flexibility, accuracy and responsiveness—characteristics not readily coupled together in the past. Indeed, under previous assumptions of economies of scale, these characteristics were traded off against one another: Control was acquired at the cost of flexibility, and automated accuracy precluded flexibility (Abernathy, 1978). Programmable controls do provide the accuracy, speed, and reliability of automation—together with flexibility and responsiveness hitherto simply not available. Moreover, the savings that result from improved control and maintenance, better waste rates and materials usage, improved machine utilization, decreased inventories, and the like themselves often fund the new equipment.

Table 1 summarizes and compares the consequences of old and new technologies.

Table 1. Assumptions Underlying Old and New Technologies.

Old Technologies	New Technologies
Economies of scale	Economies of scope
Experience-curve economics	Anomalous product life cycles
Task specialization	Multimission jobs
Market focus	Market segmentation (many market niches)
Standardization	Variety
Expensive flexibility and variety	Profitable flexibility and variety

Devising New Policies

Strategies. To attain these advantages demands a corporate strategy founded on a thoroughgoing appreciation of the strategic characteristics of the technology. Expanded time horizons, looking well beyond today's product or its associated product lines to the integrated potential of the firm's capabilities in manufacturing, marketing, engineering, and distribution, are required. Changed perspectives on capital budgeting that emphasize flexibility, change, and the benefits of alternatives, not the stability of the past, will be needed. Old marketing assumptions too must be revised.

The new technology mandates flexibility, responsiveness, and change. Programmable controls imply the capacity for one-at-a-time, irregular production that is adaptable to product changes. Simulation and experimentation are encouraged by the technology's capabilities for change and, in their turn, encourage additional product change. Custom products, tailored products, and, importantly, the simultaneous production of a range of products on the same equipment suggest new marketing and corporate strategies. Product life cycles can be short because there is little cost to variation; improvements can be quickly embodied. All these features argue for proliferated product lines and market segments, together with an increasing emphasis on quality and reliability. New approaches to marketing, emphasizing new skills in salespeople, and new expectations for change must become the norm in order to maximize these possibilities for flexibility, responsiveness, and change. (See Chapter Eight.)

The competitive strategies that play to these strengths, utilizing advanced manufacturing capabilities as a lever, result in a different way of doing business from the old identification of the company with a single product or a narrow product line. This possibility is both a threat and an opportunity. Because few comprehend the strategic options, few adopt the technology for appropriate strategic purposes (Skinner, 1984; Goldhar and Jelinek, 1983). Those who do understand the possibilities can reap rich rewards, however.

The new strategies should include deliberate efforts to proliferate product designs and product lines and deliberate efforts to truncate or shorten the product life cycle (or, alternatively, to extend it substantially by incorporating a continuous stream of improvements in order to fend off competitors). Flexible companies will deliberately use production expertise to provide responsiveness to customer needs along with quality, which also appeals to customers. Such approaches run counter to the demands of the manufacturing systems of the past (even the recent past). Previous strategies are based on assumptions about what existing factories do well: economically manufacturing long runs of standard products over an extended period of time, with slow, incremental changes in product and process tied to expensive shifts in specialized equipment.

In contrast, the flexibility of new systems makes change easy and relatively inexpensive and provides a broad set of output options. Thus, deliberate efforts to fragment the market can create useful barriers to competitors' entry. Responsiveness and quick turnaround are fundamental strengths, opportunities for competitive advantage rather than costly problems to be avoided.

Providing a variety of products and product lines is a complex undertaking. In the past, simply proliferating product lines made little sense: The economic results of widely diversified conglomerates were inferior to the returns attained over the long run by the related diversifieds, companies that used some common focus to multiply competitive advantages (Rumelt, 1982). Only a few old technologies encouraged product-line proliferation; the German dye-making industry as early as 1913 offers a historic example, with its worldwide position assured by factories that routinely made several thousand dyes. In contrast, British dye manufacturers struggled to control the manufacture of four or five dyes (Chandler, 1984). Today, once again, manufacturing technology itself frequently provides both the common thread and the basis for diversity.

Both the expanded range of products and the increased rate of change take on strategic importance, as does the increased sophistication being built into products. Complexity and change make it difficult for competitors to copy a product, so complexity and change (together with products designed for manufacturability) become desirable strategic commitments (Kanter, 1983, 1984). "Creaming" may well be the strategy of choice with new products, followed by swift introduction of new features as entry barriers. Consequently, old marketing theories about positioning, segmentation, penetration, and pricing must be reviewed and possibly abandoned. Entirely new marketing tactics must be developed to embrace and take advantage of change rather than to avoid it. (See Chapter Eight.)

Thus, the technology both commands and results from changed strategic thinking. When "What business are we in?" can have multiple answers, investment in the multimission machinery and flexible, high-capacity information systems to make it possible is no longer a luxury—nor is continued attention to business strategy and its evolution. Advanced manufacturing systems will produce their benefits only if managers exploit their flexibility, accuracy, and economy. Research, engineering, and marketing must deliver a constant stream of new products and product improvements. Distribution and marketing must aim at identifying fragmented or fragmentable market segments and perhaps at resegmenting or refragmenting the market repeatedly. Aggressive emphasis on product quality and features, as well as price, can protect market position, but such a strategy must rest on close links between marketing, product design, and manufacturing, as well as customers and suppliers (Hayes and Garvin, 1982). New organizational forms and management modes, fostering such links, will also be needed.

This sort of innovation cannot readily bubble up from the bottom; it requires a broad redefinition of mission and a companywide determination of new directions. It is a top-down responsibility. Patterns of organizational structure, communication, authority, and responsibility as well as evaluation systems all may well change in response to these new directions. To succeed, such initiatives demand the commitment of the board of directors and senior management; they are simply too broad for piecemeal approaches and carry too much risk and cost (Goldhar and Jelinek, 1983).

Assessing the success and effectiveness of new manufacturing systems will require new criteria, not simply the short-focus financial criteria of the past (Blumberg and Gerwin, 1984; Gold, 1982; Goldhar and Jelinek, 1983; Kaplan, 1984). New criteria must recognize that, rather than stability as in the past, flexibility will be the norm. Many blame the failure to recognize the strategic potential of advanced systems and continued piecemeal, short-term assessment for the delay in U.S. implementation of available technology (Gold, 1982; Kaplan, 1984; Skinner, 1984). A system's ability to deal with variety and complexity becomes a key strategic variable. Its turnaround capability, lead and surge times may be far more important than its capacity for extended runs. Accuracy and product quality, no longer simply traded off against speed and reliability, combine to create competitive advantage and to attain new minimum levels of acceptability. A system's potential for integration, and thus its potential for capturing the many advantages and economies of automated control and management at all stages of the cycle of conceive, design, make, and market, will also be important.

Implementation Tactics. The tactical side of the implementation problem seems obvious. Resistance to change has long been recognized; the word *sabotage* comes from the French *sabot*—the wooden shoes protesting workers threw into machinery to break up the wooden gears of the early textile mills. We tend to expect difficulties with employees, especially at lower levels, assuming resistance is inevitable and must be overcome. But perhaps we have misdefined the problem by classifying resistance to change as an immutable, inescapable human characteristic. Perhaps we should take potential resistance seriously and try to address people's concerns. Their concerns are legitimate; all the answers, particularly for society as a whole, have not been found. At the level of the individual organization, there are compelling reasons to take potential resistance seriously, to deal with it as an important facet of implementation. The complexity and pervasiveness of the technological impact with advanced manufacturing systems make the commitment of people across the organization and at many levels crucial to successful implementation. (See Chapters Four and Eight.) People are an absolutely central resource. The suggestions offered here are neither original nor startling. They do take seriously both the employer's obligation to employees and the employees' concerns about advanced technologies.

Four key facets of the new technology and its impacts underline the importance of considering human aspects. First, the decision process for new systems is far more complex than for older manufacturing technology. The traditional distinction between deciding what to do—formulating a solution—and actually doing it—implementing a solution—is largely inapplicable when dealing with the new technologies. To begin with, deciding on a solution is not a simple choice among a limited set of alternatives. Instead, it is an iterative process of exploring options, making trade-offs, considering the fit of components, envisioning wholly new possibilities, and changing criteria. This complexity is simply not susceptible to a single synoptic, all-inclusive decision from on high. (See Chapter Eight for a discussion of this decision process.) Senior management will have important input but will almost surely lack the detailed, hands-on familiarity with operations that such decisions require. Organizational members down to the shop floor are likely to have important insights that can assist implementation if they are brought into the decision process.

A second facet contributing to the importance of the human aspects of implementation is related: The new technology affects the business widely. People in all departments as well as at all levels will necessarily find their jobs and, importantly, their relationships with one another changed. Consequently, decisions about manufacturing systems are not simply manufacturing decisions. Instead, because these changes are so pervasive, perspectives from such diverse departments as marketing, research and development, finance, and human resources are essential. This input is desirable both because the solution that evolves should serve multiple constituencies and because these constituents will be the users of the new system. They should thus be actively represented in the decision process. Implementation will be facilitated enormously when it is seen from its initial stages not as "manufacturing's baby" but rather as "the

future of every one of us in the firm." A wide range of communication and information-gathering techniques (such as survey
feedback, brown-bag lunches with management, and cross-
departmental teams) can be used.

By the time the decision is made to proceed with a new
technology, the process of implementation has begun—wide,
early participation has already started to engender people's
commitment to success. At the earliest stages, the rationale for
adoption as well as the concerns and requirements of users must
be widely shared as part of the decision process. It is not nearly
enough to announce that automation will take place, that it will
produce many benefits, and that it is economically attractive.

The third facet of the human side of implementation occurs after the solution is decided on. A great many other difficulties, only partially predictable, lie ahead. These difficulties
flow from the many detailed arrangements, interconnections,
adjustments, and explorations required to truly utilize new
technology to its fullest. Users must try the system, consider
its strengths and weaknesses, and discover (or invent) new possibilities for exploiting it. This needed input from users, like the
decision process that preceded it, should be both broad and
deep. At the managerial level, some tasks formerly central—in
reconciling competing needs, deciding among priorities, reallo-
cating resources, and rescheduling—will be either ceded to the
computer (through an automatic schedule, for instance) or dele-
gated to others (as when rescheduling by inserting priority jobs
becomes a minor supervisory or clerical task). Managers will
find supervisors taking on many tasks that were previously important parts of the management job. Refocusing managerial
attention and reassuring managers that their jobs have not dis-
appeared are essential. Retraining or other support may be required (Foulkes and Hirsch, 1984; Zuboff, 1982).

At the supervisory level, automated systems can provide
real assistance. Especially when such systems incorporate record keeping, they can eliminate much of the drudgery of reconciling job time with time reports, tracking work in process or
inventory, and rescheduling, for instance. Supervisors may have
important, detailed insights into where previous systems com-

promised—and why new technology should not be simply an automation of previous practices. Problems can be eliminated before the new system is cast in concrete or as programming is designed. Supervisors can also play a key role in communicating to subordinates about the incoming technology, their revised roles, and how they can assist. Here, too, perhaps even more clearly than at the managerial level, a redirection of attention is needed. Supervisors can get on with managing their people and processes (Foulkes and Hirsch, 1984; Zuboff, 1982). (See Chapter Six for a discussion of successes and failures of supervisory communication.)

The shop-floor personnel are another crucial group; their knowledge and involvement can make the difference between failure and success. In particular, given the ocean of details involved in any new system, operatives, if encouraged, can provide ideas as well as insight into gaps in existing procedures. The legitimate concerns of shop-floor employees, like those of managers and supervisors, also need to be addressed. With effective communication and a commitment that shop-floor employees will not bear the brunt of the human costs of the new technology, their cooperation can be gained. As but one example of what is possible, a major manufacturer has installed an integrated manufacturing system with cooperation from its strong union; one important understanding was that computer controls would not be used to check up on people (Jelinek, 1983).

Clearly, human-resource needs become directly visible at the shop-floor level. Employees need time to become acquainted with the new equipment early on, before they must operate it, to ensure adequate training as well as input. When questions can be raised and answered beforehand, actual implementation will go far more smoothly, with less anxiety and more opportunity for success, than when concerns are not addressed in advance. Participation, training, and repeated communication seem to be the keys. Employees can be involved in designing their own training and the orientation for others, for example.

Finally, the fourth tactical aspect that affects people is the systematic integration of the new technology into business operations. To implement and operate the new technologies over time, supports beyond ad hoc teams and arrangements will be needed. Assuming that top-level commitment is in place, a series of changes in organizational arrangements will be needed to ensure widespread involvement and participation at lower levels. Some change can begin informally, with top-level backing of results-oriented team efforts across departments (in place of compartmentalized activities, for instance). Other changes, such as new sorts of performance assessment and evaluation, and new communications patterns, will likely require formal recognition. Performance can be assessed on the basis of cooperation and new-product introduction rather than simply totting up efficiency measures, for instance; decision responsibility can be moved. Ultimately, by such arrangements, the organization itself must facilitate the sort of cooperative interchange the new technology demands. Whereas older technologies offered higher returns for stability and were therefore served best by stable, change-resistant organizations, newer technologies will offer higher returns to organizations that encourage change, facilitate it, and foster it through more fluid organizational structures emphasizing flexibility and information processing (Galbraith, 1977; Jelinek, Litterer, and Miles, 1981).

Recommendations for Implementation Success

Both strategic and tactical imperatives directly suggest approaches for implementing new technologies that are radically different from the approaches suitable for old technologies. Operating assumptions must be based on the fundamental characteristics of the technology itself. Because of the complexity, the protracted and incremental process of decision and implementation, and the flexibility associated with the new systems, old assumptions cannot serve. For managers, the implications include substantial shifts in thinking about the new technology. These counterintuitive strategies for success with the new technology are outlined here.

First, invest in flexibility, despite its apparent high cost.

It no longer entails the limitations of the past, although it does carry costs of its own (especially in implementation).

Second, assume a lengthy decision process characterized by broad and deep participation. Patience and care will produce effectiveness (although the path to the decision may seem inefficient). Effectiveness here will pay enormous dividends in later efficiency; haste can be extraordinarily costly.

Third, all levels and all departments of the organization should participate and should be encouraged to give in-depth consideration to the impact of changes. Seek out democratic involvement because many viewpoints, especially on current problems, pay dividends in improvements.

Fourth, anticipate learning as you go, and prepare for incremental implementation. Plan, too, for incremental change in organizational systems to maximize benefits from the new system.

Fifth, take deliberate steps to control markets, utilizing new technological capabilities: These steps include proliferating product designs, truncating product life cycles, emphasizing quality and reliability as measures of value, customizing products to users' specifications, emphasizing product complexity, and increasing the rate of change in products.

Sixth, compete broadly across many segments by fragmenting the market. Look for opportunities to refragment or resegment, based on new developments, new improvements, alternatives, and tailoring.

Seventh, build strong engineering, market-research, and expanded distribution capacities as support for increased manufacturing abilities.

Such wholesale change does not happen overnight or without unforeseen difficulties. It is quite simply impossible to forecast all the difficulties of implementation beforehand. Even off-the-shelf systems require some tailoring to individual situations. Even companies used to change find that making haste slowly makes sense. Nevertheless, the need for progress is urgent. Technological opportunities are successful responses to developments that, not responded to, constitute threats. Difficulties with people are the outcomes of efforts too hasty, too central-ized, or insufficiently open to perceive and respond to predict-able problems.

Successful implementation is characterized by the counter-intuitive approaches outlined here. Both older businesses and in-dustries (like turbines, steel, metal working) and newer ones (electronic controls and equipment, telecommunications) have successfully implemented advanced manufacturing systems. Al-though there is no simple technological fix to problems of worldwide competition and productivity, new technology car-ries with it many possibilities that can be realized through the use of new strategies and tactics. Technology coupled with new strategic thinking and careful attention to human and organiza-tional dimensions can spell success.

References

Abernathy, W. J. *The Productivity Dilemma: Roadblock to In-novation in the Automobile Industry.* Baltimore, Md.: Johns Hopkins University Press, 1978.

American Machinist. "The Interface Challenge." *American Ma-chinist,* Special Report 772, Jan. 1985, pp. 95-102.

Barnette, J. N. "CAD System Boosts Morale and Productivity." *Industrial Research and Development,* 1982, *24,* 126-129.

Baumol, W. J., and Braunstein, Y. M. "Empirical Study of Scale Economies and Production Complementarity: The Case of Journal Publication." *Journal of Political Economy,* 1977, *85,* 1037-1048.

Blumberg, M., and Gerwin, D. "Coping with Advanced Manu-facturing Technology." *Journal of Occupational Behavior,* 1984, *5,* 113-130.

Braunstein, Y. M. "Economic and Public Policy Issues in Scien-tific and Technical Information." Unpublished paper, Depart-ment of Library and Information Systems, University of Cali-fornia at Berkeley, Mar. 1976.

Bright, J. R. *Automation and Management.* Cambridge, Mass.: Harvard University Press, 1958.

Chandler, A. D., Jr. Private communication, 1984.

Cheeseman, C. E. "One Version of a Factory with a Future—Today!" Speech delivered to the Western Metal and Tool Exposition and Conference, Los Angeles, Mar. 21-24, 1983.

Faunce, W. A. "Automation and the Division of Labor." *Social Problems,* 1965, *23* (2), 149-160.

Foulkes, F. K., and Hirsch, J. L. "People Make Robots Work." *Harvard Business Review,* 1984, *62* (1), 94-102.

Galbraith, J. R. *Organization Design.* Reading, Mass.: Addison-Wesley, 1977.

General Electric. "Leave Success Behind." Advertisement in the *Wall Street Journal,* Jan. 17, 1985, p. 13.

Gold, B. "CAM Sets New Rules for Production." *Harvard Business Review,* 1982, *60* (6), 88-94.

Goldhar, J. D., and Jelinek, M. "Plan for Economies of Scope." *Harvard Business Review,* 1983, *62* (6), 141-148.

Hayes, R. H., and Garvin, D. A. "Managing As If Tomorrow Mattered." *Harvard Business Review,* 1982, *60* (3), 71-78.

Hughes, T., and Hegland, D. "Flexible Manufacturing—The Way to the Winner's Circle." *Production Engineering,* Sept. 1983, pp. 54-63.

IEEE Spectrum, May 1983 (entire issue).

Jelinek, M. "Rethink Strategy or Perish: Technology Lessons from Telecommunications." *Journal of Production Innovation Management,* 1983, *1,* 36-42.

Jelinek, M., Litterer, J. A., and Miles, R. E. *Organizations by Design.* Plano, Tex.: Business Publications, 1981.

Kanter, R. M. *The Change Masters.* New York: Simon & Schuster, 1983.

Kanter, R. M. "Innovation—The Only Hope for Times Ahead?" *Sloan Management Review,* 1984, *25* (4), 51-55.

Kaplan, R. S. "Yesterday's Accounting Undermines Production." *Harvard Business Review,* 1984, *62* (4), 95-101.

National Research Council. *Computer Integration of Engineering Design and Production: A National Opportunity.* Washington, D.C.: National Research Council, 1984.

Rumelt, R. R. "Diversification Strategy and Profitability." *Strategic Management Journal,* 1982, *3* (4), 359-370.

Salzman, R. M. "The Impact of Automation on Engineering/

Manufacturing Productivity." In J. Mermet (Ed.), *CAD in Medium Sized and Small Industries.* Amsterdam: North-Holland, 1981.

Skinner, W. "Operations Technology: Blind Spot in Strategic Management." *Interfaces,* 1984, *14* (1), 116–125.

Zuboff, S. "New Worlds of Computer-Mediated Work." *Harvard Business Review,* 1982, *62* (5), 145–152.

Fostering Innovation: Economic, Technical, and Organizational Issues

William A. Hetzner
J. D. Eveland
Louis G. Tornatzky

The current debate over whether there should be a national industrial policy is not new, but it has recently taken on new seriousness and contentiousness. Particular concern has focused on international industrial competitiveness and on the relatively low rate of growth in productivity, especially in the traditional manufacturing sector. Since the mid-1960s, foreign competition has reduced U.S. exports and is now challenging our large domestic markets. The extraordinary strength of the dollar during 1984 apparently only served to amplify this trade deficit. Clearly, the crisis in manufacturing is becoming critical.

To some analysts, this crisis signals that the usual governmental policy levers of taxes, regulation, patent policy, trade policy, and the like have been insufficient to stem the tide of foreign products entering this country and that direct means of intervention by the government should be initiated. Others feel that the policy levers have simply been inappropriately applied and that the government's role should be confined to making

Note: Opinions, findings, conclusions, or recommendations expressed in this chapter are ours and do not reflect the views of the National Science Foundation, by whom two of us were employed when portions of this chapter were written.

sure that our foreign competitors play according to the rules while staying out of the affairs of U.S. firms.

Both sides tend to concur, however, that advanced manufacturing technology is the key to restoring economic balance, although they disagree strongly over how to facilitate the deployment of such technology. Unfortunately, the dialogue has tended to be ideological, narrow, and generally uninformed by empirical data. It has usually ignored three important characteristics of the situation that constrain what government can and cannot do to improve industrial productivity and economic growth.

First, although advanced manufacturing technologies can have significant economic benefits, their introduction and use can be a time-consuming process with significant social, behavioral, and technical costs as well as benefits. Second, significant problems are involved not only in the creation of these technologies but also in their delivery, implementation, and use. Finally, the federal government is already a major actor in the development and use of advanced manufacturing technologies but has generally failed to take advantage of its position. This chapter will describe each of these characteristics of advanced manufacturing technology in some detail and will discuss their implications for national policy.

Economic, Technical, and Organizational Dimensions

The economic advantage of advanced manufacturing technology lies in improved quality and increased flexibility. (See Chapter Nine for a discussion of the attributes of advanced manufacturing technologies and their importance to strategy.) Different models of the same product or different products can be manufactured on the same line and with uniform quality. Machines perform both physical work and information processing. Production processes can be interactively linked to design, marketing, inventory control, and other functions.

However, achieving these benefits often takes years and considerable effort. A firm must have resources—both capital and labor—and the willingness and strategic vision to stick with

its decision even though it is uncertain about the costs and ultimate magnitude of the benefits of these technologies. As Gold
(1982) and Kaplan (1983) suggest, decisions concerning advanced manufacturing technology are often more a matter of
faith than of quantitative economic analysis. Hayes and Abernathy (1980) argue that the inability of the United States to
deploy the new technological possibilities that would make the
country competitive in world markets is the result primarily of
strategic and management decisions made at the level of the
firm; U.S. managers have generally chosen not to use available
tools because of the technological, economic, and even political
risks involved. (See Chapter Three for a discussion of managerial
rigidity.)

It is clear that advanced manufacturing technologies tend
to require large-scale implementation and systematic management. (See Chapter Five for data on the adoption of advanced
manufacturing technologies.) There are currently no turnkey
advanced manufacturing systems. Each application requires significant engineering and experimentation with relatively untried
technologies, often to the point of reinvention (Eveland, Rogers, and Klepper, 1977).

Furthermore, significant software and social and organizational factors must be considered. Radical manufacturing innovations often require equally radical organizational and managerial innovations. Routine, predictable tasks are absorbed by
the technology, leaving unpredictable and complex process-
control and maintenance tasks (Davis, 1981). Traditional organizational forms with their emphasis on division-of-labor,
rigid and hierarchical authority structures, and fixed communication patterns seem to run counter to the desired flexibility of
advanced manufacturing technologies. Although direct labor is
reduced, the firm is increasingly dependent on the quality and
responsiveness of those workers that remain.

A firm must explicitly consider how the technology and
associated organizational systems are to be designed and implemented. It must make a set of explicit choices not only about
whether to retain and retrain workers but also about how workers will be organized and supervised in light of changing skill

and responsibility requirements. How managers, technical staff, and workers will interact in the implementation of the new technology and organization is also often unclear (Noble, 1979). Nondecisions or decisions by default are almost certain precursors of disaster.

Unfortunately, the backgrounds and experiences of managers and the reward systems operating in industry, government, and academia have not proved conducive to the development and application of strategic vision about either technology or human resources. Captains of industry and government are more likely to have financial and legal than technical, manufacturing, or human-resource backgrounds. Moreover, managers and corporate officers often change jobs too quickly to see the long-term benefits of introducing large-scale technical or organizational changes—although the short-range costs may be all too apparent. Decisions about organization are often left to engineers and system designers who are relatively unaware of either the range of possible choices or their economic and social implications.

Other governments, particularly in Japan and Western Europe, have been much more attentive than the U.S. government to the systemic nature of manufacturing. For example, Sweden encourages social and technical experimentation by firms and conducts case studies of those experiments that are made available to other firms. Similarly, the governments of Norway and of the Netherlands maintain staffs of consultants and researchers to work with firms introducing new technological and managerial innovations.

Implementation Dynamics

The implementation of advanced manufacturing technology lies outside the traditional macroeconomic dimensions of government policy. It involves events and people deeply embedded within organizations, both public and private. This fact does not preclude a significant governmental role in this process, although it does preclude a traditional one. But this role must be based on a clear understanding of the process dynamics involved in such technology.

In recent years, empirical studies of implementation processes have increased (Scheirer and Rezmovic, 1983), especially those concerned with manufacturing technology (Ettlie, 1985; Gerwin, 1982; Graham and Rosenthal, 1984) and the related phenomena associated with the introduction of office technologies (Bikson and Gutek, 1983; Johnson, 1985). These studies of implementation processes suggest that process technologies must be considered as collections not only of hardware but of knowledge embedded in both the machines themselves and in the software and organizational systems used to operate and control the machines. As such, the implementation of manufacturing technology is as much a problem of knowledge dissemination and utilization as of engineering (Havelock and Eveland, 1984).

Implementation is not a single decision; it is, rather, a set of decisions made at many different times and levels in the organization. Although decisions concerning the purchase of an advanced manufacturing system may be made at high levels of management, decisions concerning the implementation and use of these systems, of necessity, involve individuals and functions down to the shop floor. These decisions are often unrecognized but are crucial to the success of the implementation process.

Technological change moves through stages from initial awareness to evaluation and decision to adoption and finally to implementation and use (Tornatzky and others, 1983). The transition from adoption to implementation is as critical to ultimate success as any other but has not received as much attention as the stages leading to adoption. Up to the point of commitment of resources, which initiates implementation, knowledge dissemination is primarily a cognitive and intellectual activity that consists of learning about the innovation. Implementation, by contrast, requires the expenditure of financial, material, and human resources and calls for behavioral changes at many levels in the organization for it to succeed.

Implementation of manufacturing technology does not just happen but is a painful and stressful situation for most firms. Some of this stress can be relieved through strategic planning (see Chapter Nine). For example, advanced systems often link together diverse functions within the firm. To give leadership to any one of these functions in the implementation process could greatly limit its integration. Gerwin (1982) advocates a process champion for implementation who is not responsible to any one functional group.

Furthermore, the relationship between the equipment vendor and the user firm seems closer and much more complex than in other capital investments (see Chapter Four). The vendor has to be willing to work closely with the user and should be willing to devote resources to improve the user's understanding of the technology and its implications. Turnkey approaches to implementing advanced manufacturing technologies have not proved workable for either vendor or user (Cooke and Malcolm, 1981) any more than they have in the implementation of advanced information-processing technologies (Bikson and Gutek, 1983).

Thus, the implementation of complex technological systems demands on-site adaptation or reinvention (Rice and others, 1983)—a process in which research on complex sociotechnical implementation processes suggests that participation at all levels is critical (Tornatzky and others, 1983). Some programs have been significantly enhanced by the involvement of lower-level staff in the design and implementation of the advanced systems (Gustavson and Taylor, 1984). More of this participation may occur as management systems are replaced by structures and practices more supportive of manufacturing systems and the lower-level discretion they seem to require.

Explicit attention to implementation and participation in implementation helps workers and managers avoid surprises. The new technology is always uncertain in its effects, but many principles derived from implementation analysis can guide strategy. In general, the Japanese have been better at applying these principles than have American firms, for reasons partly cultural and partly a matter of choice. The Japanese emphasis on consensus building incorporates trials and pauses into the adoption process, explicitly recognizing that multiple decisions are complex and that all decision makers must to some degree exert rights of "ownership" over the technology. Thus adoption is a relatively long and difficult process, but when the time comes to implement the technology, the participants are already familiar with it and have accepted it.

By contrast, American managers are likely to make relatively quick decisions concerning adoption or rejection of new technology, with little understanding of or concern for the complexity of the technology and associated implementation processes. If calculations of costs and benefits are made, they tend to be "quick and dirty," without much systematic thought or basis in experience. As a result, new technologies are more likely to be rejected than accepted. Furthermore, for those technologies that are adopted, disappointment with the system tends to be interpreted as a failure of the technology rather than as the result of inadequate or incomplete implementation or management because only technical factors have much visibility to the participants in the decision.

Thus, adoption and implementation of advanced manufacturing technologies are phenomena played out in the context of the firm or some subunit within the firm and are only partially affected by interventions at the industry or sector level. The management practices and strategies essential to the successful implementation of these technologies are generally outside the direct reach of government; knowledge transfer regarding the technologies themselves is only slightly more amenable to influence than are management practices. Although government actions like taxation do have some effect on adoption, these actions probably cannot substantially alter the incentive structure for and the strategic vision of American managers so that they will recognize the importance of implementation processes. Such policies are not inconceivable, however; Hage (1985), for example, advocates the use of tax write-offs for education intended to make managers flexible and receptive to change.

Federal Role

It is frequently forgotten that the U.S. government has had a long and significant history of promoting advanced manufacturing technology, dating back to the founding of the

"Mother Arsenals" at Springfield, Massachusetts, and Harpers Ferry, Virginia, in 1794 (Smith, 1977). These arsenals, particularly Harpers Ferry, were major developers of mechanized production and the American system of interchangeable parts that revolutionized manufacturing in the mid-1800s.

A large and active government presence in manufacturing continues today. One study (Hetzner, Tornatzky, and Klein, 1983) identified approximately a dozen federal programs focused on advanced manufacturing technologies. As in the 1800s, the great bulk of support for manufacturing technology continues to be from the military; the form of this support is quite varied. Military agencies provide funding for research and development (R&D), assist contractors in purchasing productivity-enhancing technologies, provide for certain R&D expenditures as part of procurement contracts, and are major buyers of manufacturing technologies such as machine tools. Other agencies are generally limited to providing research support or assisting in the purchase of productivity-enhancing technologies, and the amount of support they provide is at least an order of magnitude less than that of the military.

Although comparisons of public and private research support are difficult (R&D data do not distinguish between product and process technologies), it is apparent that the U.S. government has been a strong supporter of the development of certain advanced technologies such as numerical control (NC). The Air Force, in particular, supported early NC research to improve the quality of military aircraft. By contrast, the suppliers of NC machine tools support little if any R&D of their own. One study (National Academy of Sciences, 1983) estimates that machine-tool firms in the United States spent about 1.5 percent of sales on R&D over five years. The National Machine Tool Builders Association places the figure at about 4.1 percent (National Academy of Sciences, 1983), which is low compared with the amount other firms and industrial sectors spend. (Some knowledgeable experts claim that the machine-tool industry reports product-development or engineering activities to come up with its 4.1 percent estimate and that even 1.5 percent may be high for the sector as a whole [Graham, 1984].)

Given this pattern, one can conclude that it is the federal government, its aerospace contractors, and the automotive industry that have been responsible for much of the innovation in the machine-tool industry. This situation is neither unique (von Hippel, 1985) nor necessarily a problem if one can assume that what is good for the Air Force, Lockheed, and General Motors is good for all discrete-parts or durable-goods manufacturing.

However, research suggests that responding to the needs of the federal government has not always met the needs of manufacturing in general. Most federal activities tend to emphasize short-term, user-oriented, relatively small-scale hardware, according to a study by Hetzner, Tornatzky, and Klein (1983). Their data showed little concern on the part of the federal government with developing manufacturing systems or even major subsystems; emphasis was largely on improving the performance of individual machines. Since their survey, certain groups in the federal government have attempted to consider issues of factory-level productivity, but these efforts have been diluted by the actions of either a larger agency or of Congress. It is apparently much easier to convince those who control the budget to "put a new coat of paint on a machine" than to try to do something radically new.

Within federal programs there is close if largely unstructured contact between an agency and its immediate industrial clientele but little or no direct contact with any other prospective developers or users. Government program managers outside the military do not even talk to each other except at meetings and conferences. This lack of integration and coordination among existing government programs is one of the most neglected issues of the industrial-policy debate and has been an impetus for various proposals to create a federal technology agency or a Department of Science. But since such a department would be unlikely to assume control over military programs, it would have little influence over the characteristics of the technologies supported by the military.

The shortsightedness of the federal government is an implicit technology policy that may be partly responsible for current industry problems. Rather than opening up radically new manufacturing possibilities, federal programs tend to reinforce the lack of strategic vision in U.S. industry. Agencies within the military, the Department of Commerce, and even the National Science Foundation that have tried to adopt a longer-term, larger-scale, and more comprehensive view of manufacturing have been thwarted by their management, by the Office of Management and Budget, or by Congress in yearly reviews of agency and program budgets that tend to emphasize limited quantitative indicators of accomplishment.

National Implications and Policy Options

We contend that if the federal government wishes to encourage manufacturing innovation and productivity improvements, it will have to go beyond the limited role already played by the Department of Defense with civilian contractors. There does seem to be a legitimate governmental role in addition to the traditional and necessary support of the basic and applied research leading to technology development.

An important area of concern is knowledge transfer and dissemination of technological information. Although the federal government plays a major role in the support of manufacturing research, efforts at technology transfer and implementation assistance are small and scattered. Federal agencies have not been given either a clear mandate or sufficient resources to promote extensive civilian applications and implementations. The knowledge required by U.S. industry is beyond the normal marketing functions—or even abilities—of equipment vendors. Furthermore, the need for information is greatest among small and medium-sized manufacturers. We cannot assume that market forces will bring the necessary information and technical assistance to this subpopulation. In fact, the extremely slow pace of technological change in small and medium-sized manufacturers suggests the contrary (Rees, Briggs, and Oakey, 1983).

Active government involvement in dissemination of information about advanced manufacturing is a radical departure from its traditional posture of staying out of technical development except where direct federal needs are involved. (The great exception, of course, is agriculture, where the extension service and the cooperative state research service have collaborated to extend the use of publicly developed technology to a vast degree.) The government has generally restricted its support to R&D, depending on market forces to enhance dissemination. However, the classic demand-pull approach seems to have been dysfunctional for manufacturing, both because of problems in adapting military and space technologies to civilian requirements and because of the limitations of management.

Some form of manufacturing-technology extension service to disseminate information about new techniques might be worth experimentation. An aggressive and coordinated technology-transfer program would imply that the government has made a strategic choice to push a family of technologies. This pattern is unprecedented in the United States in recent times, but is similar to that in both Japan and West Germany. The functions performed by a manufacturing-technology extension service might include needs assessment and aggregation, adaptation of existing technologies to these needs, packaging of the new technology for small and medium-sized users according to cells or functions, and an active interpersonal dissemination network.

At present, the leadership in manufacturing extension appears to be largely in the hands of state governments. A number of well-funded programs have been initiated by states to foster technology transfer and implementation in manufacturing. Examples include the Industrial Technology Institute in Michigan, and the Institute of Advanced Manufacturing Sciences and the Cleveland Advanced Manufacturing Productivity Center in Ohio. There is even a private-sector International Flexible Automation Center in Indiana.

Although the federal government can still play a significant and important role in this process, this role must be designed to complement rather than supplant these state efforts. Presumably the states have a comparative advantage in both needs assessment and developing an interpersonal dissemination network. But the federal government could best aggregate these needs, support appropriate research, and encourage other states to establish dissemination functions. It is not reasonable to expect that individual states take the broad view of national interests required in an economy as tightly integrated as ours.

Evidence suggests that both state and federal efforts should be directed at small and medium-sized firms. This is the pattern in the most successful parts and periods of agricultural extension (Rogers, Eveland, and Bean, 1977; Feller and others, 1984). Research by John E. Ettlie, as reported in Chapter Four, indicates that large vendors and users of manufacturing technology are already beginning to pay increased attention to the adoption and implementation of advanced manufacturing systems. Although there are certainly problems, false starts, and incomplete or inadequate implementation of new technologies by larger firms, on the whole these firms are likely to survive in one form or another. But small and medium-sized machine-tool vendors and metal-working users do not see themselves participating in the current revolution in manufacturing technologies. These firms are more than just "Mom and Pop" operations; they are a significant portion of discrete-parts manufacturing in the United States. For example, in the machine-tool industry, 8 large firms account for 42 percent of all shipments, while 428 firms account for the rest. Of these 428 firms, 20 to 35 percent employ fewer that twenty workers (Greater Cleveland Growth Association, 1984). These firms cannot individually afford even a modest investment in R&D, and they probably also could not afford either the time or money to implement any technology resulting from such an investment. The economic and human costs of restructuring small and medium-sized firms are likely to be quite large, especially in the Northeast and Midwest.

Another essential feature of a technology-push strategy is attention to the issues of worker displacement and retraining. Although it is difficult to estimate the number of jobs that will be lost as small and medium-sized firms are unable to compete or the extent of worker redundancy produced by advanced manufacturing technologies, it is certain that dislocations of labor will occur. When a company goes out of business, retraining and placement are the key issues and suggest active governmental programs. For firms undergoing technological change, dissemination of information about strategies for coping with the shocks might help. Potentially effective options include guaranteed employment, incentives to workers to retrain, and employee gain sharing in productivity improvement. National policy and governmental programs in support of advanced manufacturing technologies must recognize that these technologies abolish or change existing jobs and create new ones. Thus, management practice in this area and job creation must be recognized parts of a comprehensive technology-push strategy.

Another modest federal contribution would be to improve our understanding of dissemination and implementation processes, including an examination of current state efforts to increase the implementation of new technology and encourage economic development. The processes by which complex process technologies, for either manufacturing or offices, are adopted and implemented are not well understood and have not been translated into explicit, simple, action programs. Because advanced manufacturing systems are radical departures from both their predecessors and other better-understood technologies, there is a lot to learn about how they get implemented; industry cannot afford to be solely responsible for such research.

To date we have knowledge of some of the general dimensions of the problems and opportunities in the implementation and use of advanced manufacturing technologies. It is one thing to say that new organizational possibilities are opened by new technology; it is quite another to suggest how a certain firm can move from one organizational structure to another. Information about the kinds of strategies and programs of change that have worked or not worked in particular situations is needed, especially now that state governments are getting into the act. The implications of not doing this research are to leave the process to good will and chance, which is probably unwise in the extreme.

The experience of federal agencies with technology spin-off programs suggests that any dissemination and implementation activity cannot be easily grafted onto any existing agency responsible for supporting or conducting manufacturing research. Neither the National Aeronautics and Space Administration nor the Department of Defense has been able to sustain a comprehensive spin-off program through either the Technology Utilization Program or the Federal Laboratory Consortium, respectively.

Some rather impressionistic data indicate that the federal government has had success in certain programs that are directed at developing and transferring technologies for the private sector. One such program is the National Shipbuilding Research Program of the Maritime Administration, designed to develop and implement productivity-enhancing innovations in the ship-building industry. This program has been in operation since 1973, with about twenty shipyards participating. Other programs include the University/Industry Cooperative Research Centers and Projects Programs, sponsored by the National Science Foundation. The Centers Program generates over $13 million in private support and another $13 million from state governments, in response to a $3 million investment by the federal government. These are both rather minor programs, with little power within their agencies. The National Science Foundation, for example, rather than expand the Centers Program, developed a whole new program of Engineering Research Centers, funding six university-based centers with $10 million for the first year. The actual level of participation by state governments or industry expected or realized by the Engineering Centers is not yet clear. Clearly the federal government is slow to generalize from its own successful experience.

The bottom line of this analysis is that the federal government does not at present seem to have the capacity to respond creatively to the crisis in manufacturing. For ideological, political, financial, and organizational reasons, the government is unlikely to use its considerable expertise and leverage to support the needed industrial transition to new technology. The states can and will provide a patchwork of sometimes creative and sometimes flawed initiatives, but the overall impact of such a scattered commitment of resources is likely to be notably inefficient and ineffective. Until the federal government and its agencies come to terms with the issues identified here, government is likely to do more harm than good in the area of advanced manufacturing technology.

References

Bikson, T. K., and Gutek, B. A. *Advanced Office Systems: An Empirical Look at Utilization and Satisfaction.* Santa Monica, Calif.: Rand Corporation, 1983.

Cooke, R. E., and Malcolm, B. "Choosing and Implementing Resource Recovery Systems." *National Center for Resource Recovery Bulletin,* 1981, *11,* 35-39.

Davis, L. E. "Organization Design." In G. Salvendy (Ed.), *Handbook of Industrial Engineering.* New York: Wiley, 1981.

Ettlie, J. E. "The Implementation of Programmable Manufacturing Innovations." In D. D. Davis (Ed.), *Dissemination and Implementation of Advanced Manufacturing Processes.* Washington, D.C.: National Science Foundation, 1985.

Eveland, J. D., Rogers, E. M., and Klepper, C. M. *The Innovation Process in Public Organizations: Some Elements of a Preliminary Model.* Ann Arbor: Department of Journalism, University of Michigan, 1977.

Feller, I., and others. *The Agriculture Technology Delivery System: A Study of the Transfer of Agricultural and Food-Related Technologies.* University Park: Institute for Policy Research and Evaluation, Pennsylvania State University, 1984.

Gerwin, D. "Do's and Don't's of Computerized Manufacturing." *Harvard Business Review,* 1982, *60,* 107-116.

Gold, B. "CAM Sets New Rules for Production." *Harvard Business Review,* 1982, *60* (6), 88-94.

Graham, M. Personal communication, Nov. 1984.

Graham, M. B. W., and Rosenthal, S. R. "Learning About Flexible Manufacturing: An Action Research Approach." Paper presented at the annual meeting of the Institute of Management Science/Operations Research Society of America, San Francisco, May 1984.

Greater Cleveland Growth Association. *Great Lakes Governors' Commission on the Machine Tool Industry: Final Report and Recommendations.* Cleveland: Cleveland Area Development Corporation, 1984.

Gustavson, P., and Taylor, J. C. "Socio-Technical Design and New Forms of Work Organization: Integrated Circuit Fabrication." In F. Butera and J. Thurman (Eds.), *International Com-*

parative Study on Automation and Work Design. Amsterdam: North-Holland, 1984.

Hage, J. "Alternative Industrial Responses to Technological Innovation and Market Changes." In D. D. Davis (Ed.), *Dissemination and Implementation of Advanced Manufacturing Processes.* Washington, D.C.: National Science Foundation, 1985.

Havelock, R. W., and Eveland, J. D. "Change Agents and the Role of the 'Linker' in Technology Transfer." Paper presented at the annual meeting of the Federal Laboratories Consortium, Seattle, 1984.

Hayes, R. H., and Abernathy, W. J. "Managing Our Way to Economic Decline." *Harvard Business Review,* 1980, *58,* 67-77.

Hetzner, W. A., Tornatzky, L. G., and Klein, K. J. "Manufacturing Technology in the 1980's: A Survey of Federal Programs and Practices." *Management Science,* 1983, *29,* 951-961.

Johnson, B. McD. *Innovation in Office Systems Implementation.* Washington, D.C.: National Science Foundation, 1985.

Kaplan, R. S. "Measuring Manufacturing Performance: A New Challenge for Managerial Accounting Research." *Accounting Review,* 1983, *58* (4), 686-705.

National Academy of Sciences. *U.S. Machine Tool Industry and the Defense Industrial Base.* Washington, D.C.: National Academy Press, 1983.

Noble, D. A. *America by Design: Science, Technology and the Rise of Capitalism.* Oxford, England: Oxford University Press, 1979.

Rees, J., Briggs, R., and Oakey, R. *The Adoption of New Technology in the American Machinery Industry.* Occasional Paper No. 71. Syracuse, N.Y.: Metropolitan Studies Program, Maxwell School of Citizenship and Public Affairs, Syracuse University, 1983.

Rice, R. E., and others. "The Survival of the Fittest: Organizational Design and the Structuring of Word Processing." Paper presented to the Academy of Management, Dallas, 1983.

Rogers, E. M., Eveland, J. D., and Bean, A. S. *Extending the Agricultural Extension Model.* Stanford, Calif.: Institute for Communication Research, Stanford University, 1977.

Scheirer, M. A., and Rezmovic, E. L. "Measuring the Implementation of Innovations." *Evaluation Review,* 1983, 7, 599–633.

Smith, M. R. *Harpers Ferry Armory and the New Technology.* Ithaca, N.Y.: Cornell University Press, 1977.

Tornatzky, L. G., and others. *The Process of Technological Innovation: Reviewing the Literature.* Washington, D.C.: National Science Foundation, 1983.

von Hippel, E. *User, Manufacturer, and Supplier: An Analysis of the Functional Sources of Innovation.* Cambridge, Mass.: Sloan School of Management, Massachusetts Institute of Technology, 1985.

101 ELEVEN 101

Integrating Technological, Manufacturing, Marketing, and Human Resource Strategies

Donald D. Davis

Two premises have guided the chapters in this book. First, American firms have experienced a decline in economic power that is, in part, derived from their reliance on outmoded manufacturing and management methods. Adoption of advanced manufacturing technologies capable of increasing production has been slow. Second, advanced manufacturing technologies are not turnkey systems: their effectiveness depends on the social context of the organization in which they are embedded.

The probability of adopting advanced manufacturing technologies is determined by characteristics that affect the adoption rate of any innovation. These characteristics include attributes of the innovation and features of the adopting unit. This chapter summarizes the features that are important for the adoption and implementation of advanced manufacturing technologies. These features include characteristics of the technology itself and of the adopting organization, especially its managers, structure, environment, and strategy. Special attention is paid to management of this process. I argue that adoption and implementation of advanced manufacturing technologies are enhanced when a strategic perspective is taken. This strategic perspective must focus on technology, manufacturing, marketing, and human resources.

The Innovation-Adoption Process

Rogers (1983, pp. 163-209) has provided the most accepted general model of the innovation-adoption process. This model has five stages: knowledge of the innovation, formation of a favorable or unfavorable attitude toward the innovation, decision to adopt, implementation, and decision to retain or discard the innovation once implemented. This model describes the adoption of innovations such as advanced manufacturing technologies. One becomes aware of a new system such as computer-aided design (CAD), considers the pros and cons of the new system, and makes a purchase decision. Once purchased, the new system is implemented within the organization and its performance is evaluated through analysis of productivity, return on investment, and other outcomes. If the innovation is still viewed as appropriate, it is continued.

Barriers to adoption and implementation of advanced manufacturing technologies can exist at any of these stages. To start, potential adopting organizations may simply be unaware of these new technologies, or, when they are known, their relevance to the adopting organization may be unclear. Although one might think that few manufacturing professionals could possibly be ignorant of these new technologies, some evidence shows that such ignorance is not rare. Gerwin (1982) cites a survey reported by the Comptroller General in which 20 percent of the executives in 200 metal-working firms lacked any understanding of advanced manufacturing technologies. He further states that this problem may be particularly acute in small and medium-sized firms, where managers lack the expertise to evaluate properly their need for advanced manufacturing technologies.

Attitudes toward advanced manufacturing technologies, a precursor of purchase, are shaped by the marketing practices of technology vendors and by characteristics of the adopting unit, usually managers or groups of managers organized into a purchasing unit. Vendors must use potent strategies and practices for selling their systems. Managers must be receptive to these systems.

The decision to adopt a new manufacturing system is an amalgam of elements. Positive attitudes toward the new technology are insufficient to ensure adoption. Adoption may be denied because it is difficult to justify costs, despite managers' awareness of the benefits of the new technology and positive attitudes toward its use.

Implementation and confirmation follow the adoption decision. Potential barriers may arise at this stage because planning for implementation seldom goes beyond consideration of engineering specifications. Vendors prefer to treat these new technologies as turnkey systems to reduce the potential for costly changes in hardware and software specifications. They prefer for the burden of implementation to fall on the adopting organization. Typically, however, the adopting organization gives little thought to implementation beyond rudimentary training.

Sometime during the course of implementation the purchase decision will be reconsidered. This reevaluation may be done formally through analysis of the effectiveness of the system, or it may be done informally through discussion after interaction with the new technology; people talk to one another about the advantages and disadvantages of the new system based on their experiences with it. If the purchase is viewed as inappropriate, divestiture is possible, although this outcome is unlikely because of the large expense and high profile of such systems. A more likely outcome is continued usage at a reduced level of performance.

This adoption process for advanced manufacturing technology must be considered within an organizational context. Using the fivefold typology devised by John R. Kimberly in Chapter Two, we see that the innovation-adoption process described by Rogers (1983) characterizes the organization as user. Kimberly makes us aware of the most pertinent analytical issues. He suggests that "the right people with the right values and motivations in the right kind of organizational setting will result in an organizational system with a good potential for adopting innovations." The trick is to discover the "right" configuration. Obstacles to increased use emerge when facets of this configuration are absent or inappropriate. Kimberly goes on to state that managers must identify the innovations that are right for their organization, get them adopted, and then ensure that they are implemented successfully. Paradoxically, however, managers must not become too invested in the innovation, or they may resist future generations of it. The U.S. automobile industry's enormous investment in automating the production of cast-iron brake drums probably delayed by five years or more its move toward disc brakes (Hayes and Abernathy, 1980).

Managers must coordinate the facets of the innovation-adoption configuration in order to reduce barriers to the adoption and use of advanced manufacturing technologies. By understanding the innovation-adoption process, managers can improve their firms' adoption potential for these technologies. Organizational scholars can help in this effort by identifying appropriate adoption configurations through research and theory development.

Factors Related to Adoption and Implementation

Characteristics of Technology. Perception of the characteristics of innovations such as advanced manufacturing technologies determines, in part, the likelihood of their adoption. Rogers (1983, p. 211), after reviewing hundreds of studies, has described the characteristics of innovations that contribute most to their adoption. These include: relative advantage (the degree to which the new technology is perceived to be better than that which precedes it), compatibility (the degree to which the new technology is consistent with existing values, past experiences, and needs of the potential adopting organization), complexity (the degree to which the new technology is relatively difficult to understand and use), trialability (the degree to which the new technology may be experimented with on a trial basis), and observability (the degree to which the results of the new technology are observable to others).

In a meta-analysis of the research literature on the influence of innovation characteristics, Tornatzky and Klein (1982) state that relative advantage, compatibility, and complexity have the most significant relationships with the adoption and implementation of innovations. These characteristics of advanced manufacturing technologies should exert the strongest influence on adoption potential.

Relative advantage has economic and social aspects (Rogers, 1983, pp. 214-217). Economic reasons, including reduction in labor and other unit production costs, are frequently cited to justify the purchase of advanced manufacturing technologies. It should be noted, however, that these technologies seldom save money; they provide new opportunities for making money. The social aspect of relative advantage is the prestige and personal power associated with the adoption of advanced manufacturing technologies. Frequently, once engineers observe these new systems, they all want one. Like personal computers, new technology becomes a measure of status. Firms attempt to emulate industry leaders such as General Electric and John Deere, which implement advanced manufacturing technologies widely.

Compatibility with existing needs, values, and practices is another attribute of advanced manufacturing technologies that contributes to their adoption. When felt needs are met, the innovation is likely to be adopted. These felt needs interact, however, with other personal characteristics of the potential adopter, such as values toward change.

Complexity, a third important innovation characteristic, affects the adoption and implementation of advanced manufacturing technologies in two ways. First, the likelihood of adoption is reduced because these new forms of automation are believed to be too complex for any but the largest and most sophisticated firms. They are not purchased because they are not understood. Second, they may be adopted for inappropriate reasons. They are purchased but fail to satisfy the unrealistic expectations of the adopting organization.

Observability of the new technology also plays a role in its adoption and implementation. The production and human-resource outcomes of advanced manufacturing technologies are observable to all over time. Workers like them or do not like them; productivity goes up or down. The high observability of positive outcomes of advanced manufacturing technologies should be related positively to their adoption. Uncertainty regarding outcomes, however, will reduce the likelihood of adoption.

The ability to experiment with these new technologies on a trial basis is problematical. It is difficult to try these new systems on a small scale before making the adoption decision. Although firms may automate incrementally by starting with stand-alone equipment, only when this equipment has been integrated into comprehensive systems are the full benefits of computer-integrated manufacturing (CIM) realized. Although robots or computer numerically controlled (CNC) tools can be easily tried out, CIM cannot. The inability to try CIM on a small scale is a barrier to adoption that is difficult to eliminate. In Chapter Five, Ann Majchrzak, Veronica F. Nieva, and Paul D. Newman report that previous experience with CNC may be unnecessary for successful use of CIM, suggesting that an evolutionary approach to adoption may not be required. Clearly, additional research is needed here.

The adoption of advanced manufacturing technologies depends not just on characteristics of the technology itself. Advanced manufacturing technology is an innovation that is important to the entire firm. In order to understand the adoption of these new technologies, we must also consider features of the adopting organization.

Characteristics of the Adopting Organization. Technical progress has consistently been related to organizational form. Firms having an organic form tend to be technologically innovative and receptive to change. This organic form is characterized by informal definition of jobs; lateral, networklike, communication patterns; consultative rather than authoritative communication; diffusion of knowledge seeking throughout the firm; commitment to a technological ethos of material progress that is more highly valued than loyalty to the firm; and importance and prestige attached to extraorganizational affiliations and activities (Burns and Stalker, 1961, pp. 121-122).

Mechanistic forms of organization usually are less innovative and more resistant to change than are organic forms. Mechanistic forms are characterized by rigid breakdown of roles and jobs into functional specializations; precise definition of duties, responsibilities, and power; hierarchical control, authority, and communication; reinforcement of the hierarchical structure by the belief that managers at the top of the organization know what is best for it; reliance on vertical interaction; insistence on loyalty to the concern and obedience to superiors as a condition for membership in the organization; and greater prestige and importance attached to internal than to extraorganizational knowledge or activities (Burns and Stalker, 1961, pp. 119-120).

These relationships have received empirical support in many different contexts. Decentralized and participative forms of decision making, low reliance on written rules and regulations to govern work behavior, concentrations of professionals of different types, and complexity in general are the organizational features most frequently related to technological innovation and innovation adoption (Hage, 1980; Tornatzky and others, 1983). This relationship is evident in the analysis of the shoe industry by Jerald Hage in Chapter Three. Managers in the potentially adopting companies knew about the new manufacturing-process innovations and had the capital to support their purchase. But firms not adopting the new technology lacked the type of organizational form that would increase receptiveness— they were not organically structured. These laggard firms concentrated decision making at the top and did not rely on a wide network of managerial specialists.

Characteristics of managers also contribute to adoption of advanced manufacturing technologies. Innovations are likely to be adopted by managers who occupy central positions in professional networks (Becker, 1970a, 1970b), have positive values toward change (Hage and Dewar, 1973), and are cosmopolitan (Kimberly and Evanisko, 1981). It should be recognized, however, that decisions to purchase new technology must usually be made by many individuals in the organization. To predict the adoption of innovations such as advanced manufacturing technologies, it is necessary to know the characteristics of those actually making the decision, not just top executives. Prediction may be enhanced by defining the pattern of individual characteristics, such as cosmopolitanism, among decision makers (Robertson and Wind, 1983).

The structure of the organization does not operate independently of its managers. Structure shapes the behavior of managers and is shaped, in turn, by their behavior. Thus, the interplay between managerial characteristics and organizational structure makes the firm receptive to advanced manufacturing technologies. Hage describes in Chapter Three how this interaction can occur. Organizations that are mechanistic select and reward managers with values consistent with this form of organization—for example, those who are low risk takers. These managers, of course, perpetuate the system. Managers who have attitudes and values that are receptive to innovation and change never gain ascendancy in the organization or ultimately leave it. An incapacity for change develops.

Organizational Environment. Events external to the organization also influence the adoption and implementation of advanced manufacturing technologies. It is important to recognize, however, that the organization is not acted on passively by external events. As Starbuck (1976) points out, organizations' environments are invented largely by the organizations themselves; they select their environments from different alternatives. Decision makers "enact" these environments (Weick, 1979) by attending to some events and disregarding others. Managers make a mutual adjustment between the organization and the enacted environment. This interpretive experience affects the adoption of advanced manufacturing technologies.

The cycle of national economic activity is one aspect of the enacted environment that is likely to influence the adoption of advanced manufacturing technologies. Kimberly (1981) states that adoption tends to increase after economic recessions. The adoption rate tends to be highest "near the peak of the upside of the activity curve—that is, after recession—to level off and begin to decelerate just prior to the peak, and to be lowest on the downside of the curve" (p. 94).

Other organizations are a second aspect of the environment that affects the adoption of advanced manufacturing technologies. This network includes varying numbers of organizations linked through communication and exchange of resources (Levine and White, 1961). Closer ties often represent greater interdependence in exchange (Cook, 1977). Other organizations influence adoption primarily in two ways. First, managers of other firms act as a source of information about new technology. For this reason, extraorganizational professional activity and cosmopolitanism are often related to high rates of innovation adoption. Second, vendor organizations can be useful in facilitating adoption of advanced manufacturing technologies. This second way of influencing other organizations may be more important than the first.

A special form of interorganizational relationship exists between firms selling advanced manufacturing technologies and firms that are potential adopters. As pointed out in Chapter Four by John E. Ettlie, a good relationship between the vendor and potential user is one of the most significant factors in the successful implementation of programmable manufacturing systems. A team of at least two key people (one vendor, one user) is needed to integrate the new system into the organization. The vendor must go beyond service to help the user assimilate the new technology into its ongoing organization. Support beyond selling and rudimentary training is necessary for vendors of the factory of the future. Simple approaches to marketing are inappropriate for these advanced systems.

Marketing is the primary mechanism whereby vendor firms disseminate new forms of technology to potential user firms. Dorothy Leonard-Barton and Janis Gogan describe in Chapter Eight the special marketing features that must be considered in order to increase the adoption of advanced manufacturing technologies. They show that market segmentation should be viewed differently when marketing advanced manufacturing technologies, and they provide suggestions for using a sophisticated, nested approach instead. Also unique to the marketing of advanced manufacturing technologies is the fact that they are complex systems. Their complexity requires technical knowledge on the part of users and makes purchase justification difficult. Complexity also increases the perception of risk.

Furthermore, as pointed out by Leonard-Barton and Gogan in Chapter Eight, vendors must sell the potential of these new systems; they must sell systems into which users can grow and expand. This new way of marketing will be assisted by the development of hardware and software standards for networks so that items such as CAD and robots can be added when the firm is ready to do so. Use of integrating systems such as the Manufacturing Automation Protocol, developed by General Motors, will aid dissemination by allowing firms to adopt portions of a larger system as they can afford to do so. Firms can add additional equipment later without the integration problems experienced with the piecemeal adoption of other types of processing equipment such as microcomputers and printers. Integration is no small matter. The national survey reported by Majchrzak and her associates in Chapter Five reveals that less than 10 percent of the sampled firms have integrated most or all of their equipment. In addition, and equally important to vendors of advanced automation, users of integrated systems possess organizational characteristics and are affected by market demands that are different from those of firms in which computerized equipment is not integrated. These features may be used to segment potential users.

Joint ventures provide another event in the environment that can enhance the flow of advanced manufacturing systems from one organization to another. An organization already possessing these technologies and expertise about how to manage them joins with another organization in an effort to diffuse these processes. The joint ventures between General Motors and Fujitsu Fanuc and between General Motors and Toyota demonstrate how a firm wishing to become knowledgeable about the use of advanced manufacturing processes may join with one already expert in their use and management. This partnership accelerates the learning curve.

The actions of federal, state, and local governmental agencies are a final event in the environment that may affect the adoption of advanced manufacturing technologies. The U.S. Air Force was instrumental in developing CNC equipment and still plays an active role in the development of CIM. New legal arrangements such as research and development (R&D) limited partnerships foster the transfer of new technologies from universities to industry. Little, however, is being done by government at any level to increase knowledge concerning the organizational and management practices related to successful adoption and use of advanced manufacturing technologies. William A. Hetzner, J. D. Eveland, and Louis G. Tornatzky describe in Chapter Ten how the federal government could play an active role here.

The influence of environmental factors on the adoption of innovations is moderated by the organization's structure. The complete relationship between the organization's structure and environment and the likelihood of innovation adoption is not completely understood, although the influence of some environmental features is rather evident. When the firm's environment is turbulent and unstable, centralization and formalization may impede innovation adoption; when the environment is stable, these same characteristics may facilitate adoption (Kimberly, 1981). This reversal may also describe the relationship between organizational structure and the different stages of the adoption process. Innovation *adoption* may be impeded by centralized decision making, reliance on formalized rules and regulations, and lowered complexity; innovation *implementation,* however, may be facilitated by these same qualities (Zaltman, Duncan, and Holbek, 1973).

Organizational Strategy. Scholars and managers interested in understanding the adoption and implementation of advanced manufacturing technologies must consider the influence of strategy in different areas of the firm in addition to the values and attitudes of managers and decision makers, other characteristics of the organization's structure, and events in the organization's environment. Strategy integrates these different influences. Strategy is the process whereby the organization maneuvers in its environment. Through strategy, the firm determines what business it is in and how it intends to conduct that business. Goals and policies are selected that match the organization's resources with perceived opportunities. Organizational structure is altered to implement strategy. Strategy influences, and is influenced by, the adoption and implementation of innovations such as advanced manufacturing technologies.

Rosenbloom (1975, pp. 172-173) describes the type of interaction possible among strategy, structure, and innovation adoption by describing the development of diesel locomotive engines at General Motors. Charles Kettering, the engineering genius at General Motors, originated the idea after purchasing a diesel-powered yacht. Kettering's backers at General Motors were willing to support the project until its practicality could be demonstrated. Development was augmented by the purchase by General Motors in 1930 of the Winton Engine Company, a large manufacturer of diesel engines, and the Electro-Motive Engineering Company, an engineering, design, and sales organization that had a close business relationship with Winton. These organizations became the basis for the General Motors Electro-Motive Division. As Rosenbloom points out, receptiveness to this new idea grew out of the strategy formulated during the 1920s by Alfred Sloan and his associates and the new organizational structure they created to implement it. This new, decentralized structure, consisting mostly of autonomous divisions, released upper executives from management of operations sufficiently so that they had time to appraise new ventures that were different from the major business thrust of General Motors. Rosenbloom raises the intriguing question of whether the idea would have arisen at General Motors if it had retained the traditional functional form of organization.

In this brief example we see how strategy led to change in organizational structure, which made the firm receptive to new ideas. Innovation adoption was facilitated through purchase of other organizations. Strategy guided the development of a low-priced, mass-produced diesel locomotive backed by an established service network and standardized parts for repairs to compete with custom-designed, expensive, traditional steam-powered engines. Strategy, structure, and new technology carried the day. Strategy may be the most important element for making organizations receptive to advanced manufacturing technologies.

Strategies for Implementation

Strategy binds together the firm's potential for adopting innovations such as advanced manufacturing technologies. Strategy forces the organization's decision makers to consider opportunities and threats and to structure the organization to optimize adaptive potential. At least four types of strategy are important in the adoption and implementation of advanced manufacturing technologies: technology strategy, manufacturing strategy, mar-

keting strategy, and human-resource strategy. The role of each
is discussed here.

Technology Strategy. Technology strategy emphasizes
the importance of new technology to the firm and its contribution to overall business strategy. Technology strategy results
from the firm's attempt to respond effectively to technological
threats and opportunities. All technological choices are also
business choices (Maidique and Patch, 1982). Maidique and
Patch (1982) suggest that technology policy "involves choices
between alternative new technologies, the criteria by which
they are embodied into new products and processes, and the deployment of resources that will allow their successful implementation" (p. 274). Technology policy is distinct from manufacturing strategy, which tends to involve decisions regarding the
location, scale, and organization of production resources.

Maidique and Patch (1982, p. 275) state that firms must
make technological choices in at least the following six areas:
(1) selection of which technologies to invest in, determination
of how these technologies should be embodied in existing products, which performance parameters should dominate, and how
these new technologies should be evaluated; (2) level of competence required to become proficient in understanding and using
the new technology, proximity to technological state of the art;
(3) extent to which external or internal sources should be relied
on as sources of the new technology; (4) level of R&D investment considered optimal; (5) competitive timing of the firm,
extent to which it wishes to lead or lag behind competitors in
the introduction of new products; (6) type of R&D organization and policies.

Choices will be influenced by the general business strategy of the firm. For example, firms choosing to be first to market with highly innovative products will require an aggressive
technology policy that leads to the adoption of state-of-the-art
process and product technology. Competence levels must be
high in order to take full advantage of these new technologies.
Both internal and external sources of new technology may be
used. The level of R&D investment will be high, and efforts will
be made to organize the R&D function for optimal perfor-

mance. The corporate emphasis will be on leading competitors to the market with new products. Zilog, Inc., as described in Chapter Seven by James C. Taylor, Paul W. Gustavson, and William S. Carter, employs this type of technological strategy.

Firms vary in the degree to which they have a long-range strategy for the adoption of process innovations such as advanced manufacturing technologies. Ettlie (1983) describes data from the food-processing industry that suggest that long-range strategies for technology may be associated with perceived uncertainty about environmental events such as capital supply, competition, and new-product requirements of the industry. Firms with aggressive long-range technology strategies are likely to adopt radical innovations. The form that such a strategy must take remains unclear.

Firms wishing to be receptive to new ideas and practices such as advanced manufacturing technologies must think strategically about technology and develop long-range plans for its adoption. Because technological choices are also business choices, firms must search for technological threats and opportunities. Firms fail to think about technology strategy at the risk of losing their business. An example shows how such market losses can occur. The development of reliable, small semiconductors was relevant to the watch industry, but few traditional watch-making firms understood or were aware of this development. This failure allowed new firms such as Texas Instruments and Casio to gain large shares of the watch market. Many traditional watch-making firms have yet to recover from their oversight.

Manufacturing Strategy. Managers have been bombarded increasingly with the idea that manufacturing must be viewed as one of the firm's most formidable competitive weapons. Skinner (1969) led this assault. Buffa (1984) and Hayes and Wheelwright (1984) have made additional contributions. Manufacturing, it is said, must be viewed as more than simply a production function. Manufacturing managers must play an active role in establishing a manufacturing strategy that contributes to larger corporate strategy. Only in this fashion can manufacturing provide the competitive advantage of which it is capable.

Buffa (1984, pp. 15-19) provides a model of manufacturing strategy stressing six activities. These include decisions regarding positioning of the production system, capacity and location, product and process technology, work force and job design, operations, and suppliers and vertical integration. These features focus the attention of manufacturing managers on all the activities associated with material flow—from suppliers to production to distribution.

Just as products have a life cycle, manufacturing has a cycle of its own. Managers must position the manufacturing system with this cycle in mind. Abernathy and Townsend (1975) delineate three stages of the manufacturing-process cycle—early, middle, and late periods. Each of these periods has different implications for parts and materials, technology, labor, manufacturing scale, product characteristics, and modes of production-process change. During the early stage of the manufacturing-process cycle, characteristics of the job shop dominate. Raw materials are available from suppliers, and the firm has limited influence over the supplier; technology consists of general-purpose equipment, with equipment modifications made by the user; workers have a broad range of skills, and there is great flexibility in the tasks performed by each worker; short-run economies of scale are acquired through learning-curve improvement, although the scale is not sufficiently high to act as a barrier to entry; a great variety of products is produced with different features and quality, making possible frequent design change; there is little automation. During the early stage, the process is flexible and able to deal with low volumes.

During the middle stage of the manufacturing-process cycle, suppliers become more dependent than they previously were, and more tailored specifications may be demanded of them; some process automation is evident, although the level of automation varies—there are islands of automation; automated processes are linked manually; tasks are highly structured and standardized, with labor continuing to be a significant production cost; scale increases to compete in an industry segment; product segmentation becomes possible, with significant volume in some product lines; processes that are difficult to automate are separated from those that can be automated; process flow begins to hold sway.

The most mature stage of the process cycle reveals greater control and integration. Suppliers are integrated; automation is used, with automatic materials handling and stress on integrating the entire system; workers spend time on monitoring and maintenance tasks, with rigid labor classifications; great economies of scale are possible, to the point that they may be limited by antitrust laws or logistics; product variability is low and volume is high; there is product and process alignment to meet changing markets.

Mariann Jelinek and Joel D. Goldhar point out in Chapter Nine how advanced manufacturing technologies can have important implications for positioning the production system—the first component of manufacturing strategy. Advanced manufacturing technologies blur the distinctions between early and mature stages in the manufacturing-process cycle. It becomes possible to combine the flexibility and low volumes of the job shop with the economies of scale made possible through the automation of the production and materials-handling system. A new economy of scope becomes possible.

A second component important in formulating manufacturing strategy is capacity and location decisions. The capacity component of manufacturing strategy must be based on long-term predictions concerning markets, technology, and expected incursions by competitors (Hayes and Wheelwright, 1984, p. 46). Excess capacity is sensible only when mushrooming demand is foreseen. When it is not, the high costs associated with excess capacity are unjustified. Advanced manufacturing technologies may contribute to overcapacity, although this is not an inevitable consequence. Flexibility in capacity is one of the unique advantages of these new technologies, making production and schedule changes less costly. Often, however, to justify investment costs, additional capacity must be projected, sometimes through the addition of shifts. Capacity, then, becomes a strategic decision with financial considerations.

Capacity may lead demand, stay approximately equal to demand, or lag behind demand. Resulting strategies may include the following: "(1) Don't build additional capacity until the need for it develops; (2) outguess the market by following a countercyclical strategy; (3) buy for the long haul; and (4) follow the leader" (Hayes and Wheelwright, 1984, pp. 69-70).

Development of facilities that meet the long-term needs of the firm is important as well. Location decisions include consideration of traditional factors such as shipping and production costs. In some industries—for example, electronics and computers—other factors become equally salient. In these cases, geographical characteristics such as climate, access to university resources, and attractive community amenities become important. As additional firms in the industry stress these locational features, they become necessary to attract and keep the best employees.

Advanced manufacturing technologies have a great impact on capacity and location decisions. As Jelinek and Goldhar point out in Chapter Nine, with this new equipment, "the economic order quantity approaches one because variety has little or no penalty at the production stage. . . . The equipment does not 'care' whether it makes an extended run of many units or an extended run of a wide range of units. The changeover costs are small because tool changes are typically automatic, and program change electronic." Capacity becomes easy to manage because flexibility and change are simple and relatively inexpensive. Location decisions are also simple because the exchange of information is electronic, reducing spatial and geographical limitations. Bylinsky (1983) reports that Yamazaki Machinery Works Ltd. has completed a flexible manufacturing system outside of Nagoya, Japan, that uses sixty-five computer controlled machine tools and thirty-four robots linked by fiber-optic cable with the CAD center twenty miles away at company headquarters. The automated factory can be directed to manufacture parts, and make tools and fixtures to produce the parts, from control of the CAD data base. The ability to communicate information at such speed may begin to render obsolete traditional notions about location planning.

Product and process technology is a third aspect of manufacturing-process strategy that is important. Decisions here focus on whether and when to adopt new process and product technologies, to what uses they may be put, and so forth. Reluctance to adopt new process technology is a major weakness in the manufacturing and corporate strategy of many firms. Several perspectives on this problem have been provided in this book. Jelinek and Goldhar in Chapter Nine describe many of the strategic implications of new forms of process technology. Primary among these are economies of scope, new forms of control, flexibility, accuracy, responsiveness, variety, different product life cycles, and relatively inexpensive capacity for multiple missions. Unlike old forms of automation, where these features are traded off against one another—for example, increased accuracy and control often reduce flexibility and responsiveness to customer demand—new forms of automation allow their joint accomplishment. These new possibilities represent competitive advantages. Exploitation of these advantages will require awareness of their possibility and willingness to integrate manufacturing strategy with long-term corporate strategy. Few firms, especially small and medium-sized ones, have grasped these strategic possibilities.

The fourth aspect of manufacturing-process strategy focuses on the work force and job design. The acquisition and deployment of the work force is critical to the successful use of advanced manufacturing technologies and must be considered an important element in any manufacturing-process strategy. This component will be discussed in detail later, in the section on human-resource strategy and practices.

Operating decisions are a fifth component of manufacturing-process strategy. Operations managers frequently are a barrier to effective use of advanced manufacturing technologies because they view themselves simply as a means of meeting output targets and performance goals (Hayes and Wheelwright, 1984, p. 172). Because of their specialized technical training in areas such as industrial or materials engineering, they tend to lack a comprehensive understanding of the capabilities of process innovations. Operations managers must consider these questions (Hayes and Wheelwright, 1984, pp. 173-174):

How does a new process work? Inputs, outputs, and processing time; flow pattern; delays or inventory accumulations; capacities and bottlenecks; balance among resources; balance between various stages in the process; flexibility in the process; trade offs—for example, set-up time versus running time; major uncertainties; likely errors.

What are its economics? Original versus operating costs; life time and payback characteristics; costs versus volume and economies of scale; cost breakdown by ingredients—for example, materials, labor, supervision; cost of product changes.

What are the key operations and manufacturing problems associated with it? Changes in volume or products; cost control; work-force management; planning, scheduling, and balancing; maintenance; purchasing materials; materials handling.

Operating decisions such as those regarding attempts to control quality have major strategic implications. When the responsibility for quality rests with those who produce the product rather than a separate group whose function is quality control, important strategic possibilities emerge. This realization provides the foundation for quality circles and explains their effectiveness.

The final component in the model of manufacturing-process strategy provided by Buffa (1984) focuses on suppliers and vertical integration. When considering the strategic implications of suppliers, one must study suppliers of raw materials or subassemblies important to production and suppliers of the technology itself—that is, vendor relationships. Issues important when considering suppliers of raw materials include how much of the supplier's business is provided by the focal company, whether to use multiple sourcing, how much R&D and other forms of engineering are to be done by the supplier, and whether to pursue full-scale vertical integration. Negotiations are typically at arm's length, with the constant threat of changing suppliers.

Vertical integration is an attempt by the user to exert as much control as possible over uncertainties in the source of supply. In the case of vendor relations, the supplier of new process technology plays a considerable role in the success with which the new technology is used. This new role places the user in a different, more dependent position vis-à-vis the supplier than is traditional. Ettlie describes this relationship quite clearly in Chapter Four. Successful implementation of advanced manufacturing systems is usually accompanied by a close and personal relationship between user and vendor, a relationship often described as being similar to a marriage. Thus, in contrast to the traditional distancing between the user and supplier, an interdependent and closely connected relationship is necessary for the successful implementation of advanced manufacturing technologies.

Marketing Strategy. Two aspects of marketing are important in the adoption and implementation of advanced manufacturing technologies. First is the role marketing plays in their dissemination. Several chapters in this book discuss this issue. Leonard-Barton and Gogan in Chapter Eight describe how the special features of new technologies must be considered by vendors when trying to disseminate them broadly. Some of these features include the characteristics of technology described previously. Majchrzak and her associates describe in Chapter Five some of the organizational features that might be used for market segmentation. Ettlie in Chapter Four describes some of the special features of the vendor-user relationship that affect the success of adoption and implementation.

A second important aspect of marketing strategy is selling products manufactured with new forms of automation. How do advanced manufacturing technologies, once they are implemented, affect existing marketing strategies and practices? Advanced manufacturing technologies have as dramatic an impact on marketing practice as on production. Time-worn tactics such as market segmentation must be reexamined in the light of these new technologies. Advanced manufacturing technologies make possible the simultaneous production of high-quality, multiple products, with great variety and complexity because of software-determined flexibility and precision (Jelinek and Goldhar, 1984, and Chapter Nine). Skinner's (1974) advice that manufacturing be focused can be followed at the same time that a policy of flexibility is pursued; a multiple focus is both possible and economical. Because change is easy, firms can frequently update products, making differentiation an inexpensive tactic to pursue; product variety costs less. Understanding these marketing opportunities will assist in justifying the adoption of these new technologies. Because advanced manufacturing technologies have a pervasive effect on the full range of business activities, marketing strategy must consider them.

Suggestions for a link between manufacturing and marketing and sales are often met with grimaces by those asked to cooperate. Differences in professional training, orientation, norms, and practices lead members of each group to see the world differently. Yet their individual success is inextricably bound to each other's. Without manufacturing there is nothing to sell; without marketing a firm has overflowing warehouses. Marketing strategy must be integrated with manufacturing strategy.

Hayes and his colleagues (Hayes and Schmenner, 1978; Hayes and Wheelwright, 1979, 1984) provide a framework for effectively joining manufacturing with marketing strategy. This framework links stages of the product life cycle with the manufacturing-process cycle described previously in the section on manufacturing strategy. The idea of a product life cycle is patterned after human growth and refers to a product's evolution over time. Stages in this cycle are introduction into the market, rapid growth, maturity, and decline. An innovative product is introduced into the market during the first stage. Growth is slow and relatively flat while buyer inertia is overcome. Rapid growth occurs as many buyers rush to purchase the product once it has proved successful. The market eventually becomes saturated as it matures and most potential buyers have purchased the product. Finally, growth declines as new replacement products are introduced.

Porter (1980, pp. 159-161) describes how strategy, competition, marketing, and manufacturing practices change at each stage to capitalize on opportunities. During the product-introduction stage, marketing typically uses a "creaming" strategy (aiming at purchasers with higher than average income) and tries to compensate for the high marketing costs associated with high advertising for low sales volume. This is the best period to increase market share by stressing product characteristics. Marketing during the growth stage still employs considerable advertising, but higher sales occur than during the introductory stage. It is practical here to change price or quality image; product quality and availability are stressed. Once the market for the product has matured, markets are usually segmented, product lines are broadened, and service and deals are stressed. It is difficult here to increase market share. Competitive costs and dependability become the key strategies. Finally, as purchase of the product declines, advertising-sales ratios are low and marketing is reduced. Because price continues to be important, cost control becomes paramount.

Manufacturing concerns are different during each stage of the product life cycle. The first stage is characterized by short production runs of low volume, high production costs, overcapacity, and high skilled-labor content. During the growth stage, there is a shift toward mass production; undercapacity exists. Manufacturing during the mature stage experiences optimum capacity or some overcapacity; manufacturing processes become stable; low labor skills are needed; long production runs with automation are stressed. Finally, during decline, there is substantial overcapacity, with automated mass production being used.

The manufacturing-process cycle of Hayes and Wheelwright (1984, pp. 205-207), described previously, meshes with the product life cycle. During the first stage of product introduction, manufacturing processes resemble a job shop; general-purpose machine tools are used, and special adaptations of these are made by the user. Small batches of products can be produced. Producing a variety of new products with different features and quality is possible. During the growth stage, some process automation emerges. Although islands of automation may exist, these are linked by manual operations. Scale economies begin to become possible with increased volume. The mature stage is characterized by automated mass production with computerized integration. This configuration complements reduced product variability and high volume. Significant economies of scale favor price competition.

Hayes and Wheelwright (1979) recommend use of the product-process matrix to assist in matching manufacturing and marketing strategy (Table 1). Rows represent the manufacturing-process stages, moving from jumbled flow through continuous flow. Columns represent stages in the product life cycle, moving from low volume, low standardization, and innovative products to high volume and highly standardized products. A company or strategic business unit usually occupies a region of this matrix depending on the match between its process technology and product life cycle. Commercial printers are typical of firms located in the upper left corner of the matrix. Because each printing job is unique, a jumbled-flow process is best for meeting market requirements. The market requires equipment and personnel flexibility and product variety and does not allow sufficient volume to permit economies of scale. Far down the diagonal, we see sugar or oil refining. Here the product is a commodity; price provides the primary competitive advantage. High product consistency and low prices are made possible through reliance on highly automated, continuous-flow technology, resulting in low flexibility and variety.

The upper right and lower left corners have been left blank in the model because of their scarcity. For example, production of a commodity with a job-shop process would be uneconomical in most cases. A similar mismatch is the use of a continuous-flow process to manufacture small quantities of products. Diagonal locations are most common and preferred; a firm may opt to locate itself in another cell in order to distinguish itself from its competitors, but it does so at great risk.

Advanced manufacturing technologies offer new strategic advantage because they increase the likelihood of success with deviation from the diagonal of the product-process matrix. The flexibility and variability provided by these new technologies allow the firm to gain economies of scale with small-batch runs. The equipment does not "care" whether it produces a thousand runs of one part or one run of a thousand parts, once the software has been programmed. Flexibility and variety no longer require elimination of standardization. Traditional trade-offs between custom design and cost are no longer important.

Table 1. The Product-Process Matrix for Manufacturing and Marketing Strategy.

Manufacturing-Process Stage	Stage in Product Life Cycle			
	1 *Low Volume,* *Low Standardization,* *One-of-a-Kind Products*	*2* *Multiple Products,* *Low Volume*	*3* *Few Major Products,* *Higher Volume*	*4* *High Volume,* *High Standardization,* *Commodity Products*
Jumbled flow (job shop)	Commercial printer			
Disconnected line flow (batch)		Heavy equipment		
Connected line flow (assembly line)			Auto assembly	
Continuous flow				Sugar or oil refinery

Source: Adapted from Hayes and Wheelwright (1979, p. 135).

Furthermore, reliability does not have to be sacrificed for customization. Advanced manufacturing technologies thus allow a hybrid manufacturing process with characteristics of the job shop and assembly line. The link between manufacturing and marketing must be reconsidered to take into account these new possibilities. Understanding of this potential will facilitate the adoption and implementation of advanced manufacturing technologies.

Human-Resource Strategy. The final type of strategy important for the successful adoption and implementation of advanced manufacturing technologies focuses on human resources. Human-resource strategy and practices are important because workers and managers act as a major barrier to the success of new technologies. Several chapters in this book address different aspects of this issue. Knowledge, attitudes, and values of decision makers have frequently been associated with resistance to new technology (Tornatzky and others, 1983). It is, in part, for this reason that having a variety of managerial specialists is positively related to the adoption of new process technology. Gatekeepers and process and product champions are also important (Allen, 1977; Tushman, 1977). As Hage suggests in Chapter Three, it would be advantageous to the organization to identify the individual characteristics related to these activities and to incorporate this information into the selection system so that the organization can be assured of having a plentiful supply of the gatekeepers so important to the innovation process.

Important components of any human-resource program must include job analysis, recruitment and selection, training, career development and succession planning, performance appraisal, linkage of compensation and reward systems to performance, and organizational development. These practices are important at three levels—operational, managerial, and strategic (Devanna, Fombrun, and Tichy, 1981). The operational level focuses on the short term and includes the day-to-day management of people, such as setting up monitoring systems and making staffing and recruitment plans, administering the wage and salary program, providing specific training, and, in general, managing the interface between the individual and the organization, with special attention to matching individual differences and the goals of the organization. Individual workers must be matched effectively to advanced manufacturing technologies. The managerial level takes a more aggregate view than the operational level, focusing on intermediate-term issues such as longitudinal validation of selection devices, compensation plans, performance appraisals to guide and develop employees, organizational and employee development, career paths, and succession planning.

The strategic level focuses on the human-resource system at its most aggregate and abstract level. Important issues include identification of the knowledge, skills, and abilities required in the long term to work successfully with new technologies; adaptation to changing work-related needs and values evolving in the larger population; linkage of the compensation and reward system with long-term human-resource strategy regarding the type of individuals required to fit the anticipated organizational culture; determination of the basis for performance appraisal in the long term; identification of potential management "stars" for special grooming; design of the organization to facilitate adjustment to anticipated environmental demands; development of a long-term system for mutually satisfying the needs of the organization and its employees; and linkage of the human-resource system and strategy to general business and corporate strategy.

Human-resource factors important to implementation include staffing and training. The survey of vendors and users of programmable automation reported by Ettlie in Chapter Four revealed that bumping is a frequently cited human-resource barrier to optimal use. Bumping occurs when someone with greater seniority takes the place of someone with less seniority because of a lay-off or preferred access to overtime. Unfortunately, the older worker typically has less expertise about the new technology than the younger one. Union rules and frequent turnover can amplify this problem.

The education and training required for these systems will present an obstacle to their optimal use for some time. An entire generation of those trained in the skilled and semiskilled trades is becoming obsolete. Tool and die makers and machinists must now possess greater cognitive abilities than at any time before. Machine operators must adapt to jobs requiring less manual labor and more time spent monitoring equipment. These changes are aggravated by the fact that less than half of the American firms using computer-aided design/computer-aided manufacturing (CAD/CAM) in the manufacture of transportation equipment, electric and electronic equipment, and industrial and metal-working machinery—those industries most likely to use computerized automation—have any type of education and training program for these new technologies, although about half subsidize training provided by external sources (Majchrzak and Nieva, 1985). Several strategic questions must be faced. Should older workers be retrained or should only younger workers with the prerequisite skills be hired? How often should those who use the new equipment be retrained? How can the need for new knowledge be reconciled with seniority practices? How can hiring practices and training anticipate technologies only now being developed? How can workers be selected when the required abilities and skills cannot be specified before the new technology is adopted? How can the human-resource requirements of a new technology influence early decisions about its design, purchase, and implementation?

Additional human-resource concerns focus on preparation of the organization for the new technology. Changes in information flow and control, power and authority, supervision and performance appraisal almost inevitably accompany the use of advanced manufacturing technologies, especially for integrated systems. This new technology affects the business widely. For example, over twenty departments were identified as being involved in the implementation of a robotics system at General Dynamics (Helander, 1983). Manufacturing decisions inevitably become business decisions. Formerly central managerial tasks such as deciding among priorities, allocating resources, and scheduling are easily subsumed into software. Expert systems, natural-language processing, and other forms of artificial intelligence may further decentralize knowledge and decision making (see Shwartz, 1985). Authority and responsibility may even be located in the equipment itself. Zuboff (1982) describes the effects of a new computer controlled monitoring system in the Volvo plant in Kalmar, Sweden. A feedback device was programmed to flash a red light when a defect was detected. The workers protested, insisting that this function be returned to the supervisor, with whom they could negotiate and whom they could cajole, rather than the computer, whose decision was not subject to discussion and debate. In this instance, the computer became the authority, and the workers subject to this authority had no recourse. Many managers and supervisors are ill prepared for such changes in their role. Furthermore, with production merging in a computer-integrated system, in contrast to the traditional system where each person operates a single piece of equipment, appraisal of individual performance becomes more burdensome. Responsibility for errors becomes difficult to ascertain because of the system's complexity and the interdependence of its elements. Merit-based compensation systems become impossible to administer fairly and accurately for individual workers.

Another human-resource concern is the effect of advanced manufacturing technologies on individual workers. Certain communication strategies may be effective here. The study of the implementation of robotics reported by Linda Argote and Paul S. Goodman in Chapter Six provides evidence. The study discovered that the method of communication about the installation of a new robot was significantly related to how well workers accepted the robot. Although their research focused on production workers, the need to communicate effectively about new automation is equally important for middle managers. Middle managers frequently resist advanced forms of automation. At Boeing Aerospace, for example, middle managers fought the installation of a flexible manufacturing system designed to manufacture parts for air-launched cruise missiles; they were afraid of relinquishing authority (Brody, 1985).

Workers with low-level skills are also fearful of process innovations such as robots (Chao and Kozlowski, 1984). This fear is fed by knowledge that escalating wages can be used to justify new technologies. Roger Smith of General Motors once stated that every time the cost of labor goes up one dollar per hour, a thousand more robots become justified ("G.M. Shift," 1981). Although retraining will allow many workers to adapt to new technologies, efforts must be made to address these fears directly.

Other deleterious side effects are associated with the use of advanced manufacturing technologies. Finne (1983) found that the negative effects of a CAD system in a mechanical-engineering firm included eyestrain, muscular tension, fatigue, stress, and mental exhaustion. Feelings of stress and reduced control also accompany the implementation of robots (Argote, Goodman, and Schkade, 1983; Office of Technology Assessment, 1984). Although the impact of stress and lack of control on organizational commitment, absenteeism, and turnover among workers using advanced manufacturing technologies has not yet been studied extensively, sufficient evidence exists in other settings to expect these linkages to exist (see Mowday, Porter, and Steers, 1982). These effects could be reduced considerably with appropriate human-resource strategy and practice.

Finally, an important element in any human-resource strategy is a focus on the implementation effort itself. Standard organizational-development approaches lend themselves to this approach. Participative decision making can be used in the early stages of adoption to reduce resistance to change (Davis, in press; Davis, Catanzaro, and Greene, 1985). Team building might be a useful strategy for strengthening the vendor-user relationship in order to enhance the transfer of technology (Ettlie and Eder, 1984). Survey feedback is useful for monitoring employee attitudes such as perceived role conflict and role ambiguity, task perceptions, job satisfaction, and organizational commitment, which may change as a consequence of interacting with the new technology. Principles of sociotechnical systems can be used to redesign units, as pointed out in Chapter Seven by Taylor and his associates. Jobs can also be redesigned to enhance their perceived psychological characteristics; autonomous work groups may replace individuals as the job-performance unit of analysis.

Human-resource concerns must be considered early in the technology-implementation process. Interaction with other units such as engineering and product design is essential. For example, AT&T's training staff participate in new-product planning so that they can become aware of training needs and design training programs six to nine months before equipment goes on line ("Retraining Displaced Workers," 1982).

The impact of changes in human-resource practices on functioning in other units must also be considered. Majchrzak (1985) cites an example of a plant endorsing participative decision making through an employee suggestion plan. They neglected, however, to prepare the engineering group for the impending volume of suggestions, only to have the engineers feel overwhelmed, ignore the suggestions, and stifle worker initiative. Team building would be useful for integrating functional units such as engineering, manufacturing, marketing, and human resources. This increased collaboration would simultaneously make the organization receptive to new ideas and practices and ensure smooth implementation once these ideas were adopted.

Conclusions

American manufacturers are experiencing unprecedented change. Change provides both opportunity and danger. Whether change is opportune or dangerous depends on decision and action. Failure to act is as harmful as false action.

Advanced technologies such as CAD/CAM and CIM provide new competitive opportunities. They make possible a hybrid form of manufacturing that simultaneously possesses characteristics of small-batch, mass-production, and continuous-process forms of production. Traditional trade-offs between standardization and customization are no longer necessary. An efficient, multiple manufacturing focus is possible. Yet few manufacturers, especially small and medium-sized ones, have appreciated these new strategic possibilities. American manufacturers have been slow to adopt these new technologies. Factors contributing to this slow rate of adoption are the same as those that determine the adoption of any innovation—features of the innovation, the adopting unit, and its environment.

Simple purchase of advanced manufacturing technologies, however, does not guarantee that their productive potential will be realized. These are not turnkey systems. Rather, they are systems that affect the very foundation of the business itself. The entire organization must be prepared for their implementation. Responsibility for adoption and implementation cannot rest in a single department.

Effectiveness of the technology is constrained by the surrounding social system. Successful implementation of advanced manufacturing technologies requires that attention be paid to this social system, which includes human-resource practices and vendor-user relationships. Adoption and implementation can also be guided by strategic planning in the areas of technology, manufacturing, marketing, and human resources.

Danger arises from failure to adopt advanced manufacturing technologies as well as from failure to appreciate their systemic nature. Failure to adopt them is certain to ensure continued loss of market share because of higher costs and poorer quality. Failure to consider the social system providing the context for their implementation and use is sure to limit their potential.

References

Abernathy, W. J., and Townsend, P. L. "Technology, Productivity, and Process Change." *Technological Forecasting and Social Change*, 1975, 7 (4), 379-396.

Allen, T. J. *Managing the Flow of Technology: Technology Transfer and the Dissemination of Technological Information Within the R&D Organization.* Cambridge, Mass.: MIT Press, 1977.

Argote, L., Goodman, P. S., and Schkade, D. "The Human Side of Robotics: How Workers React to a Robot." *Sloan Management Review*, 1983, *24*, 31-41.

Becker, M. H. "Factors Affecting Diffusion of Innovations Among Health Professionals." *American Journal of Public Health*, 1970a, *60*, 294-304.

Becker, M. H. "Sociometric Location and Innovativeness: Reformulation and Extension of the Diffusion Model." *American Sociological Review,* 1970b, *35,* 267-283.

Brody, H. "Overcoming Barriers to Automation." *High Technology,* 1985, *5* (5), 41-46.

Buffa, E. S. *Meeting the Competitive Challenge: Manufacturing Strategy for U.S. Companies.* Homewood, Ill.: Dow Jones-Irwin, 1984.

Burns, T., and Stalker, G. M. *The Management of Innovation.* London: Tavistock, 1961.

Bylinsky, G. "The Race to the Automated Factory." *Fortune,* Feb. 21, 1983, pp. 52-64.

Chao, G., and Kozlowski, S. W. "Employee Perceptions on the Implementation of Robotic Manufacturing Technology." Paper presented at 92nd annual meeting of the American Psychological Association, Toronto, 1984.

Cook, K. S. "Exchange and Power in Networks of Interorganizational Relationships." *Sociological Quarterly,* 1977, *18* (1), 62-82.

Davis, D. D. "Designing Organizations for Productivity, Technological Innovation, and Quality of Worklife: A Human Resource Perspective." In D. Gray, T. Soloman, and W. A. Hetzner (Eds.), *Strategies and Practices for Technological Innovation.* Amsterdam: North-Holland, in press.

Davis, D. D., Catanzaro, D., and Greene, V. *Management Innovations and Organization Improvement.* Vol. 2: *Impact of Participation in Decision Making on Productivity, Quality of Worklife and Technological Innovation.* Washington, D.C.: National Science Foundation, 1985.

Devanna, M. A., Fombrun, C., and Tichy, N. "Human Resources Management: A Strategic Perspective." *Organizational Dynamics,* 1981, *9* (3), 51-68.

Ettlie, J. E. "Organizational Policy and Innovation Among Suppliers to the Food Processing Sector." *Academy of Management Journal,* 1983, *26* (1), 27-44.

Ettlie, J. E., and Eder, J. L. "The Vendor-User Relationship in Successful vs. Unsuccessful Implementation of Process Innovations." Paper presented at the annual meeting of the Institute of Management Sciences/Operations Research Society of America, San Francisco, May 1984.

Finne, H. "The Designer and His Job in the Face of Integrated CAD/CAM Systems." Paper presented at a workshop sponsored by the International Federation of Automatic Control, Karlsruhe, Federal Republic of Germany, 1983.

Gerwin, D. "Do's and Dont's of Computerized Manufacturing." *Harvard Business Review,* 1982, *60* (2), 107-116.

"G.M. Shift: Outside Suppliers." *New York Times,* Oct. 14, 1981, pp. D1-D2.

Gold, B. "CAM Sets New Rules for Production." *Harvard Business Review,* 1982, *60* (6), 88-94.

Hage, J. *Theories of Organization: Form, Process and Transformation.* New York: Wiley, 1980.

Hage, J., and Dewar, R. "Elite Values Versus Organizational Structure in Predicting Innovation." *Administrative Science Quarterly,* 1973, *18,* 279-290.

Hayes, R. H., and Abernathy, W. J. "Managing Our Way to Economic Decline." *Harvard Business Review,* 1980, *58,* 67-77.

Hayes, R. H., and Schmenner, R. W. "How Should You Organize Manufacturing?" *Harvard Business Review,* 1978, *56* (1), 105-118.

Hayes, R. H., and Wheelwright, S. C. "Link Manufacturing Process and Product Life Cycles." *Harvard Business Review,* 1979, *57* (1), 133-140.

Hayes, R. H., and Wheelwright, S. C. *Restoring Our Competitive Edge: Competing Through Manufacturing.* New York: Wiley, 1984.

Helander, M. G. "Human Factors Aspects of Computer-Integrated Manufacturing." Paper presented at the 27th annual meeting of the Human Factors Society, Norfolk, Va., 1983.

Jelinek, M., and Goldhar, J. D. "The Strategic Implications of the Factory of the Future." *Sloan Management Review,* 1984, *25* (4), 29-37.

Kimberly, J. R. "Managerial Innovation." In P. C. Nystrom and W. H. Starbuck (Eds.), *Handbook of Organizational Design.* Vol. 1. New York: Oxford University Press, 1981.

Kimberly, J. R., and Evanisko, M. J. "Organizational Innovation: The Influence of Individual, Organizational, and Contextual Factors on Hospital Adoption of Technological and Administrative Innovations." *Academy of Management Journal,* 1981, *24,* 689-713.

Levine, S., and White, P. E. "Exchange as a Conceptual Framework for the Study of Interorganizational Relationships." *Administrative Science Quarterly,* 1961, *5* (4), 583-601.

Maidique, M. A., and Patch, P. "Corporate Strategy and Technological Policy." In M. L. Tushman and W. L. Moore (Eds.), *Readings in the Management of Innovation.* Boston: Pittman, 1982.

Majchrzak, A. "Effects of Computerized Integration on Shopfloor Human Resources and Structure." Paper presented at AUTOFACT conference, Detroit, 1985.

Majchrzak, A., and Nieva, V. F. *CAD/CAM Adoption and Training in Three Manufacturing Industries.* Washington, D.C.: National Science Foundation, 1985.

Mowday, R. T., Porter, L. W., and Steers, R. M. *Employee-Organization Linkages: The Psychology of Commitment, Absenteeism and Turnover.* New York: Academic Press, 1982.

Office of Technology Assessment. *Computerized Manufacturing and Automation: Employment, Education and the Workplace.* Washington, D.C.: Office of Technology Assessment, 1984.

Porter, M. E. *Competitive Strategy: Techniques for Analyzing Industries and Competitors.* New York: Free Press, 1980.

"Retraining Displaced Workers: Too Little, Too Late." *Business Week,* July 19, 1982, pp. 178-185.

Robertson, T. S., and Wind, Y. "Organizational Cosmopolitanism and Innovativeness." *Academy of Management Journal,* 1983, *26,* 332-338.

Rogers, E. M. *Diffusion of Innovations.* (3rd ed.) New York: Free Press, 1983.

Rosenbloom, R. S. "Technological Innovation in Firms and Industries: An Assessment of the State of the Art." In P. Kelly and M. Kranzberg (Eds.), *Technological Innovation: A Critical Review of Current Knowledge.* Vol. 2. Washington, D.C.: National Science Foundation, 1975.

Shwartz, S. P. "Artificial Intelligence Technology in Manufacturing." In D. D. Davis (Ed.), *Dissemination and Implementation of Advanced Manufacturing Processes.* Washington, D.C.: National Science Foundation, 1985.

Skinner, W. "Manufacturing—Missing Link in Corporate Strategy." *Harvard Business Review,* 1969, *47* (3), 136-145.

Skinner, W. "The Focused Factory." *Harvard Business Review,* 1974, *52* (3), 113-121.

Starbuck, W. H. "Organizations and Their Environment." In M. D. Dunnette (Ed.), *Handbook of Industrial and Organizational Psychology.* Chicago: Rand McNally, 1976.

Tornatzky, L. G., and Klein, K. J. "Innovation Characteristics and Innovation Adoption-Implementation: A Meta-Analysis of Findings." *IEEE Transactions on Engineering Management,* 1982, *EM-29* (1), 28-45.

Tornatzky, L. G., and others. *The Process of Technological Innovation: Reviewing the Literature.* Washington, D.C.: National Science Foundation, 1983.

Tushman, M. L. "Special Boundary Roles in the Innovation Process." *Administrative Science Quarterly,* 1977, *22* (4), 587-605.

Weick, K. *The Social Psychology of Organizing.* (2nd ed.) Reading, Mass.: Addison-Wesley, 1979.

Zaltman, G., Duncan, R., and Holbek, J. *Innovations and Organizations.* New York: Wiley, 1973.

Zuboff, S. "New Worlds of Computer-Mediated Work." *Harvard Business Review,* 1982, *60* (5), 142-152.

Index